# THE OTHER
# SIDE OF
# THE RAINBOW

· · ·

# THE OTHER SIDE OF THE RAINBOW

## MÁIRE BRENNAN

**With Angela Little**

Hodder & Stoughton
LONDON SYDNEY AUCKLAND

British Library Cataloguing in Publication Data
A record for this book is available from the British Library

ISBN 0 340 75613 6

Typeset by Avon Dataset Ltd, Bidford-on-Avon, Warks

Printed and bound in Great Britain by
Clays Ltd, St Ives plc

Hodder & Stoughton
A Division of Hodder Headline Ltd
338 Euston Road
London NW1 3BH

For Tim, Aisling and Paul.

Thank you Angela and Phil.
Thank you Mammy, Daddy, Auntie Bríd,
Columba, Catherine and León.

# Preface to the New Edition

Writing *The Other Side of the Rainbow* ranks as one of the most difficult, challenging and emotional experiences of my life. At the time I was first approached to present my autobiography, neither the publisher nor anyone who encouraged me along the way had any idea about the real truth behind Máire Brennan. Despite the turmoil in my personal life, I had been largely successful in my attempts to keep it privately locked away. I speak honestly when I say that I have never had so many doubts about a project and would happily have presented four or five albums before tackling anything so personal and painful. What made me do it then? You might well ask. I still wonder about this myself. With the hindsight of publication, though, I now rejoice in confidence that this was an important step forward in my life's destiny.

August 2000 was a big turning point. The book was complete and being prepared for publication in October. Few had read the manuscript, but many of my friends and family were concerned. We knew there would be a big reaction to the book in Ireland and everyone was deeply troubled by how it might affect my career, my family and, most of all, my children. At that time I was back home in Donegal for a concert, which was attended by my good friend Father Bartley, who was visiting from America. Father Bartley, Mammy's cousin, had brought me home from Dublin when I was two years old and all my life I had remained close to him. In many ways he has taken my grandfather's role as a kind of mentor to the family. Everyone respects his opinion and, though he has now lived in the USA for several years, we all feel a great respect and fondness towards him.

With trembling hands and a heavy heart I handed Father Bartley the manuscript, knowing it carried the full weight of my family's doubt and concern. Back in Dublin I worried. Was it too late to pull out? Wouldn't it be easier on everyone if my story was never published? Two long weeks passed and as every day went by without me hearing from America I feared the worst for Father Bartley's reaction. Then one evening, when Tim was out and I was putting Aisling and Paul to bed, the phone rang. My heart leapt into my mouth when I heard Father Bartley's familiar voice.

'Máire,' he paused. I held my breath. 'I think you're very brave and I think this book is going to help a lot of people.'

Tears pricked in my eyes and I could barely talk. Father Bartley continued, with nothing but encouraging words. After thanking him profusely, I put the phone down and leapt up the stairs two at a time, shrieking with joy and relief – so much so that the children jumped out of bed to see what all the excitement was about.

Father Bartley's approval gave me a fresh confidence for what I had known in my heart to be right all along. Although the shadows of doubt had constantly haunted me and so many things had come my way to make me stumble, I knew that my story could be of much encouragement to many others who had made mistakes and struggled with guilt and feelings of failure. The publication would go ahead as planned and I would face all the consequences this would bring day by day, one at a time. If it could help just a few people to find forgiveness and freedom, then it would be worth the suffering.

More and more I am seeing a deep spiritual hunger in the people I meet through my music and I have been privileged with countless opportunities to perform at events that are great testimony to God's people coming together in unity. At the peak of my doubts about the book's publication I was invited to Rome to perform for World Youth Day. It was an incredible experience. Almost three million young people represented just about every nation of the world and I was one of only two solo artists invited to perform for the final concert in the presence of Pope John Paul II. The day before, the band and I had played at a festival in Poland in a beautiful setting in the woods just outside

Gdańsk. As we flew into Rome we were met by a police escort to lead us at high speed through the streets of the city, out to the purpose-built auditorium where the three million people gathered. I have never seen such an awesome sight. At nine-twenty in the evening we walked out onto the huge stage. It was dark, with a low moon, and all I could see was a blanket of candles, shining out for miles and miles across the sea of shadows. For the next four minutes it felt as though I held my breath, but somehow I looked up to the sky, thought of home and let my voice fly. It was one of the most precious experiences of my performing life and a joy to be part of positive Christian fellowship on such a worldwide scale.

The summer had been full of great festivals and I was loving being out on the road with the band, with festivals in places as far flung as the Spanish Pyrenees to an island off the coast of Japan. There was talk of another album and rumours of a possible invite to record for a film soundtrack. Meanwhile work was afoot on a new Clannad album that had been recorded live on our last British tour. Musically things could not have been better. However, September brought a shock. Though the official release date for *The Other Side of the Rainbow* was October, it hit some of the shops in Ireland early. I panicked. This really was it. It had been scheduled that I would appear on Ireland's prime chat show, *The Late Late Show*, just as the book was released. That was an important thing for me. I wanted to be able to prepare people for some of the revelations of my story and to make it absolutely clear to them why I had felt the need to write so honestly, before the terrors of the tabloids got there first. Thankfully the show was able to reschedule and within two days I was set to appear.

In the thirty years of my time with Clannad I have stood in the wings of *The Late Late Show* on numerous occasions, but I have never felt so sick with nerves as I did that night. With a tight knot in my stomach and perspiration on my palms, I listened to Pat Kenny's introduction and prayed that I might be able to say the right things:

'Now, ladies and gentlemen, my next guest is no stranger to *The Late Late Show*. She is the girl from Donegal, the one we all know and love as the voice of Clannad. But tonight she's here to talk to us about her autobiography and let me tell you, there are some shocking revelations. Do we actually know the real Máire Brennan? Let's meet her.'

I took my seat to the audience's welcoming applause, taking a moment's comfort as I made out the silhouette of my husband, Tim, sitting on the front row. As expected, Pat Kenny honed in on the darker aspects of my story, particularly the abortion. I knew that this would be a terribly shocking revelation to some people, especially those who knew me, but I wanted to get across my message about God's forgiveness and to share how my broken life has been healed through turning to Him. It was difficult, but I knew that it would be over soon and that I would be able to regain my composure and professional self when I began to sing. That was the bonus about the interview as I had been invited afterwards to perform a song from my album *Whisper to the Wild Water*. But as I was talking, the production assistant, off camera, pushed a note at Pat. It read 'cut the song'. The previous guest had run over and whilst that wasn't uncommon with the show, this time there was no flexibility to extend my slot. The channel had booked satellite time in order to broadcast the Olympics live from Australia, so the programme had to run absolutely to schedule that night. There would be no song and I would leave the audience with the images and message of the book. There it was; stark, real and out in the open. I tried my best to get the positive side of my story across, but I left the theatre feeling less than happy.

Most members of the family couldn't bring themselves to watch the show live. Few of them had had the opportunity to read the manuscript, so they were particularly fearful of its contents and the inevitable reactions from the public and the press. For the next few days I felt like I wanted to hide. Sure enough, I found myself on the front pages of Ireland's newspapers. That was OK. I was prepared. What I feared the most was an adverse reaction from my family. One by one the telephone calls and visits came. As each read the book, or saw a recording of the show, I received the most beautiful, warm, emotional reactions. Of course they knew many of the gritty details, but even those closest to you don't share your innermost thoughts, the things I had revealed for public viewing. The positive response of my family gave me a new confidence and again affirmed in my mind that I had been right to follow that little voice of encouragement all along.

The tabloid publicity in Ireland was as expected, but I had a little respite from the front pages through Paula Yates' sudden death. Then I did another interview and there I was again, the terror of my past blazed across the gossip columns. But I also enjoyed some wonderful reviews of the book in other newspapers and magazines. The Irish magazine *Woman's Way* was particularly complementary, and with this and the many ensuing personal testimonies I received, I began to realise that my story had touched a chord in many people, particularly women. While my imagination had everyone focussing on the 'big issues' of my story, I found that individuals picked up on many of the subtleties. Numerous times I was stopped while out shopping when a woman would thank me for my honesty and tell me how encouraged she was by my story. One woman in particular really touched my heart. Seemingly, because of some family situation, she had not spoken properly to her mother for more than thirteen years. After reading the book, she picked up the telephone and they shared an emotional reunion. Stories such as this, and many more besides, continue to flood in, making me more and more grateful for the things God has done in my life and the opportunity I have, through my story, to help others. Just before Christmas I was invited to go to Romania with the charity Samaritans Purse. Over there, among the children, I could have been anybody. All they needed was a smile and the hand of love. We can all help others by giving a little of ourselves in some way, whether it's simply putting our hands in our pockets, or through the personal giving of time. Beyond all my early doubts, I realise now what a precious opportunity I have been given; a public platform to reach out further in sharing this, my 'love' story.

I thank God that, so far, I have received little adverse reaction to this book and am especially pleased to have received many encouraging letters from nuns, priests and church leaders from varying denominations. So easily we wrongly fear the judgement of these people who, perhaps more than most, might reveal compassion and forgiveness. Many readers, I am sure, might be wondering what effect this publication has had on my own children. As I write, my daughter Aisling, now nine years old, is reading the book. The other night she got to chapter seven and we sat and talked about the mistakes of my past. It hurts me to reveal these things to her, but, in telling my story, I have had to face the skeletons of my previously firmly-closed closets and, though it has been hard, I have also experienced something of a greater healing. Now I can explain to my daughter some of the realities of life and how easy it is to make mistakes, especially when you're walking alone, without faith. I can also face those difficult 'parent' issues with a new bravery. My friend Steve Chalke points out in his book *The Parentalk Guide to Sex* that we should not leave it too late to talk to our children about this subject. There are few other things that we leave them to discover by themselves, only to address the issue later, perhaps too much later.

I have a feeling 2001 is going to be another good year. It opened with the news that I had been nominated for a Grammy Award (the highest accolade in the music industry) for *Whisper to the Wild Water*. I am also very proud to have received a number of other awards for my solo work and am enjoying the thought that my solo music career is still only in its embryonic stages. Above and beyond all these things, the real excitement in my life is the stream of weddings and births that fill our family. My brother Leon, who married Anne last year, is an expectant father, and my sister Olive gave birth to her second child, a daughter, Maeve, at Christmas. Our youngest brother Bartley is to be married next year, and I am immensely proud of my sister Brídín who, in the midst of preparation for her own wedding, is working hard at the launch of her first album with a single already doing well in the charts. Meanwhile Enya continues in high acclaim with her latest project and who knows what's in the musical pipeline for me.

Each season brings its ups and downs, its loves and losses, its challenges and celebrations. We all continue to chase the gold at the end of our rainbows, being sure not to miss out on the colours of our lives.

Máire Brennan, February 2001

# Chapter 1

'Listen, listen! I'm sure they're talking about us.'

My brother Pól was leaning over into the front seat trying to tune in the radio.

'It could be anything,' I said, taking over control of the dial. 'I can't hear enough for the crackle.'

'Leave it Pól,' said Ciarán, 'we're getting too near the mountains, you won't get anything.'

It was cold and dark, but as our van bumped along Donegal's rocky roads we were all awash with excitement as each mile took us nearer to Gweedore – our home.

'I'll need to call Mammy and Daddy again when we get to Letterkenny,' I said.

'What's going on?' asked Noel from the back of the van. 'All these calls, Monaghan, Omagh, now again. Do they think we can't find our way home or something?'

'I'm just doing as Mammy told me,' I said. 'You know them, they're probably just excited and want to know how far away we are.' But Noel was right, it did seem a bit odd. They'd asked us to contact them from some of the main towns en route and seemed very concerned that we should take the coast road rather than the shorter mountain pass. Still, the weather had been fairly wild and the mountain area was pretty remote. It probably was safer this time to go the long way around through Cresslough.

I was happy enough to jump out of the van again at Letterkenny. It had been a long drive from Dublin and I was glad to stretch my legs. The boys stayed in the van while I ran into the service station and phoned home. I could hear excitement in Daddy's voice as he answered.

'Ah, we can't wait to see you, Máire. Only an hour now, eh? Now, you will take the coast road, won't you?'

'Yes Daddy, just like Mammy said. We'll be seeing you soon. Gotta go now.' The pips were sounding and by that time I had very little money left for the phone – just as well, as any longer and my hands might have frozen to the receiver. Breathing into my cupped palms I quickly scampered back to the warmth of the van for the final leg home.

Murty Kavanagh was our driver on that trip and as he put his foot down I smiled to myself, seeing the mountains up ahead and knowing that the fires would be warm and welcoming in Gweedore.

'There seems to be a lot of traffic on the road,' said Murty.

He was right. In the distance we could see dozens of sets of headlights coming towards us. That was certainly unusual. Even in the tourist season you can travel for miles on that road without seeing another soul. It was one of my favourite stretches on earth, filled with many happy memories of me and Daddy travelling out to Derry for my dancing class. I looked out into the darkness – the untamed landscape, peat bogs and dark silhouettes of the glorious mountains, looming over the windswept landscape and governing all that is precious and proud to be Donegal. And yes, just about now, if I squinted into the darkness, I could see the spot where the tiny little sweet shop once stood. It was really nothing more than a box at the side of the road – the smallest, most remote shop in the whole of Ireland, where Daddy and I would always break our journey to buy orange juice and crisps.

The first of the stream of cars seemed to slow down as it came towards us and we squinted as the headlights lit up our van.

'Hang on a minute,' said Ciarán, 'wasn't that one of the McFadden's cars that just went by?'

Pádraig's surprised voice came from the back of the van. 'Yeah, I think it is . . . and it looks as though it's turning around.'

Sure enough, the car did a u-turn and began to follow us. Stranger still, the next car did exactly the same thing. And the next.

'There's definitely something going on here,' said Pól with excitement. Within minutes we were astonished as twenty or more cars turned to follow us, all then sounding their horns and flashing their lights. We recognised both family and friends as they hung out of their car windows shouting at us.

'Hey Clannad, welcome home . . . see you down at Leo's.'

Murty picked up the speed, with our van full of laughter and astonished chatter as we realised what was going on. These cars had come out about twenty miles to greet us. In each village we passed through people came out of their houses to see what was going on. We must have made an extraordinary sight as our white van – with 'Clannad' painted on the side – rumbled through with a cavalcade of cars behind, all sounding their horns and making a commotion.

'Hey guys, look at this,' I exclaimed as we approached Dunlewey junction. Up ahead we could see a huge bonfire, more cars and a bunch of local people gathered. 'I bet you Maggie Gallagher had something to do with organising this,' I said, as we slowed down to briefly exchange 'hellos'.

It was then that we noticed Mammy and Daddy's car, with Daddy leaning out of the window, motioning us to follow them. 'Looks like they want us to drive right through the parish,' said Ciarán with a grin. As we drove on, past the peat-burning station, towards Derrybeg, it seemed the whole of Gweedore was alight with bonfires. All along the roadside there were families out in the cold, waving to us and cheering as we went by. 'I don't believe it!' We all drew our breath in astonishment. 'Surely this isn't all for us?' Half a mile from our home, the Dore Fife band (that the boys played with) were out in full force. There was Dick Sally and Michí Eoin Fheargail, and Donie Green on the big drum with Barney Doogan keeping them all in order. The boys couldn't contain themselves and before I knew it they'd jumped out of the van to march with the band towards our home.

Murty and I couldn't help laughing as we continued up through an avenue of torches. We heard later that Annie Doogan had run into her mother's house and picked up her best new broom. Wrapping an old rag around it, she dipped it in oil and set it alight. When some of the other women saw it, they too headed for their broom cupboards and, after our torch-led procession, it is said there wasn't a single broom to be found in Dore the next day.

Our home stands anchored at the foot of the Grogán

mountain, looking out over Gweedore and beyond to the raging waters of the Atlantic. That night it was shrouded in a mass of activity.

Uncle Lala's huge juggernaut trailer was parked in front of my grandparents' house. It had been transformed into a stage with microphones and seats where I recognised some of the area's most prominent personalities waiting to greet us.

'I don't believe it,' I said to Murty, 'that's Teddy Kearny from Radio na Gaeltachta! So that's why they wanted to know where we were. They must have been broadcasting about our coming home.'

'Pól was right then. That must have been what we were picking up earlier,' said Murty as the van ground to a halt and he threw open the door.

It seemed as though every soul in the area had come out to greet us. Everyone was shouting, cheering and calling our names.

'Hey, Moyabrennan, welcome home.'

'We saw you on *Top of the Pops*.'

'Well done, well done for "Harry's Game".'

Making our way through the crowds, everyone wanted to shake our hands and at one point I stopped to greet Annie Doogan – still carrying her torch – with her young daughter who handed me the most beautiful bouquet of flowers.

My eyes scanned the crowd as we pushed nearer to the stage. There was Uncle Columba with Catherine and their little baby Mairín, all wrapped up to protect her from the cold. I recognised Séimí Diver and Threasa Boyle who I knew would have had something to do with organising this magnificent welcome.

It was a sight to behold. Mammy and Daddy were grinning from ear to ear. I flung my arms around them and was instantly smothered in the hugs of my younger brothers, sisters and Aunt Bríd. Bríd was crying. 'Oh Máire, if only your grandparents could have seen this. They'd be so proud.' Before I had the chance to join in the emotional reunion I was being dragged up towards the stage. The boys were pushing me to say something on behalf of the band and I wasn't being given much choice. Once on the stage I looked out at the sea of familiar faces, friends and loved ones. Teddy Kearny was talking into his microphone and I knew his broadcast was going out all over the West of Ireland.

'Here they are, back home, Donegal's own success story, fresh from a tour of Germany and of course their appearance on *Top of the Pops* with that lovely tune "Harry's Game". Of course we know them as the Brennans and the Duggans, a local family whom many of us have seen singing in Leo's Tavern . . .'

I shook hands with everyone on the stage – local dignitaries and politicians, Sheámus Rogers, Dinny McGinley, Pat 'The Cope' Gallagher, Father Bonnar and Annie McBride. Like Aunt Bríd, Annie told us how proud my grandparents would have been to see this triumphant homecoming. Now in her late seventies, Annie was an authoritative, staunch figure in the community who, along with my grandparents, had always worked to keep Irish culture alive in the area. She was one of the founders of the Gaelic theatre (Amhraclan Gaothdobhair) – where, as children, we had performed in the Irish pantomimes – and was a high-profile campaigner for the promotion of the Gaelic language and Celtic arts.

After my brief address some of the crowd started shouting for us to perform 'Harry's Game'. I looked at the boys in desperation. It was freezing cold and there was no way we could set up the equipment quickly.

'No, no, the sing-song's down at Leo's,' I shouted to everyone.

Gradually the crowd dispersed. There would be a heck of a party down there, where my wonderful sister, Olive, had spent the whole day preparing an amazing spread. We couldn't believe all these people – young and old alike – had braved the cold to give us such a welcome. There were people there who I am sure had never even heard of *Top of the Pops*, but nonetheless we had put Gweedore on the map and, for that, they were proud. We were Clannad, the band from Gweedore, County Donegal who, in a 'strange tongue', had charmed a nation and beyond with a bit of a song. We had made it. This was the stuff we hadn't dared to dream, but now we were home with our people and it felt more than good.

I would spend my life coming 'back' to Donegal, but this was one special kind of homecoming.

Donegal always has been, and I guess always will be, 'home'. My very first memory was of going 'back' to this remote Irish county.

I was actually born in Dublin, but somehow, in the moment of my birth my whole being recognised its belonging to the open space and mountain air of Donegal.

Memories from the tender age of two are hardly more than conceptual flashbacks, but I am certain I can quite clearly remember being on the train leaving Dublin. At that age I understood little about what was going on but I sensed an excitement in my parents and I knew they kept talking about 'when we get home'. That day they had kissed me goodbye and put me on a train in the care of Father Bartley (a cousin of my mother) and Gran Duggan. Gran cooed over my baby brother Ciarán in his Moses basket and Father Bartley pointed out all the strange animals in the fields. It was a real adventure, but I fought against the cradling motion of the train as it ambled on into rural Ireland and the next thing I knew I was being put down on the platform.

'Ahh, little Máire.' All of a sudden I was scooped into the arms of a huge man with thick-rimmed glasses and a big smile. 'My beautiful granddaughter. Come with me now. Don't worry, Mammy and Daddy will be here in a few days. Another wee while and we'll be home.' Still holding me, he took the Moses basket from my Gran, kissed her, and we all headed off towards his car.

I took my name from my mother and grandmother – three generations of Máire. That isn't unusual in Ireland and you often find that children are frequently addressed in a combination of both parents' names. Growing up I often found myself called by my full name all rolled into one. 'How ya doin' Moyabrennan?'

My mother goes by the name 'Baba'. It was something she'd called herself as a child and somehow it had stuck. It made it easier for people to differentiate between her and her own mother – my Gran Duggan.

Knowing what I know now, there must also have been a certain anxiety mixed with the lighter spirit of my mother's return to Gweedore. For the first time she was going home as a married woman, with me and my brother Ciarán, a babe in arms.

As a young girl I loved to hear my parents tell the story of how they eloped to be married – Mammy still slightly bashful, and Daddy still glowing with pride at the claiming of his bride.

My mother was the eldest daughter of Hugh and Máire Duggan. Both were teachers, and he, being the local headmaster, was highly regarded and bestowed with a great deal of respect and honour by the people of the area. Although it wasn't common for a country family, it had always been expected that their daughter would go off to further education. Then the world would be her oyster and one day she would bring back to Donegal a love for learning that would infuse the next generation. No one expected that in her early twenties she would fall in love with a musician and secretly marry. Still, in many ways she had her own father to blame for the untimely introduction to her sweetheart.

Hugh Duggan was a great socialiser who enjoyed the odd tipple and many's the time my mother was sent to retrieve him from the pub where he whiled away the hours ensconced in lively debates and listening to the local musicians do their turns. One young lad – Leo Brennan – was a particular favourite. He had come to the area with his parents' band and they rented a large house at the bottom of the road, not far from one of Hugh Duggan's favourite haunts. Often came the call . . .

'Leo, Hugh Duggan's up at the pub asking for the boy with the accordion, hurry up, don't keep him waiting.'

So Leo Brennan would drop what he was doing and go play. He loved an audience and especially warmed to the man called Hughie who would love to hear the old songs.

One such time Máire Duggan was up at the house, watching the clock, fearing for the meal getting cold.

'Baba, go find your father from the pub, tell him his dinner will be ruined if he doesn't get here soon.'

So off my mother went, the half mile down the hill to retrieve her beloved father. But before she could drag him away, much to her embarrassment, he insisted she sing one of his favourite songs, 'Danny Boy', with Leo accompanying her. And there, as in the traditions of all great love stories, Leo's and Baba's eyes met. It was the beginning of a great romance.

Of course the idea of the headmaster's daughter with a showband musician was slightly frowned upon. So as it happened, my mother was sent off to Dublin, post haste, to continue her education, leaving the love-sick Leo to pour his heart into songs of loss and woe.

But sometimes, some things are just meant to be. Cupid's arrow was well and truly embedded and it wasn't long before Leo took off to Dublin to claim Baba as his bride.

One thing I learned from an early age about my grandparents was their constant love, acceptance and inclination to put 'family' above all else. Mammy has always been quick to tell me how her parents, once they recognised her mind was made up about Leo, soon accepted him into the family. Though Leo was not the teacher or the lawyer or doctor the Duggans might have hoped for their daughter, they secretly admired him for his musical prowess, his art and free spirit, and quickly grew to love him as a son. In fact I am told that there was a time when Hugh Duggan would not go anywhere without his son-in-law to drive him. Along the way they would swap stories, sing songs and generally put the world to right, enjoying each other's company. In many ways Leo Brennan was a great catch. He became the leader of the family band that his parents had started, The Slieve Foy, which became a popular show band, and I guess my grandparents could see the light in my mother's eyes as she watched him perform, sometimes joining him on stage. She was, and still is, a beautiful piano player and singer and I've always loved sitting alongside my mother as she leads the choir in the chapel in Gweedore.

My grandfather, though he didn't play a note, had music in his head. He was passionate about the arts, music, story-telling and folklore and it was a love he nurtured in all his charges. As soon as I was old enough to go to school I'd walk down the path from my parents' house and in through the back door of my grandparents', which was also the local school house. By the time I'd been at school for two years we were moved out of their house to a smart new purpose-built place, but it was still no more than one hundred yards from our house. It smelt of paint and new wood, but still it felt like home, because Gran and Gog were there. Everyone in the immediate family knew my grandfather as 'Gog'. At three years old it was the nearest I could get to saying 'Grandfather' and somehow the name stuck. I didn't get any special dispensation in class for being their granddaughter –

many's the time I had the ruler slapped over my knuckles for misbehaviour. They treated everyone equally and their warmth, enthusiasm and inventiveness for our learning made everyone's National School days a delight.

There were just two classrooms in the school. In one my grandmother taught both junior and senior infants and first and second class. Then you moved into my grandfather's class for years three to six. Both rooms had high ceilings and huge fire places. Gog made up the fire each morning and we all had to take turns to bring in the peat. There we'd sit, two by two, our desks linked by the seating bench – twenty to thirty empty vessels waiting to be filled with knowledge, eager to learn, our scrubbed faces reddened in the fire light and our nostrils filled with the smell of earth.

I loved being in Gran Duggan's class. She was a gentle, softly spoken lady, slim, with wavy brown hair that was always neatly groomed. She was special to me, of course, because she was my Gran, but all the children warmed to her twinkling eyes, gentle smile and seemingly endless patience in helping us to understand something. She would often have us sewing, making things or doing little dramas. Every year both classes would join together for a drama or music production which we put on in the local hall. Once we did a Gaelic version of Snow White. It was my first time on stage. I was, of course, Snow White. Our language was Gaelic. That's what we spoke at home and school. In many ways back then it was considered a 'poor man's language'. Some areas in the West of Ireland have always remained strong Gaeltachts – where Irish is the main spoken language – and these days they are treasured by those who recognise the wealth of Ireland's precious culture.

Gog's classroom fascinated me. It was the larger of the two rooms with a big blackboard along one wall and a large globe on my grandfather's desk. I would spend ages turning the globe, dreaming of all the places, imagining far-off people in far-off lands. As for most children at that time, my world was a small place. We didn't have a car in the early days and rarely strayed beyond the perimeters of the house. We didn't need to. My two uncles, Pádraig and Noel, were only a couple of years older than me and they were my main playmates. Then, throughout my early years, there was always a new brother or sister in the house. There was plenty of open space and a myriad of adventures to be had just outside the front door.

My grandfather was quite unique in his belief about teaching in those days. Years later people tell me how they learnt so much more than basic education in his classes. Music wasn't taught in schools at that time. There was great pressure to teach and mould children with strong academic skills to embrace the modern world, but my grandfather balanced this with his love of music, Greek mythology and the heritage of our land. Hundreds of years before, Ireland was full of travelling Bards. These men would roam the countryside, going from village to village, sharing stories and songs. That was one of the ways folklore and music were passed around, and our land has developed a world-renowned wealth of rich stories. My grandfather loved and treasured that kind of thing and I remember every year he would invite one of these story-tellers into the school. We never really knew who he was or where he had come from. He never arrived in a car, so I assume he just walked around from place to place. I think Gog recognised him as one of a dying breed, so he would always allow us the treat of listening to this man as he shared stories and taught us new songs and rhymes.

Outside school the stories would continue. Gog loved nothing better than to gather his grandchildren round him to listen to his tales. He would sit in his big chair in the front room and fill our heads with stories of roguery. The tales were usually based on people getting up to no good. One of his favourites, that I heard him tell many a time, was of the farmer and the three rogues.

One day Paddy was heading to the fair. There were three rogues in town who knew he was taking his best cow to the market. So the first fella meets him and says, 'That's a great goat you have there, Paddy.'

Paddy, in astonishment, says, 'That's not a goat, it's a cow.' Paddy goes on his way and soon he meets the next fella.

'How' ya Paddy, that's a great looking goat you got there.'

'What do you mean a goat? It's a cow!' says Paddy, this time beginning to wonder himself. As Paddy gets nearer the town he meets the third rogue.

'Ah, Paddy, what do you want for that goat, I'll take it off yer hands,' he says. Paddy starts looking at the cow. Now he's thinking, well three people say it's a goat, and I don't want to make a fool of myself at the market. So Paddy decides to sell the cow to the man. Obviously he only gets a third of the price of what he would for a cow.

Eventually Paddy goes home to his wife and tells her the story. '... When I met the first fella, then the second, then the third fella, I really got to thinking that perhaps it was a goat.'

'You're the silly old goat,' his wife scolds. There are three rogues in town and you've been well and truly done by them.'

So Paddy starts to think. He goes back into town where he sees the three fellas.

'Oh you made a real idiot out of me,' he says.

'Ah well, Paddy, a deal's a deal.'

'OK,' he says. 'Well, I'm just here to buy some shoes.'

He'd already been into the cobblers and paid for a pair of shoes, but knowing the three fellas are watching he goes into the shop, chooses some shoes and says, 'Yes, I'll take these please.' With that he waves his hat and the cobbler says, 'OK, Paddy, they're paid for, see ya next time.'

Now the fellas, seeing this, are quite astonished.

Next thing, Paddy calls them over and invites them to eat with him in the local restaurant. He's gathered together his wife and his friends and orders a huge feast. Everyone eats their fill and when they are done Paddy waves his hat and the restaurant owner says, 'Thank you Paddy, that's paid for.'

By now the boys' curiosity about the hat is getting the better of them.

Meanwhile Paddy has secretly arranged with his friend to put some sheep's blood in a skin under his jacket. When they get outside Paddy and his friend start arguing. As the three rogues look on, Paddy pulls out a knife and sticks it into his friend. Of course the friend falls on the floor and there is blood everywhere.

'He's really in trouble now,' say the three fellas to each

11

other. But no, Paddy takes off his hat, waves it over his friend and his friend gets up again, perfectly well.

The three fellas are so amazed and plead with Paddy to sell them the hat.

'Oh no,' says Paddy, 'the hat's not for sale.' But the fellas are persistent, so Paddy enters into lengthy negotiations and finally settles on a good price for the hat.

The fellas go away happy with their prize and go off to order a huge banquet. Then one of them takes a sword and pushes it into his friend. 'It's OK,' he says, and starts waving the hat. Of course nothing happens. The man dies and the other two are taken off to jail. So Paddy gets his own back!

My grandfather would laugh and laugh at the end of the story. It was one of our favourites. Not all of them were so gruesome, but they usually ended with people getting the come-uppance they deserved. I suppose in a way they reflected another very striking feature of my grandfather's character. He always stood up for the underdog and for certain rights to be upheld. With a keen interest in public affairs he was both a member of the Donegal County Council and Chairman of the Western Board. He campaigned to keep the local railway going and tried to provide jobs for the people on Tory – the bleak island inhabited by less than one hundred and fifty people, just off the coast of Donegal.

There were always people in my grandparents' house. The parish priest Father Bonar was a regular visitor and he and Gog would debate for hours about religion. Gog read loads of books, many of them exploring and questioning his faith. I remember he would rile against many of the religious practices. Many a time I'd hear him say to my grandmother, 'Pray directly to God, he'll hear you. You don't always need to intercede through the saints.'

Gog was passionate about prayer. One of my biggest regrets is that I never got to share with him my own experience of faith and religious freedom. I owe so many of the good things in my life to my grandfather's influence and I always remember his wisdom and gentleness, especially now when I perform the old hymn 'Be Thou My Vision', which he translated into Irish.

One of the other men that would frequent my grandfather's

sitting-room was the King of Tory. I loved to hear Gog recount the stories this man brought. I suppose he was a Robin Hood-type character. They called him the 'Uncrowned King of Tory' because of all the good works he did for the people there. Tory lies approximately twelve miles out in the Atlantic. It is easily seen from the north coast of Donegal, but woe betide anyone who tries that short sea crossing without knowledge of its depths and volatile currents. I was always fascinated by the fact that fishermen who worked these waters never learned to swim. Better that they died quickly if they fell overboard than suffer trying to fight the overpowering might of the ice-cold, unforgiving waters.

Very little grows on Tory. Maybe a little turf, but otherwise it is just a big rock with a lighthouse at one end. The King of Tory lived there when life was very basic and bleak, but somehow he always managed to keep himself and his people just above the level of basic existence. He was a real mischievous character, a rogue in every sense of the word, which is what made him so fascinating to me as a young girl. He would make frequent visits to Dublin where he would meet with investors or large stores, convincing them that he owned a large shipping company or hotel. He would persuade them to invest large amounts of money, and the stores would have furniture – beds, tables, chairs – all packed up, supposedly for his hotels. Invariably he would go on a Friday, pay by cheque, take the goods, and of course by Monday morning, when the store came to cash the cheque, he was long gone. No shipping company, no hotel, no money. Everything he could get was taken back to Tory and divided among the people. He was a clever man and somehow always seemed to cover his tracks. It is said that the postman and the locals knew him by several different identities, depending on who was looking for him.

I remember, when I was older, going to visit him one time on the island. Tory is the kind of community where everyone knows who's who and what's going on. I have relations there whom I still occasionally visit if the weather and tide allow. The funny thing is that by the time I get from the little pier up the cobbled street hill to their house, Jenny already knows I've arrived on the island and am on my way. People look out for each other and news of any stranger whips round the community faster than the Atlantic wind.

Visiting the King of Tory was something of an honour for me. He was a gracious character, loved by his people for all the kindness he showed them. For all his big antics, he was a small, rather spindly looking man with a sad face. I think he regretted some things in life. I remember he showed me a picture of his wife – a beautiful woman who died young – and I was struck by the thought that he believed she deserved better than the life he could give her.

Yes, the King of Tory, the parish priest, the passing story-teller and many other characters, would all keep my grandfather's repertoire of stories alive. Little did we know that their influence would be a foundation on which to build our music.

# Chapter 2

Our house stands just behind my grandparents' home. When we moved back from Dublin it was nothing but an outhouse in Gog and Gran Duggan's garden. But there were plenty of people happy to lend a helping hand and it wasn't long before a basic structure was built that would be the Brennan family home. In no time at all there was a sitting-room, my parents' bedroom and a little kitchen out the back. As the family grew, so did the house.

We'd not been in the house a year when another little brother, Pól, came along. Being the baby of the family, he slept in the cot in Mammy's and Daddy's room while Ciarán and I spent our early years sharing a bed in the living-room. By day it was a sofa and we loved it when Mammy and Daddy had visitors in the evening because it meant we had to stay up until they left.

I clearly remember the day the builders turned up to work on our extension – Jimmy McBride, Lucky Phaddy Jimmy and Michael McGee. There was lots of smoking, laughter and leaning on spades and Mammy seemed to spend the entire day making tea and sandwiches. Slowly but surely they built another two bedrooms, a bigger kitchen and a little bathroom. It was a huge undertaking and very exciting for Ciarán and me to watch. In a way it was the end of an era – I still have rather fond memories of the Saturday night bath tub in front of the fire. I always went first, followed by the boys. For the rest of the week Mammy used to make us scrub our necks, hands and knees at the kitchen sink.

Ciarán and I moved into the first bedroom while the building work was still going on. It was exciting to be in the new part of the house, with the smell of mortar and dust and the half-painted breeze blocks. It was one big adventure. I was about six years old

15

at the time and Ciarán would have been nearly five. We weren't often allowed sweets – only occasionally on a Sunday after chapel when Daddy would bring some back in a little paper bag with the Sunday newspaper. One particular night, however, I thought I knew where there was a sweet jar. I tiptoed out of our bedroom and into the living-room. All was quiet, except for the muffled voices of Mammy and Daddy talking with Gran and Gog outside the kitchen door. I tiptoed over to the dresser, climbed up on the armchair and reached up to where I'd seen Mammy hide the jar of colourful little sweets. Scampering back to our bedroom I gave one out to Ciarán.

'Two for you and two for me. That's all for now,' I said, in my best Mammy voice.

Then one slipped out of the jar and rolled across the bedclothes. Ciarán snapped it up.

'OK, then I have to have another one to make it equal.'

As I tipped the jar, two sweets came jostling out. That meant Ciarán had to have another one as well, followed by another for me. By then it was getting funny. Each time I tipped the bottle, more sweets would fall out and so it went on until the bottle was empty and we'd divided the contents between the two of us.

The sweets tasted bitter, but they looked good as they kept escaping into the bedclothes. It seemed as though they were alive as we jostled and kicked and it became a game to catch them quickly and push them in our mouths. We laughed and laughed until we were dizzy.

The next morning was Sunday. Mammy came in to wake us as usual and found the jar of Junior Aspirin completely empty and me and Ciarán in a deep sleep. Mammy shouted at Daddy to go fetch Gog. He was up at the house like a shot, followed closely by my Uncle Eoin, the eldest boy in the Duggan family.

I awoke in terror, choking on Gog's fingers as he tried to push them down my throat, all the time shouting at me to wake up. I was confused and frightened and could see Uncle Eoin doing the same to Ciarán. Gasping for air I tried to call for Mammy, but she was nowhere to be seen. It turned out she and Daddy had gone off to chapel. Sunday Mass was never missed and I'm sure they went that morning to pray for our lives, knowing little else to do. When they returned Ciarán and I were still vomiting the pills. All I wanted to do was go back to sleep, but Gog and uncle Eoin wouldn't leave us alone. Every time we thought we could be sick no more they'd force their fingers down our throats again in desperate attempts to clear the poison from our bodies.

Looking back now it's a wonder we even survived. We had taken the whole jar of Junior Aspirins. There was no being rushed to hospital in those days either. I remember one time hurting myself very badly. The council in those days would leave old tar barrels at the side of the road. They were large metal things with a big 'V' shape cut in the middle. This particular day my twin uncles, Pádraig and Noel, had dragged a barrel into our garden, pinched themselves a plank of wood from the building area behind our house and made a seesaw. Great fun. I was dying to have a go. However, being somewhat smaller than the boys and more eager than my own strength allowed, it wasn't long before I came off the plank, landing myself right in the centre of the open barrel, ripping my leg on its jagged edge. In that moment time stood still. I didn't cry. I was in shock. I don't remember what happened to my uncles, perhaps they went running to fetch Gog, but I limped over to our house.

'Mammy,' I said feebly, at the kitchen door.

When my mother turned around her face so instantly filled with horror that it frightened me. By that time my leg was gushing with blood and it seemed like the world went into total panic. My leg started to throb with pain. Then came the tears. Big heart-wrenching, streaming-down-the-cheek sobs.

I don't remember exactly what happened next, but since I have no recollection of doctors or hospitals I guess my grandfather must have patched me up. He always knew what to do. He had three huge medical books – *The Household Physician* vols 1 and 2, and *Harmsworth's Home Doctor* – that he always consulted. Some of the descriptions in them frightened me, but I was always intrigued by them and couldn't help taking a peek when I was able to reach them off the shelf.

Another time when I was slightly older we were staying with Gran and Gog while our parents were with the Slieve Foy in Glasgow for the St Patrick's Day celebrations. It was the day they were due home and much was the anticipation among us children about what delights they might bring back. I was playing with a huge ball of string in the garden, letting it roll down the stone steps into the kitchen. No sooner had I touched on the second step down when my foot got entangled in the string and I found myself hurtling towards the hard kitchen floor, head first. I hit the floor with a thud and, for a few moments, the world turned silent. Then, in no time, Gog was there, scooping me up into his arms as the kitchen filled with commotion. Gran made me drink warm milk while Gog fixed me on his knee to clean and press together the gash in my head. Ciarán and Pól made much fun taunting me that they would get all the sweets Mammy and Daddy would bring. After the initial shock my head really started to sting, but as I flinched from Gog's hold he employed his most useful tactic – distraction.

'Now Máire, you just weren't concentrating, were you? And you know what that can mean. It reminds me of that time I found the leprechaun and his pot of gold at the end of the rainbow.' I smiled up at Gog. I'd heard this story before, but my brothers and I were always fascinated by it. We didn't quite know whether it was true, but our young imaginations still preferred to believe every tale our grandfather recanted to us.

'I'd followed the rainbow all day and there he was, the cheeky leprechaun sitting on his crock of gold. It was all gleaming and bright and shining in all the different colours, but you know the little rogue, he wouldn't let me anywhere near it.'

We listened with wide-eyed wonder as Gog continued the story.

'That's the thing about leprechauns, Máire. You see, they know you're after their gold. And you mustn't take your eyes off him for a second, not even to blink or he'll vanish. And that's what happened that day with me. That cheeky little leprechaun started dancing around and singing and running about the place so fast that he made me dizzy and before I knew it, I'd taken my eyes off him. Whoosh! They were gone – the crock of gold, the leprechaun, the rainbow – they all vanished into thin air.'

Gog released me from his knee just as his tale came to an end.

'I'm going to look for that leprechaun next time I see a rainbow,' exclaimed Pól.

'Don't be silly,' said Ciarán, 'there's no such thing.'

I looked at Pól's distressed face. 'Shut up Ciarán,' I said, 'of course there is. Everyone knows that if you chase a rainbow and find the crock of gold, all your dreams will come true.'

Just then Mammy and Daddy came in through the door. Mammy fussed around me like a mother hen when she saw my head but it didn't hurt anymore and I was keen to hear of their adventures in Scotland. As expected, there were sweets for us all and Mammy made sure I got my fair share.

Daddy spent a lot of our childhood going off to play music. The show band was very popular and when he wasn't busy with them, there was always a string of people queuing up to book Daddy and his accordion for their party or wedding reception. At the time I guess we just thought everybody's Daddy did that kind of thing, but it must have been tough on Mammy. When you live in Gweedore, getting to most other places constitutes a long journey, even now when the roads are in a better state (anyone who visits there will probably laugh at the idea that the roads today are considered 'good'). So it wasn't unusual to find Daddy leaving early in the afternoon for an evening's dance. He travelled all over Ireland and invariably wouldn't arrive home until after four o'clock in the morning.

One morning when he came in – it can't have been much later than 5 a.m. – he woke me up. Pulling myself around from my sleep all I could see was the huge grin on Daddy's face and excitement in his eyes.

'Guess what, Máire,' he said. 'Last night when I was at the dance they were selling little babies and I got a little girl for you to play with.'

With wide-eyed wonder I let Daddy lead me out of my bed, imagining the scene at the dance – shelves of babies and Daddy there pointing, saying, 'Can I have a look at that wee girl?'

'Sshh, go quietly now,' said Daddy, as he carefully pushed open the door to my parents' room. Mammy was laying on the bed holding a tiny bundle in her arms, all wrapped up in Pól's baby blanket. I stared and stared at the little pink sleeping face.

'Ah, Daddy,' I said, 'she's a lovely one. How much was she?'

'Two and six,' he replied.

So entered into the Brennan household my sister Deirdre. It was lovely to have another girl. My circle of playmates up until then had consisted of my two uncles and two brothers. There are six years between me and Deirdre, but throughout our childhood we were best friends and in those years I couldn't have imagined how my little sister would have to look after me in our adult life.

In the first sixteen years of my life Mammy blessed the family with five more children. After myself, Ciarán, Pól and Deirdre came Leon, Olive, Eithne, Bartley and Brídín. There never seemed to be any fuss about Mammy being pregnant. She'd just get on with things, looking after us with the help of Gran Duggan and Auntie Bríd. Pól, Deirdre and Leon were born at home in what is now the music room. Both grandmothers were on hand as midwives when Leon was born. He was a big baby and seemingly it was a very difficult birth. There was much excitement among us, but in truth it had more to do with the fact that Gog had just taken delivery of a television. It was probably the first one in Gweedore and we were all absolutely fascinated to see the fizz and pop of the picture as Uncle Eoin and Uncle Columba set about putting the aerial up on the roof. Meanwhile, in the middle of this excitement and commotion poor Mammy was struggling in the full force of childbirth. Finally the job was done . . . we drew the curtains and settled down to an episode of *Wells Fargo*.

By the time Eithne, Olive and Bartley were born I thought I was really smart. I knew that when Mammy went off to the hospital she'd come back with another brother or sister. I was sixteen when Brídín was born. By then Mammy shared more openly with me about the pregnancy and I knew she relied on my help looking after the others while she was in hospital. Of course at sixteen I could have even been a mother myself, but we didn't talk about those kinds of things. We led a very sheltered, innocent life. Growing up in Donegal was free and safe.

We were, and still are, a very close family. There was never room for arguments or jealousy. We all doted on Brídín, being the baby. I, being the eldest, took on a motherly role, especially with the younger ones. I was also quite bossy at times.

I look back on hours and hours of playing together. In my memory the sun was always high in the sky and the days were long and warm. It's amazing really when I think of it now. Donegal is the most northern peninsula of Ireland – not exactly renowned for its fine weather. At any time of year, even midsummer, a front will stir in the Atlantic, with little predictability, bringing harsh winds and lashing rain. Any wonder that most of the land is fit for little other than bog-growing turf!

But that is not the memory of my childhood. They were good days. My birthday is in August and the sun always seemed to shine. From the beginning of the school holidays I looked forward to my party. My brothers and sisters all joined in and some of my school friends came around, all dressed in their party frocks with ribbons in their hair. Bella McGee, Margaret Sweeny, Bríd McGee, Sadie Diver – they were my main school mates. Then I had 'summer' friends, Mary McBride, who didn't go to my school, and Máire Lee whose parents brought her every summer to spend the holidays in Gweedore. When she turned up, it was a sign that the holidays had really begun. In those days there were no magicians or puppets or trips to theme parks or McDonalds. We simply played out in our garden. Of course there would be presents, that was the important bit, and Mammy always made a special tea with a birthday cake and candles to blow out my age.

It was lovely to have friends at the house. Usually it was just us brothers and sisters and Pádraig and Noel. There were no other houses near ours and families didn't have cars to ferry children around the way they do now. Still, we didn't need much. We had our freedom, our imaginations and each other. We were always inventing things. We played at houses and shops and pretended we were lost camping up in the mountains. Gran Duggan used to keep chickens and one of my favourite things was to collect the eggs and put them in my pretend shop. Aunt Bríd then had to come and buy them from me with imaginary money. That was my own special game, just me and Aunt Bríd. Sometimes we would all trek part way up the mountain at the back of our house. It was a delight to take off our boots and feel the soft peaty ground beneath bare feet as the wild heather tickled between our toes. I guess it could have been dangerous with the bogs, but we never came to much harm.

Most families had their own piece of bogland for the turf. Every summer it would be cultivated, then left to dry, ready to be stored for fuel in the winter months. On good days all the family would go up the track behind the house and dig at the land. The men worked bare-backed and at the end of the day Mammy would rub cream on their sunburnt skin. The bog lands were rife with little streams and we would fish for tiddlers using sticks. Of course our catches weren't large, but sometimes there'd be a fish that was big enough to cook on the fire the men made. It was the tastiest fish ever. We always took a pan up there to boil water in. The water was taken straight from the streams and the tea it made was wonderful. There was nothing like it – Mammy's sandwiches and fresh-caught fish, washed down with rich, peaty tea.

It was hard work for the adults, but there was lots of laughter as they worked. Everybody mucked in: uncles, cousins, local families. The turf was stacked up in blocks of ten or twelve and left to dry. Later in the year the family would rent a tractor and load up the dried turf. We all wanted to ride on the tractor down to the old garage where the turf was stacked. The smell in there was rich and pungent. A heady mix of earth and sweat, it spoke to us of comfort and security. The turf was in and the family would enjoy roaring fires throughout the winter.

As the colder, dark days drew in we still had plenty to occupy our minds. We'd spend a lot of time at Gran and Gog's house. Aunt Bríd – Mammy's younger sister – lives there. Bríd never married and to this day she treats us as her own. She is a hairdresser and in those days there'd always be a string of women visiting the house for their weekly wash, set and gossip. We would be upstairs and we used to peep down through the floorboards into the room where the women performed their rituals. Their conversation was always about births, deaths, marriages or the weather. 'Poor Maggie down the road, the fags'll kill 'er yet and have yer heard about Mary? Oh, that son of hers, shocking 'tis . . .'

Every night we had 'radio'. It was a human radio in the girls' room. We would all sing a song and as it finished you had to carry on straight into another one. You couldn't run out of songs. You just kept going, each one of us taking the lead as a song came to mind. Then, when we were close to exhausting our repertoire or Mammy had come in to tell us to go to sleep, we would end the session with a little jingle – 'And that's all for tonight'. We had to sing that on cue and in harmony and I remember getting very cross if one of the girls didn't get it right. I suppose I could be a bit of a bully with them. I needed the show to be exact and finish right on cue. If it didn't, I'd make them do it again.

One of the best things about winter was coming in from the cold to Mammy's chicken soup. There wasn't a lot of money, but we always had a pot of something ready. Being so many of us we'd usually have a couple of sittings at the table, except on Sunday. Sunday was very important in our house and we'd all cram around the table for the roast. There'd always be loads of fluffy white potatoes and cabbage and gravy. Daddy would give thanks to God and it would be one of those special family times – lots of noise and chatter, all trying to talk at once, Mammy laughing at our stories as she told us not to talk with our mouths full. We all had to take our part in the cooking and clearing up and with Mammy's encouragement the girls became good cooks. I only remember Daddy cooking once or twice – he made wonderful sweet omelettes.

When it came to culinary delights we'd look forward to visits from Uncle Eoin, Mammy's younger brother. In 1962 he'd gone to sea as a radio officer and it was always a treat when he came home. He would bring strange things from far-off lands. I remember one time he brought spaghetti and rice and we all stood around the cooker watching as he showed us how to cook it.

The chore we hated most was the washing. It was the girls' job and we all had to take turns. The wash tub was outside. It was a huge old tub with a hand wringer. I remember struggling with the heavy wet washing until my back ached and my fingers were raw with cold after hanging them on the line. Then there was the ironing, loads of it, all done on the kitchen table. Even with eleven of us in the family Mammy was determined we would all be well presented. It was a chore and there was little getting out of it, but it was a good apprenticeship. Mammy is a stickler for doing a job properly.

The winters could be long and harsh, but looking back now I don't remember any misery in our household. There was always Christmas to look forward to; then, after Lent, came Easter. Before we knew it, the spring flowers were popping up in our garden and it wasn't long before the heather was back in bloom up on the bogland. Lent was an important time in the Brennan home. It meant giving up something. I think we felt special that we were grown-up enough to do what the adults were doing.

They usually gave up sugar in tea, butter on bread, or some other such 'nicety'. In our case it was usually sweets. Great Aunt Sarah from Calhame used to bring us bars of chocolate and all kinds of goodies from her family shop. We'd love her to visit, but when she came during Lent the sweet delights would have to go into a box until Easter Day. Good Friday was also an important day. The grown-ups would fast, then eat fish in the evening. Everything closed and we weren't allowed to run around or make much noise from midday until three o'clock in the afternoon. We'd all go to church together and do the Stations of the Cross, remembering the path that Jesus took on the way to his crucifixion. I was fascinated by the pictures and sad that Jesus had to die. Then we'd all line up – grown-ups and children – to kiss Jesus' feet. The statue of Jesus was mounted up on the wall and Daddy had to lift each of us up to kiss his feet. I'd look at his sad eyes, nails through his hands and red blood trickling down his face. Sometimes it made me want to cry.

Come Easter Day, we'd be up early tucking into our sweet boxes. The whole day was a celebration. We'd all dress up and go to chapel. The marching fife bands would be out and after mass we'd follow them. Mammy would go straight home to prepare the roast, so when we got home it was there on the table. Then we'd go out following the bands again for the rest of the day. Sometimes Mammy would come too. I loved that. She looked so graceful, marching along, smiling and singing.

*As down the glen one Easter morn*
*To a city fair rode I . . .*

The next big event was our annual summer holiday. We'd go for a day to Bundoran. I suppose you could say it was like a Blackpool equivalent in Donegal. There wasn't the huge pleasure beach or anything, but there were amusement arcades and a few children's rides. I loved the merry-go-round and the helter-skelter. We'd save our pennies all year and as the day grew closer we were beside ourselves with excitement. Daddy often arranged to play at a wedding in the area. We'd all turn up at a church and have to sit in the car while Daddy played in the service. It was desperate. The time just seemed to be endless as we waited for him to come out and take us the rest of the journey to the delights of the sea and amusement arcades. Finally the church bells would start to ring. Ah, that wonderful, sacred sound that signalled to us that the service was over and our pleasure was about to begin. Within minutes, the bride and groom would come out, followed by a mass of smiling people in their finery. We'd all laugh at the ladies in big hats and men in uncomfortable shoes. For a moment my imagination was caught. I pictured myself in a big white dress, flowers in my hair and my sisters all in pink bridesmaid dresses. But the moment was soon over. Daddy jumped in the car, giving us the accordion for our knees, and we were off towards Bundoran. Daddy would then leave us there all afternoon while he went back to play at the wedding party.

I must have been eleven or twelve the last time we went on this family outing. There'd be seven of us children, plus Gran Harden or Gran Duggan, one of whom always came along. I don't know how we all got into the old Austin car, but somehow we managed.

Gran Harden was loads of fun. She was Daddy's mother. Now you may wonder why she's not called Brennan. The truth is, my father wasn't really a Brennan by rights. Gran married a Brennan and had three girls and a boy. Then she remarried a Harden and had three boys and a girl. The first to come along from that second marriage was my father. In those days people used to take a baby to be baptised straight away. I'm sure Gran Harden was there, but being weak from the birth, it fell on her elder children to take care of the official business. The baby was to be named Leo. That was the only discussion regarding the name, so of course, without thinking, the Brennan girls took their new brother and registered him with their surname. My father grew up Leo Harden, but when he planned to get married himself and needed his birth certificate he discovered the name he was legally given. He has remained Leo Brennan ever since.

Gran Harden was a totally different type of grandparent to Gran and Gog Duggan. Her husband died when I was still very young and she went off to America where two of her daughters had emigrated. When she came back I was about seven years old. She was going to stay with us for a while and I was delighted when she ended up sharing my bedroom. We had loads of fun together and I will always remember her insisting we go all the way up to Sligo to buy my First Communion dress. Gran Harden always had cod liver oil and a glass of orange juice, followed by a glass of hot water in the morning. To me she was very grand. I knew Gran Harden had come from England and she was very different to everyone else in my world. She had some beautiful jewellery and loved the fine things in life. When she later moved in with her youngest daughter, Rosemarie, who lived just down the road, she would still visit regularly. 'Ooh look, Máire, I can still touch my toes,' she'd say, and down she'd go with her fingertips almost touching the floor. She was very fit, having spent most of her life as a dancer. Later on she also ended up playing the drums in the family band.

Gran Harden had a wonderful approach to life. I suppose I inherited some of her nature, her love of performing and being on stage. Music ran deep in the veins of the family on both sides. In one sense our future had a certain inevitability about it; though in many ways, it was a future we hadn't even dreamt about.

# Chapter 3

'Máire, Máire, come quickly, there's somebody wants you at the back door,' Mammy shouted. She was excited and smiling and I knew something good would be afoot. I loved to see Mammy's face light up with her big broad smile and twinkling eyes. I jumped out of bed and ran through to the kitchen. There, with its head sticking around the kitchen door, eating cream crackers, was a beautiful donkey. He'd been left behind by some travelling tinkers and he instantly became a much loved member of the family. We named him Neddy. Our new playmate opened up a whole realm of new games. Now we could really get down to the business of cowboys and Indians. The boys would climb up on Neddy's back, but I, being the squaw, was always the one being tied up to the washing pole.

Our house in those early years was something of a menagerie. Along with Neddy, we also had a goat and there was always a variety of cats and dogs at the back door. Somehow they just used to arrive. The first cat that came along was a big black moggy. I can't remember how we first came by him, but he was adored by all the children and was the only one ever allowed in the house. His name was Peewee and I suspect he was the father of the many cats that came after him. The goat was the biggest nuisance. She ate everything in sight and we were forever having to rescue some item of clothing she had pulled from the washing line. The stream of dogs was pretty much continuous. I suppose it helped in that we didn't get too attached to them. Our house, though in what you might call a remote setting, is on a main road and the dogs were always running out and getting knocked over as cars went flying past.

Consequently there were a lot of funerals in my childhood. We had a little graveyard at the side of the house where we buried all the deceased pets and any other dead animal we might have come across. We'd go through a huge ceremony of crying and singing songs. Despite our tender years we knew about death. In Irish Catholic families – especially in the country – a body is rarely sent to a funeral home. Rather, the deceased vessel of a loved one is brought back to the family home and displayed in its coffin in the best room of the house. Some families – especially in years gone by – had a room especially reserved for deaths or visits from the priest. Everyone in the area, children and grown-ups alike, is invited to pay their respects. They pray over the coffin, then some kiss the cheek of the poor deceased. This was always a big cause of intrigue and fear for us children. Would you dare to kiss the body? I went many times to a wake with my mother. It was a large parish and there was always someone dying. As the women made the tea the men would have the odd glass of whiskey and prepare to stay up all night. That was always the tradition – it was just something the menfolk did – all in the name of respect for the dead, of course.

Every time we buried an animal we'd go through the pretend ritual of a mass. Whether it be one of the dogs or just a dead bird we'd found, we gathered together as many of the clan as possible for the funeral parade. It was very important to do the right thing. Somehow we thought it would be blasphemous to say the words of a mass so we would follow the form, but not say the real words. We had our own language. It was complete gobbledygook. Similarly with the songs, we'd sing the melodies, but the words were not real. We often played at going to mass. Of course, one of my brothers would have to be the priest and the rest of us, along with an assortment of animals and stuffed toys, would be the faithful parishioners.

Everyone around our way was Catholic. All the kids went to mass; you weren't allowed to miss it. Every Sunday morning, and whenever it was a holy day (there were many), we would pile into the car and Daddy would drive us up the mountain-side to the little chapel in Mín a Bhaoill. A simple structure made from sheets of green painted corrugated iron, its grandeur is purely in the warmth of its people. The service starts at ten o'clock, but we used to get there early to chat and meet with other people of the area. When it was time for the mass to begin we would go down to the front. There before us was the altar and the priest's chair, with a statue of the dying Jesus mounted on the right-hand side of the wall and the Virgin Mother on the left. In the early days the mass was in Latin, but when Pope John XXIII decreed that people should worship in their own language – so they could understand it better – our mass was then conducted in Gaelic. The choir stood at the back of the church. A valiant crew, they were recruited and kept going by my mother. Music wasn't actively encouraged in church at that time, and many an evening I would go with Mammy and one of my other sisters to choir practice only to find one other of a small band of faithfuls there. But Mammy has always been one determined lady and year after year she would encourage and cajole some of the other parishioners until she built a fine choir that today goes from strength to strength. In fact, there are not many things in my life which make me more proud than being able to use my mother's choir on one of my recordings.

The first Holy Communion is an important milestone in the life of a young Irish Catholic. I was about eight years old when it came to mine. We took communion classes in school, learning the catechism, prayers and stories from the Bible, but I struggled to remember some of the prayers and all the rules of what you could and couldn't do. The idea was that if we learnt them by heart, we would understand what we were doing on the day of communion, but at eight years old it's hard for a girl to get beyond the distraction of the pretty dress you get to wear. Still, in later life I would appreciate the value of those daily lessons in religious instruction. At least as a world-weary adult, when I began to search for meaning in life, I knew where to look. Also, the discipline it gave was a good thing. We grew up with a strong sense of right and wrong. I think it's sad today that children don't seem to be taught these things. It is as though we have become scared to assert any sense of righteousness and our children suffer at the hand of moral liberality.

On the day of the first Holy Communion there was a great sense of celebration. Before you could take the sacrament you had to go to confession and say the Act of Contrition, a prayer about being sorry. It was nerve-racking, but we were well prepared with a list of our little sins in our heads, ready to recite by rote. It was a special day. You might get a couple of treats, sweets or a few pennies, but the excitement came from the sense of achievement. Growing up in church, I'd watched the big people line up waiting their turn with their tongues held out ready to receive the mysterious-looking wafer. Now it was my turn. No more staying in the pew. I was a grown-up, a fully fledged member of the Holy Catholic Church.

I'm not saying that my childhood religious practice was purely ritual. In fact I am certain that I had a strong innate sense of spirituality. When I remember the things that ran through my young mind I now recognise a certain sense of 'want', even in those early years. Perhaps it was something to do with the prayers of my grandparents and the sense of faith I recognised in Mammy and Daddy; or maybe the priest's special anointing when I was still very young. I was only six or seven years old when I developed some kind of fever. Despite my tender years I have always lived with the memory of the dreams. It was as though I were hallucinating. The dreams came fast, wild and jagged as my body burned. I can also quite clearly remember Father Moore's kind face as he came to anoint me with oil and pray over me. His prayers were warm and thoughtful. Some were from a prayer book, but Father Moore would also close his eyes with his gentle hands on my head and talk to God as if he was in the room with us. Father Moore wasn't our usual parish priest, but visited our house quite often, becoming a close friend of the family. I always thought of him as a very special, holy man.

I know that you shouldn't judge what is in people's hearts, but, sadly, the parish priest during most of my early years was about as far removed from Father Moore as you can imagine. Father Boyle was short and round. His bald head was white and his breath heavy. When he spoke, his voice was harsh. He didn't seem to like children. He was very strict and didn't approve of women who wore trousers. I remember one occasion when we spotted Father Boyle's car coming over from Crolly, we dived into a nearby ditch until he passed by so that he did not see our ungainly attire. When I got into my teenage years this became my little rendezvous with rebellion and I remember once going to a dance in a pair of the boys' pyjama bottoms that I had adapted into fashionable flared trousers. I thought I was the coolest girl in the parish!

Father Boyle literally put the fear of God into me. On one occasion, not long after my First Communion, he threw me out of the confession box in anger. It was always a scary thing going into the box. Trembling, I sat on the hard wooden bench, trying to remember my sins and the correct way to say the liturgy. Feeling Father Boyle's sharp, irritated breath through the holes in the partition veil, I clasped my shaking hands together in anguish as I confessed the biscuit I had stolen last Monday and the little lie I had told to protect Deirdre. It wasn't her fault. Neddy had distracted her at that crucial moment when the clothes were going through the wringer and, to our horror, Mammy's best white sheets had come tumbling down into the muddy puddle. Deirdre started crying, so I told Mammy it was Neddy that pulled the sheets out of the tub. When it came to say the Act of Contrition my mind just went blank. Father Boyle's breath became heavier and he barked at me to get out until I could learn to be a good Catholic girl and not make God angry.

I was so upset I cried all the way home. It took a lot of consoling from Gran Duggan to ease my distress. She was very understanding and from that day she took me with her to Ards where there was a monastery of Capuchin monks. It was there she found her own peace, refuge and a priesthood of compassion. I loved those special outings with Gran. The monastery was about thirty-five minutes' drive away, between Falcarragh and Cresslough. I always felt a tingle of anticipation at the point where we turned off the main road and started going up the winding track through the forest. I used to imagine all the creatures that lived there and the fairies and leprechauns that would come out to play at nightfall. Perhaps this was where the rainbows started. Before too long the trees cleared and there stood the beautiful old monastery, usually shrouded in sunlight. In my mind it had an aura of holiness, like the light that shone around the Virgin Mary in the pictures on Gran's wall. It was a place of security.

Thankfully my bad experience with Father Boyle did not sour my developing awareness of spirituality. Though I feared God, I also searched for him in my childlike way. I was never in any doubt that he heard me when I said my prayers, the way I was taught, from my prayer book. Yes, it was liturgy, but it was deeper than just a procedure I was compelled to undertake. My prayer book was all I knew. That's how you talked to God and I was sure he heard me. I remember organising some of my friends to go to the huge rock that stood just down the hill from our school. It was a strange-looking thing, long and in the shape of a 'V'. For some reason I identified it as a special place and I made the girls all kneel in a line and say prayers. When I was about nine years old I heard Aunt Bríd talking to Mammy about a girl not far from our home who had a visitation from the Virgin Mary. That afternoon I went off into the clump of trees beside our house. I took candles and a little vase with some very carefully picked flowers. There was a clearing in the middle of the trees and it was there that I set up my little shrine and read from my book in full expectancy that the Virgin Mother would visit me. She didn't appear, but I sat there until it grew cold and I heard Mammy calling us all in to tea.

The Virgin Mary was important to me. My grandfather's encouragement to pray directly to God, rather than through Mary, rang in my ears, but for me, especially in my younger years, I took great comfort in her being. I know that it is a criticism against Catholics that too much emphasis is put on the Blessed Virgin, but even today, when I have left much of my practice behind, I find it hard that little reverence is bestowed on her outside the Catholic Church, except perhaps at Christmas. Surely all mothers must share a certain empathy. Imagine being the mother of Jesus. Imagine the fear and uncertainty surrounding the birth. Imagine then watching your son grow only to see him die a cruel, harsh and unjust death. Jesus could have just appeared ready for his ministry at age thirty, but no, the Bible gives us a precious and glorious birth story. Why was it so important that God's son be born through a virgin woman? Surely it was because his birth was important, and there can be no other woman worthy of greater honour.

As a child, I loved dancing and music. I did Irish dancing from an early age, as did all the girls, but in my head I was a supreme ballet dancer, with my hair in a bun, a tutu frock and points on my toes. To say there wasn't much ballet in Gweedore is an understatement. I got all my ideas from my comics. It was always a big treat when Daddy would pick up his newspaper from the little shop down the road and bring me back a *Bunty* or a *Judy*. I absorbed myself in the ballet page. It set my imagination alight. I knew all the big-name dancers and used to dream of joining them on the stages in London, Paris and Moscow. I was mad about ballet. I think my parents thought I would forget about it, but my passion just grew and eventually they decided I could go for lessons. This was no mean undertaking. There was no one in the area who gave lessons and the nearest class we could find was out in Derry, Northern Ireland. Every second Saturday Daddy would take me on the three-hour journey to do my ballet class. We'd chat most of the way, Daddy telling his stories. My father has always been a great talker. As we drove along the back road past Dunlewey and out through the mountains he'd always tell me of his adventures in Glenveagh Castle. At that time it was owned by McLlhenny whose family had made their fortune in Tabasco sauce. McLlhenny used to throw elaborate parties every year and, as children, we'd watch the helicopters fly over to deliver the esteemed guests. Sometimes we'd get limousines pulling up outside our house and a posh accent would ask the way to Glenveagh Castle. For years Daddy had been invited to play at the parties. He always had to stay downstairs to eat with the servants but he was full of stories of the hoi polloi guests and was proud to entertain the likes of Grace Kelly and other celebrities and dignitaries from around the world. Daddy performed at these parties until the early seventies when the troubles in Northern Ireland made people much too anxious to visit and the parties came to an end. I loved to hear Daddy's stories, but I also knew of the estate's sinister past – a story that disturbed and saddened me. Around the 1840s, dozens of Irish peasant families were evicted from their homes on the edge of the lake so that the grand castle could be built in its idyllic setting. The peasant homes were burnt and pulled down and the families were left to starve. As Daddy drove along chatting in his merry way I had pictures in my head of haunted faces and grief-stricken families begging for their homes.

The Glenveagh estate stretches for miles and today the castle and gardens are open as a national park. A herd of deer roam in the grounds and another of Daddy's favourite stories recalls the night he was driving home late from a dance and was faced by a huge stag that had become free of the park's boundary. Startled by the headlights, it nearly ran Daddy off the road as it leapt in front of the car.

My father knew so many people through his work with the band and almost every house we passed he'd tell me something of those who lived there. When we finally got to Derry he'd stay waiting for me in the car, then after our lunch, he'd wait again while I had a private lesson. It must have cost my parents a small fortune, but of course I had no idea of that at the time. When Deirdre was old enough she wanted to start ballet as well, so then there were the three of us on the special drive over to Derry. After a while Deirdre and I started going by ourselves on the bus. That same Lough Swilly bus still passes the house at eight o'clock every morning. Every second Friday night we'd leave a chair upside down outside the front of the house. This acted as a signal for the bus to stop. It was a rackety old bus, with solid seats, and we used to have to cling on tight for fear of being thrown off our bench. Poor Deirdre used to get terribly travel sick – three hours there, then three hours back, with sleepy heads and achy limbs. For years it was always the same conductor on the bus. He was called Manus and had red hair and a cheeky, bubbly face. He was a welcome sight. I've never been much of a morning person, even in my childhood, and it took all my enthusiasm for ballet to get me out of bed on a non-school day. Manus could always bring a smile to our faces. It wasn't such a bad way to start the day. He always took care of us and I suppose our parents trusted him to keep a look out for us getting the bus back home. He always had the same jokes and sometimes we found them very tedious. We'd heard them all before, and no one laughed at the punchlines as much as Manus did.

Then there were the music lessons. Mammy by that time was teaching music herself but it's never a good idea to try to teach your own, so she sent us off for piano lessons with Sister DeSales at the convent in Falcarragh. Despite ballet being my main distraction, I still loved going to Sister DeSales because it also meant an adventure with my brothers and sisters. We went in twos, threes or fours for a one- or two-hour lesson. None of us wanted to go first. Sister DeSales would often get so caught up in her first lesson and if you were lucky she'd run out of time before your turn. There was only one room, so if we weren't being taught at the piano we'd play dominoes on the floor. We tried to keep as quiet as possible so she might forget we were there, but of course children trying to keep quiet is always a recipe for disaster. Eithne was a terrible giggler. I would get cross and tell her to 'shush'. Then Deirdre would start and before long we'd all be rolling on our tummies, stuffing our hands in our mouths to try to stifle our snorts and giggles.

Sister DeSales was a lovely nun. She was small and old and her wiry white hair sprung out from under her veil. She'd rap you on the fingers with a pencil if you didn't have your position correct, but we weren't scared of her and we didn't mind doing a bit of practice to get by. We always looked forward to going because it was also the day we got our pocket money so we could go to the sweet shop straight afterwards. We had ten pennies each. We always ended up buying the same things as each other. Sometimes I would choose first and the girls would want the same. But if Ciarán or Pól were with us they'd often find something different. Then we'd all change our minds and want what they chose. The shop woman was very patient, weighing out quantities of sweets from the big jars, then putting them back again when we were convinced we wanted something else. One thing we often bought was a packet of sweets called 'Charms'. They were flat little fruit sweets that would last for ages if you sucked them. We used to have competitions to see who could make them last the longest, but I was never a winner. I would always bite into mine. If you kept sucking sometimes you could make a hole in the middle of the sweet. That was the best thing.

Throughout the summer we'd be busy with competitions, known in Ireland as Feis. On the whole, we loved it. We got to travel around the area and we'd meet lots of friends. One of my best dancing friends was Rosaleen Diver. We did Irish dancing classes together in Middletown Hall. Michael Quigley was our teacher. He was a very animated teacher and we always laughed at the way the change in his pockets used to rattle when he danced. Through my enthusiasm for dancing I, along with

Rosaleen, became one of his main pupils. He used to keep us and a couple of other girls back after class to give us extra lessons. It kept us busy. I remember several times coming from Derry having done a ballet performance and changing in the back of the car into my Irish dancing costume to do a Feis in one of the towns on the road home. I always won medals in Irish dancing and I was Donegal Champion at one time, winning a huge silver cup. I still have the photograph of me and Rosaleen. It was nice in a way that we both got to win. She was a year older than me so she won the senior division and I the junior.

Then there were the singing competitions. Choosing the right song made a lot of difference and I won quite a few medals. One of the Feis we travelled to was just outside Donegal, over the border in Strabane. The competitions in Northern Ireland were different, in that the song was chosen for you and everyone had to sing the same one. Can you imagine? There were about seventy children taking part, all singing the very same song.

One particular time I was number sixty-three and I didn't come anywhere in the winner's list. That was all right. I was disappointed, but I was only twelve years old and there were some great singers, many of them older boys and girls. Wherever you came, you always went to the judge's board afterwards to collect their appraisal. They would make notes on your overall performance for constructive criticism. Things like, 'Great posture, but watch the long notes. Work on tuning.'

I collected my notes and one of the comments from one of the judges was, 'need to work on your Irish a bit more'. I was confused and when Mammy saw it she gasped, then laughed. She took the piece of paper from my hand and waltzed up to this particular adjudicator, Michael Hynes.

'A-hem, excuse me, Mr Hynes,' she said with her face full of mischief. 'I feel I should point out your mistake here.' He turned around to look at her as though thinking, 'Oh no, not another over-protective mother'. But Mammy's face was filled with nothing but amusement. 'I think you just need to know that you have told my daughter Máire Brennan to work on her Irish a bit more, yet she's a native Irish speaker!'

Michael Hynes was extremely embarrassed and came to apologise to me. The trouble was that all the other contestants had learnt the Irish song phonetically, not having a true word of Irish in their heads. Yet there I was, born and bred with Donegal Gaelic in my tongue, singing the song naturally, the way I knew it. To Michael Hynes it just sounded different from all the other young hopefuls. At least we saw the funny side of it, and from that day Michael Hynes became a good family friend.

Little did we know then that in years to come there would be much to sing in this poetic language. It speaks of the Donegal mountains and the Atlantic Ocean, the little harbours, sweeping beaches and the sand dunes; it is the language in which stories are bold and secrets best told.

# Chapter 4

At fourteen years of age I went to the Ursuline convent, Sligo.
I suppose it was quite a late age to start boarding school, but life
in the country was relaxed and there didn't seem to be any
urgency to perpetuate my education – or perhaps, more
pertinently, my departure from the family fold. My parents and
grandparents had always nursed a dream that I would have a
good education and, as a young girl listening to Mammy and
Aunt Bríd tell stories of their own boarding-school days, I often
let my imagination dance with fantasies of what might eventually befall me. Still, throughout my childhood, such musings
were always of a time in the far-off future. I'm sure Mammy
and Daddy were also happy to delay the reality of their
ambition. It would be hard to see their first-born go off into the
big wide world, and in many ways it signified the beginning of
a new era in the Brennan household. Certainly, they were as
apprehensive about my absence as I was about my new life
surrounded by strangers.

Still, what would be, would be, and during that final blissful
summer of 1966 Daddy set about finding an appropriate school
where I would be enrolled for the next four or five years. I'll
never forget first hearing about the convent. Daddy was so excited
to tell me of his visit. I trembled a little, realising that my time
had finally come, but I put a smile on my face and soon his
enthusiasm caused a thrill of excitement to allay my anxiety. My
parents were so proud to be able to send me to this special place
and I knew that they had already made many sacrifices to bless
me with the opportunity. Daddy was especially keen on the
Ursuline convent because of its reputation for music. It was one

of very few places that taught the harp and he had always harboured a little dream that I might take to the instrument. Gog too was very encouraging. He'd always talk of the value of a 'good education', how it would open up the world to me. He'd fuel my imagination with stories of faraway places and people who spoke many different languages, but at heart I was very much a home bird.

When you're seven or eight years old your world is a small, safe place, but at fourteen the responsibilities of looming adulthood can lay heavy on your shoulders. The time had come when I had to go shopping for my school uniform. Usually shopping with Mammy was a treat. There weren't any clothes shops in our area, so if Mammy wanted something special she'd go the twelve miles to Falcarragh or further to Letterkenny. The trips always involved stopping for tea and cake along the way so she was never short of a volunteer to accompany her. Otherwise we relied on 'Johnny the Jew' and his mobile shop who turned up in the parish about once a month. He was known to everyone as 'Johnny the Jew' but I don't know why because he was a Pakistani man! His van was a deluge of delights. It might not always be the best quality, but we usually bought from him because Mammy and Aunt Bríd said he was 'so reasonably priced'. My sisters and I loved rummaging through the goodies. It was packed to the roof with shoes, socks, stockings, skirts, blouses and lots of children's clothes. It was amazing that no matter what you wanted, Johnny seemed to stock it, and he always had your size in the shoes or boots you picked out.

But neither Johnny the Jew nor the finest stores in Falcarragh or Letterkenny could equip me with my school uniform. That day we had to go all the way to Sligo, a good two-hour journey, to the special shop that proudly catered for the Ursuline convent and the equivalent boys' school in the town. Mammy clucked around me, telling me how smart I looked, but I just felt silly in the unfashionably long pleated tunic, jumper and blazer. Dark green – imagine wearing this every day of my life for the foreseeable future! To top it all the shop assistant then completed my humiliation as she neatly crowned my locks with the convent school hat. Mammy wiped away a tear from her eye.

I'll never forget my first day at the Ursuline. Mammy and

39

Daddy drove me to Sligo. The convent lay just beyond the heart of the town, past the docks. It was a huge old granite stone building with a long double driveway – one way in and one way out. Mammy turned to look at me in the back seat as we drove down the tree-lined drive, past the basket ball and tennis courts, towards what seemed like the most enormous building I'd ever seen.

'Just you wait 'til you come home Máire,' she laughed, 'our little house will seem even more tiny after living here.'

I swallowed hard. I didn't want to think of home – my cosy bed and my sisters playing our night games without me. Mammy reached for my hand. She knew what I was going through, she'd been there herself. She also knew that many great days lay ahead.

Before I knew it I found myself standing in a long corridor full of girls. The noise was deafening, all high-pitched English chatter and squeals of delight as girls flung themselves into each other's arms like long-lost friends. Mammy spoke soothing words of encouragement in Gaelic, keeping the safe bond of home alive. You could tell the new girls a mile off. They were the only ones wearing the awful hats and their uniforms were starchy and uncomfortably large. Like me, they had the wide-eyed composure of frightened animals and stood close to their parents, watching in awe as whirlwinds of green-clad gigglers decimated the sterility of the pristine corridors. At one time a loud bell pierced the noise and the older girls disappeared in varying directions. It obviously meant something, but it was one of the rituals yet to be revealed to the eighty or so new students. It was all so new, so enormous, so frightening, yet there was an excitement about the place that sent tingles down my spine.

'Leo Brennan?'

We turned around to a pretty girl with fair curly hair, pale skin and a delicate smile. She recognised Daddy from his playing at her sister's wedding up in Ardara. I warmed to her instantly and it was nice to find someone from near my home town. Her name was Mairéad Kennedy and we were to become great friends.

I stood with Mairéad in a line waiting to be greeted by a nun who told us what dormitory we would be allocated. I'd always loved to hear Mammy and Aunt Bríd recall their dormitory days – the midnight feasts and girlish hilarity – and I was excited to see where I would be sleeping. Still, when the two flights of wide wooden stairs finally opened up to an enormously long bed-lined room, I once again swallowed on a hard lump in my throat, shocked by the magnitude of it all. The beds seemed to stretch for an eternity down the chamber and each end housed an intriguing private cubbyhole where – Mammy explained – a nun would sleep. I counted the beds as we wandered down the row looking for my name tag. Twenty-six, twenty-seven, twenty-eight . . . It was one thing to share a room with four sisters, but quite another to swap sweet dreams with twenty-nine fellow dormers.

Mammy followed close behind with my suitcase and chatted away as she helped me unpack my belongings into the little locker beside my bed. She laid out my linen and underwear, every piece labelled with my name. Two nights ago I had watched as she had laboured over each item, meticulously stitching my identity into each sock and pair of knickers. Even then it had all seemed so far away and unreal, but now here I was about to be abandoned to the company of strangers, all suitably labelled, lest they too be lost in a sea of green.

It was a sorry moment as I watched Mammy and Daddy set off down the long drive. The noise from the other girls filled my ears and I bit my lip, trying to hold back the tears. That night there was lots of crying under the sheets in the dormitory, but no one moved; we were all too scared. Some of the girls were only twelve years old and I told myself to be brave and grown-up. It didn't help. I hated that first week. It was all just so foreign and different and I missed everything about home. It was a big shock for me. Everybody spoke in English and even the Gaelic lessons were different to the Donegal Irish I was used to. Most of the nuns were sweet-tempered characters whom I grew to love, but that first week – still in reverence and fear – I thought I encountered something of an attitude towards my native tongue from the Sister who took us for Gaelic classes. 'OK Máire, since you speak Irish, let's see if you can translate this for us.' She made me stand up in front of all the class. I looked at the page in my book. I fully understood the meaning of the Gaelic words, but really struggled to translate it properly into good English. It wasn't that I couldn't do it, but I was so nervous at being put on the spot that I stuttered and stumbled, making the other girls snigger behind their hands.

Every day of that first week, I wrote a letter to my mother pleading with her to come and take me home. Mammy told me later how hard it was for her. She was all for jumping in the car to come and get me, but my grandmother said, 'Give her another week and if she's still writing letters, we'll go up and see her.'

Sure enough, the letters stopped and I began to settle down and enjoy my new life, even though the discipline of the daily routine was hard. For a girl who went to school just a hundred yards down the road and was still often late for the nine o'clock start, the six-forty-five rise time was nearly unnatural! Every morning when the bell went I would long to turn over and go back to sleep, but no, the dormitory was alive with the hustle and bustle of my new friends and by seven-thirty we were all neatly arranged in the chapel ready for mass. One day a week we were allowed a lie-in as one dormitory at a time was excused from having to attend mass. On those days I'd leave it until the very last minute to get up and then rush down to catch the eight o'clock breakfast.

Communal living was not too much of a shock for me. Coming from a large family I was used to queuing for the bathroom and to a general lack of privacy. We were allowed a bath once a week. Everyone was on a strict half-an-hour rota. Whenever your time was nearly up there would always be the next girl knocking on the door and you had to be sure to leave a clear five minutes to scrub the bath with 'Gumption' after you'd finished. Everyone hated that, but it had to be done. Similarly, our clothes were sent to the laundry only once a week so you'd always find girls trying to wash out their underclothes between laundry runs. We found that if you wrung them out tightly in a towel and then laid them between the bed blankets, they would be dry the next day – it was one of many basic survival techniques.

I very quickly grew to love my time at the Ursuline. Within a few weeks I, along with most of the other new girls, had taken the scissors to my skirt and stitched up the hem to more than just a little above my knees. The hat remained in my suitcase under my bed and the blazer was only worn when absolutely required. A few of the nuns would shake their heads disapprovingly, especially when we pushed the limits on make-up, but even a convent school couldn't avoid a gentle sway in the height of the swinging sixties.

I enjoyed most of the lessons and became involved in all sorts of extra-curricular activities, especially music, sports and art. One term I was captain of the camogie team. Camogie is the girls' version of Ireland's national sport, hurling. It is a notoriously 'rough' game and I constantly had bruises on my shins from being hit with an opponent's stick, or caught in the line of the hard ball. If I wasn't on the sports field I could usually be found in the art department, drawing up a poster for our latest musical or theatre production. I loved drama and with the help of a friend I once produced an Irish play that had everyone in stitches. Obviously my early days in the pantomime at home had given me good training! The school also had a wonderful music department, helped by the fact that the music teachers were some of the most popular nuns in the school. There was a strong operatic group, but I was only ever given a small solo part or place in the chorus due to me not having a very strong voice.

For a couple of terms Mairéad and I were given the prestigious charge of the sweet shop. To us it was like a holy appointment. It meant we didn't have to queue with the six hundred or so other girls, but more than that, I loved the responsibility of working out the stock orders and getting to chat to everyone as we served. It consumed every moment of the afternoon break but we loved the job.

All the girls had a regular supply of goodies sent from their families. Everyone tried to ration out their feasts, storing the treasures in their little tuck boxes which were kept in a large cupboard. Mammy and Daddy would send me a parcel every two weeks or so. I could hardly wait to open the package in afternoon break. Usually there would be buns or little cakes that Mammy or Gran had baked, and my sisters would fill the space with my favourite sweets. One day Mammy sent a real treat – some portions of home-cooked barbecue chicken. It was all wrapped in tin foil and, even though it was cold, there was still a wonderful homely aroma emanating from within. I placed it carefully in my tuck box and smiled as I imagined the scene at home, my brothers and sisters licking their fingers to clean off every last morsel of the family favourite.

A few days went by before I gathered some of my best friends together promising them a wonderful treat. I took the box from the cupboard and we all headed off, up past the sports fields to where there was a little shrine. We often gathered there. It was a peaceful hollow where the sun broke through the trees and you could sit looking down on the tennis courts and camogie field. It was a warm afternoon and we looked forward to sharing the delights of our tuck boxes in an hour of blissful girly fellowship. The chicken felt heavy as, with gleeful anticipation, I lifted it from the box and tried to peel back the paper. It was sticky and I struggled with the foil, finally plunging my thumbs into the package in a bid to separate the layers. There was an unnerving squelch and in that moment I screamed and threw the parcel to the floor in complete terror. A maggot stuck to my thumb and the chicken was a lively squirming mass on the ground. My stomach retched and there were howls of laughter from my friends who were all gripping their sides and wiping tears from their faces as they tried to control their convulsions. Soon I too was rolling around in pain through laughing too hard, but even now I can feel physically sick at the memory of that chicken. I can't believe I was stupid enough not to consider that it would go off, especially kept in a non-refrigerated room for three or four warm summer days.

Time passed quickly and the holidays soon came around. Even though I was limitlessly happy with my school life, I always counted the days as it got near the end of each term and couldn't wait to see my family back in Gweedore. Mammy was right, the house did always seem tiny when I first got home, but the welcome couldn't have been larger. For days my brothers and sisters fussed around me wanting to hear stories of my life in Sligo.

I enjoyed my lessons but I was only ever an average student, so if there was something I was interested in, I would work hard to get good marks. I remember when I was fifteen we were given an essay to do over the Christmas holidays on the European

Economic Community. Ireland was entering the EEC and the nuns said it was important that the Ursuline girls understand what it might mean for Ireland's future. 'The European Economic Community' – I repeated the words over and over. It sounded very important and grown-up to me and I was eager to get to work. Over the holiday I collected papers and all the footage I could get my hands on. I spent hours working on my essay, delving into my dictionary for new words that would make the essay sound like a professional report. After the holiday I handed it in to Sister Maria with a real sense of achievement and every expectation of top marks. The next day I was quite excited as she came around handing the essays back.

'Now girls, I would like you to know that one of our pupils has excelled herself with the holiday project.' My heart beat with excitement. It had to be my essay she was holding. Sure enough she walked towards me with the paper in her hand.

'Máire Brennan. You have handed in a fine piece of work, extremely well written. In fact, I think you should read it out to the rest of the class.'

The smile drained from my face and my excited beating heart jumped in terror.

'Stand up, Máire, and come to the front of the class,' I heard Sister Maria say through the haze that had descended upon me.

As I walked out to the front my legs shook so much I had to grasp hold of the Sister's desk. I began to read, but when I got to the new big words I stumbled so badly that Sister Maria became very cross.

'Máire Brennan, you can't read those words, because you don't know what they mean. And you don't know what they mean because you didn't write them. Who did this work for you?'

'No one, Sister,' I stuttered, 'I . . .'

'Then what's wrong with you?' she barked. 'It is quite clear to me, Máire Brennan, that this is not your work.'

I was so flabbergasted that I couldn't speak. My eyes pricked. I was hurt and humiliated and all I could do was stand there, biting my lip and staring ahead lest one of the tears should escape down my cheek. I had tried so hard to prove that I could be above average and I knew my essay was good, and wholly by my own hand, but yet again when it came to standing up and speaking in front of an audience I had badly let myself down. I was angry at Sister Maria's reaction, but more than anything I was frustrated at my own inability to prove my worth.

That was a bad experience, but on the whole the nuns were lovely and not at all the strict mistresses that some might imagine in a convent school. Sister Declan – we called her 'Decky' – had a great sense of humour and she was often party to our girlish pranks. Looking back I know the girls at the Ursuline were very privileged to have such role models. There was a peace, dedication and lust for life about many of them and I know that the thousands of girls who have passed through their care carry with them valuable assets, far beyond basic education. At one stage I thought I might like to be a nun. That wasn't unusual at the school. I suspect many of us imagined we had the 'calling'. We were all well practised in the traditions and disciplines of the Catholic faith and it gave us a strong value system and identity. In the senior school years, though always encouraged, it was no longer compulsory to go to mass every weekday. I must admit, I was relieved to be able to stay in bed a little longer, but there were times, particularly during Lent and October devotions, that it was important to me to go every day. It gave me a certain peace and comfort. Perhaps some of it came from knowing that Mammy and Daddy would be at the chapel near our home doing the same thing.

Every year the school had a retreat. I used to look forward to them. It was very different to the normal school routine. School was so busy, what with lessons, then all the other extra things in which I was involved, so I suppose the three-day retreats brought some much needed space into life. For me it was a wonderful indulgence just to walk by myself in the grounds of the convent. It was a big place so you could easily lose yourself and I cherished the opportunity to be alone with my thoughts and prayer-book devotions. The library would always be restocked around this time and I would spend hours reading books about missionaries in far-off lands and people who gave their lives in the service of others. Of course, not all the girls took such pleasure in the peace and solitude and we all knew the prearranged place where a regular gang would meet to engage in the usual banter.

There were no formal lessons during the retreats but often a visiting order of priests would lead lectures on basic life matters, especially for the more senior years. They were usually a little dry, but I remember one particular occasion very well. One of the priests from an order in Roscommon caught the attention of the girls immediately. He was quite young, tall, slim and undeniably good-looking. That set some of the girls giggling and nudging each other before he had even started the lecture. His mission was to educate us about the 'facts of life', as the nuns called it. As he began to speak, we were rapt in attention. He was very specific about sex and at first it had us in hysterics, especially when he drew very explicit pictures on the blackboard. The nuns sat along the side of the room, all looking rather hot and nervous, obviously worried at just how far this priest would go. Yet it was the first time that many of us had heard anything like this. He explained the facts very clearly and in a way that we could begin to understand. Although I was the eldest of a large family, the making of babies was something that was just never talked about. (Indeed, after reporting back to my mother on these lessons, she engaged me to talk to my sisters about sex!) Until then I had never been privy to an explanation of just how a baby came to be and, since I had opted to do Domestic Science instead of Biology, I had no idea of the function of certain bodily parts or the mechanics of procreation. When we had all got over the shock and hilarity of having a giant penis drawn on the blackboard we each sat in silent fascination as the priest then showed an excellent film about two young people. The message warned of how a simple courtship could easily lead on to further things. There were no more giggles until we discussed the details a few nights later at one of our midnight feasts.

At sixteen years old there was much to learn from the dormitory talk. It seemed that everyone was obsessed with boys, though sometimes I would grow tired of the endless and intense altercations about the opposite sex. I didn't quite understand what all the fuss was about. I'd grown up with a house full of boys and, to me, they weren't worth the bother. I certainly wasn't nervous of them. Around this time my brother Pól was sent to Summerhill College, the boys' boarding school down the road, and I would often meet up with him and his friends in the local coffee bars. Pól was popular at school and – particularly through his own music and drama interests – often found himself in the company of older boys. I enjoyed being with Pól. It was refreshing to be able to relax and talk about music and sports with him and his friends, instead of the usual banal 'boy talk' at the convent. How many more times could I bear to hear Bernadette Sweeny's direction on how to French kiss? Unbeknown to me, however, I was earning a reputation for myself among some of the other girls. Inevitably, through hanging out with my brother, I got to know a lot of the boys at Summerhill – many of them around my own age – and this had not gone unnoticed. I began to suspect something when I once walked into a room and the bunch of girls laughing and chatting there instantly went quiet. It was quite obvious they had all been talking about me. I just waltzed through the room, picked up my bag and left. I wasn't going to let it bother me. I was tougher than that.

Then another time one of the girls came up to me sobbing her eyes out.

'Well, if you're going to make him happy, and that's what he wants, I don't mind,' she sobbed. I looked at her. She was completely crazy, her eyes red with crying and her face all blotchy.

'What are you talking about?'

'Kevin. You were with Kevin,' she muttered.

I was aghast. 'Stupid girl,' I thought, but I didn't say it. 'Mary, I was only talking with Kevin. He's a friend of my brother Pól. We were talking about the band that's playing in McGlynn's on Saturday night, I know the fiddle player from Derry.'

If you'd have asked Kevin, he undoubtedly wouldn't have had a clue who Mary was. She'd never spoken to him, but only admired him from afar and, in her head, he was the boy for her. That kind of thing used to happen all the time. I just thought it was funny. I couldn't understand why the other girls assumed so much. To me it was immature and silly and I found myself more comfortable in the company of girls in the older years who shared my enthusiasm for music. One of them was Pauline Ryan. She was the year above me at the convent, but I often bumped into her on a weekend when we were allowed out in Sligo. Pauline's brother was in a very cool band called 'Granny's Intentions'. We often watched them on TV and Pauline and I could talk for hours about what was happening in the music scene.

Of course, I did end up with a few sweethearts in Sligo, but it was all very innocent. Myself and Mairéad were prefects, so we couldn't get up to much mischief, but I remember one night when we had to sneak back, long after the school gates were closed. We'd been in town with these boys – two brothers who took quite a shine to us. We drank coffee and milkshakes and put record after record on the juke box. When the coffee bar closed they wanted to walk us back to the convent. We took the long way and every so often we'd stop for a kiss. Ten-thirty came and went and we knew the main gates to the school would be long since locked. Our only chance was to sneak in down the long dark side road by the music rooms. From there we could make our way around to the back of the school in the hope that the sports hall door had been left unlocked. Our luck was in. Thankfully, we were able to scamper back to our room completely undetected. That was about as mischievous as I got at school. It was all just innocent fun.

Mairéad and I were close and she knew what I was really like. She'd found herself party to some of the gossip-mongering about me, but I knew she was loyal and stood up for me when the other girls were furtive with their speculations on my love life.

Much more distressing to me was the discovery that I had also gained an unseemly reputation for myself at home in Gweedore. In the holidays I would always tag along with my uncles and brothers to the local dances. My sister Deirdre was still too young to be allowed out and I thought nothing of going along with the boys. Once in the dance hall, however, it was still very much a case of boys on one side and girls on the other, so when I spent most of the night in the company of Ciarán, Pól, Pádraig, Noel and their friends, certain people drew certain conclusions. We all shared an enthusiasm for music and I loved hanging around with them after the dance talking to the bands. Music was my passion and I was far more interested in what new keyboard the guys used than the smell of their aftershave.

One day, only a week after returning to the convent from the summer holidays, I was in class when the head nun came in.

'Máire Brennan, your mother and grandmother are downstairs. Leave your books and go and see them.'

My heart leapt. It would be lovely to see them, but what were they doing turning up here only a week after they had brought me back to the school? I knew there had to be some kind of problem and I feared what kind of news they might be bringing.

Mammy and Gran Duggan sat in the parlour, drinking tea from the head nun's best china. They were both very smartly presented, Gran in her long tweed coat and matching gloves. We exchanged hugs and kisses and then Mammy pulled a letter out of her handbag.

'Máire, I want you to read this,' she said.

Her eyes looked deep into mine as she handed me the white envelope with a Donegal postmark. As I read, I was absolutely horrified. It was an anonymous letter, addressed to my parents. It said I had been seen drunk at the dances and that I was throwing myself at the boys in the band. There were some horrible things detailed. I was nothing but shocked. It was so completely untrue. At my Confirmation I had taken a vow not to drink until I was twenty-one and – certainly at that point – I had remained committed to it. Yes, I had hung around the boys in the band but it was always just to talk about music, and always with my brothers and uncles.

'Máire, is this true?' my mother asked.

'No,' I replied, still reeling with shock and bewilderment.

With that she took the letter from me, folded it up and put it back in her handbag. Nothing more was ever said about it and I never saw the letter again.

This was very like my mother. She put the onus completely back on me. I guess she knew that if I had lied to her, my own guilt would give me more grief than telling the truth. There was no accusation or warning. Just a question and trust in my answer. I was so thankful that I was able to deny the charges with all innocence. I've always valued that in my parents. In later life I was to realise how they would stand by me no matter what mistakes I made. It is something all of us children appreciate. Mammy and Daddy have always been there with a shoulder to cry on, always accepting, despite our many failings and disappointments. This was the first time my parents had really had to stand by me. There were to be many times as I grew older – times when I could not face them in such innocence.

# Chapter 5

When I was sixteen years old, my Father bought a derelict bar that was to become Leo's Tavern. It had been a difficult few years for him. The dances were losing their popularity and Daddy realised that the days of the Slieve Foy band could be numbered. For years the dances had been the heart of the social scene. They were usually organised by the parish priests and served as a way of keeping the community together. People of all ages went to the dance and for years the form was the same – girls on one side, boys on the other and the mineral bar at the back of the hall. The dances were usually in sets of three – three waltzes, three foxtrots, three jives. In between, you could chat and get to know your partner while the band changed their music. If a boy took you for a mineral after a set of three dances you knew he really liked you.

Daddy took me to my first dance when I was fifteen. I was shy and embarrassed, especially when the only dance I got all night was with my father. He was on the stage most of the time with the band, but took pride in whirling me around the dance floor towards the end of the evening. I had no idea how precious such a time was to him and just felt humiliated at not being asked to partner anyone else.

Daddy loved the dances and still talks about the huge ballrooms throughout Ireland with the fondest of recollection. But in the mid to late sixties the tide was turning and people were heading more into the pubs, preferring to sit with their drinks and be entertained.

Music was Daddy's trade and he had a large family to support. He found himself a regular gig in a hotel in Gorthork. Before

51

long he became so popular that word got around and people travelled for miles to enjoy Leo's accordion playing and sing-songs. In the meantime he was still always in popular demand to do weddings and private parties. My father therefore began to nurture an idea. In many ways it was an obvious move – he should look at opening his own bar.

It wasn't an easy decision. Daddy never drank nor smoked, so the general pub culture was alien to him. He thought long and hard before deciding to buy a place. Then one day he heard of a pub not too far from our house that was for sale. The building was dilapidated and in need of serious repair, but it already had a licence, so it was worth something to any prospective publican. My father put in a bid and, almost before we knew it, the sale had gone through. Daddy didn't mind that the old pub was falling down around his ears. In actual fact he was more than happy to knock it down and start again, redesigning it in a fashion that would more easily fulfil his dreams for the place – a long, spacious structure with a bar at one end, seating around the edges and a stage at the other.

I came home for the school summer holiday to find my father, brothers, uncles and a bunch of workmen up to their eyes in cement as they rapidly tried to finish the building in time for the tourist season. They were exciting days and all the family got involved. On 16 July 1968 Leo's Tavern officially opened. Of course, there was a ready crowd of locals who had caught the buzz of the new bar opening. I was thrown in at the deep end with a job as a barmaid. I knew nothing about drink and there I was with a tray in my hand and a room full of noisy people shouting their orders at me. It took me all of half-an-hour to do my first order because I had to keep checking it to make sure I'd got it right. There was much raising of eyebrows and tutting among the customers, especially the older men, but still everyone came back the next night, and the next, and Leo's Tavern quickly became one of the busiest bars in the area – though I'm sure that had more to do with Daddy's hospitality than the bar service.

As the weeks wore on I got the hang of it. I soon discovered that the more I smiled and was nice to people, the bigger the tips. I made stacks of money by getting to know the orders really well so that when they said 'same again' I could produce the round and at the same time handle three or four other orders. The down side of my job was brushing the floor at the end of each night. The place wasn't completely finished when we opened and the floor had been left with just concrete. The dust was unbelievable and it felt as though you could brush all night and not get anywhere. We quickly discovered that if you poured water on the floor you could stop a lot of the dust flying up in your face as you brushed, but still I used to find a grey residue on my skin each night and the place always smelt bad with the stale water, beer and general after-effect of a packed bar. Still, it was the smell of 'good nights' and Daddy – leading the sing-a-long from his own stage – was in his element.

Since those days Leo's Tavern has seen many a carpet worn threadbare and replaced for another season, but the basic structure of the place and the warmth of Daddy's show hasn't changed. People now travel from all corners of the world and Daddy's bar has an international reputation – not only for being the place where Enya and Clannad began their careers – but as an example of Irish entertainment and hospitality at its finest.

In our younger years, of course, neither I nor my brothers could have dreamt what beginnings would come from that little stage in the Tavern. In that first year Daddy would often get us up to do a party piece. My brother Pól – only just into his teenage years – would do a mime to a Peter, Paul and Mary record called 'Candy Bar'. Pól had such a confidence about him and his act would have the audience in stitches. Sometimes Daddy would persuade me to get up and sing a song. We were all heavily into the Eurovision Song Contest at the time and I loved singing some of the songs – 'Puppet on a String', 'All Kinds of Everything' and even the Italian song 'No Ho L'eta', which my grandfather helped me learn phonetically.

Daddy's face always lit up when I started to sing and I felt a swell of pride that quashed my nerves and embarrassment. Even in my younger years I recognised this bond we shared and I loved performing with him. I remember when I was twelve years old Daddy took me with him and the band on their annual trip to Glasgow and Edinburgh where they performed for the St Patrick's Day celebrations. This particular year he had decided that it would be good to introduce some Irish dancing into his show, and since I was doing so well in the Feises he asked me if I would like to take part. I, of course, jumped at the chance and, taking Pól along as company for me, we set out on the big adventure across the sea. To help make ends meet Daddy usually took a dance somewhere on the way to the boat and this year it was to be in Termon. Mammy was also coming along this time to play the piano. (She would occasionally join the Slieve Foy for special dates, leaving my brothers and sisters in the care of Gran and Aunt Bríd.) Pól and I were beside ourselves with excitement in the back of the van, but it soon began to seem like an eternity until we reached Termon. When we finally arrived we were allowed in for tea and sandwiches while the band set up, but once the dance started we had to huddle together outside in the van while Mammy and Daddy performed with the band. It was great fun at first – all covered up in coats and blankets listening to the laughter and sounds of the dance from inside the hall – but we must have both fallen asleep because the next thing I knew it was two o'clock in the morning and we were being woken up by the band loading the van, ready to head off to Larne to catch the ferry. Once in Scotland I loved taking part in the shows. Daddy had me do my Irish dancing, but then didn't allow me any time to change my clothes before I sang my party piece, 'My Boy Lollipop'. It was my favourite song at that time and I knew I could sing it well, but I felt stupid and embarrassed performing it in my Irish dancing costume.

By the summer of 1969, when the bar had been open for close to a year, we each seemed to be joining Daddy on stage more frequently to do our various party pieces, and music was a huge passion. My uncles and brothers were buying loads of records – spending all their money in Letterkenny's music shops – and we all listened to Radio Caroline and Radio Luxembourg to keep in touch with the latest pop sounds. There was no shortage of instruments around the house left by the Slieve Foy band; before long the boys got together and formed their own group – Pádraig and Noel on guitars, Ciarán on bass and Pól singing and tapping out a rhythm on the bongos. They'd always fancied themselves as a 'cool' band, even in our days of the Irish pantomime when they would perform pop songs they had translated into Gaelic. I always remember the first time I heard the Beach Boys' 'Surfin'

USA' in Gaelic. It didn't quite translate! Very occasionally I'd join them to do a Joni Mitchell song or a ballad, but on the whole, it was the boys' band. Of course they could only play in the holidays but they loved performing and Daddy was happy to let them go on stage early in the evening before he took over around nine-thirty. They became very popular among the locals and the summer tourists loved to hear them perform their Gaelic translations. Very soon we found that the place was practically full from eight o'clock in the evening and the boys' set was getting longer and longer.

It was a great summer but, like all great summers, it went by very quickly and before I knew it I was leaving the family behind and heading back to Sligo. I quickly immersed myself in school life, but in the meantime the boys had become more serious about the band. It was quite difficult, with Pól also being away at school, but when the opportunity arose they put themselves forward for Slogadh – a new Gaelic competition that set out on a local level and then went on to national acclaim. The aim of the competition was, I suppose, to promote Irish culture, and there were all sorts of categories, including one for a pop group, which my brothers and uncles duly entered. By that time they had a reasonable repertoire but realised that performing Gaelic transla-tions of popular songs would not get them very far in the competition. Instead they chose to perform their own arrange-ment of a traditional Gaelic song from Donegal and also set about writing a pop song of their own. Their self-penned attempt was a song that I thought was really great, called 'Liza'. There was much excitement about the whole thing and I was delighted to hear from one of Mammy's letters that the boys had won the local competition and would be going on to the county-level event with high hopes for the regional and perhaps even the national.

In the meantime I was beginning to get more involved in performing myself, albeit reluctantly. I was involved in all sorts of music, but my main instrument was the Irish harp. I loved to play, but I also had a certain complex about it. I hated the image of the Irish girl – we called it the 'Irish Colleen' – with the harp. I admired the famous players like Mary O'Hara and Deirdre O'Callaghan, but it was just so 'Irish country girl' at a time when everyone was heavily into the Beatles and the Rolling Stones. Daddy especially loved to hear me play, but I wouldn't have dreamt of getting up on the stage with it in Leo's. My excuse always was that the harp was too difficult to tune.

In the spring term of 1970 word went around that RTE, the main television channel in Ireland, was looking for new talent. They had a team of researchers going around the country to schools and town halls, where local auditions were being organised. The posters went up around the convent and everyone who was involved in music got really excited. I wasn't interested. There was no way I was going to go on national television and play the harp. The day of the auditions came and from the dining-room I could see the queue of excited girls waiting outside the main hall where the try-outs were being held. Mairéad and I had just sat down to lunch when two of the nuns came into the hall and rushed towards us. 'Máire, Máire, you have to come with us. Please, it doesn't look as though they are interested in anyone so far,' said Sister Rosario, almost begging me and trying to physically lift me out of my seat. 'They're not taking anyone. Please, just for the sake of the school, don't let us down!' Sister Rosario knew that my native Irish tongue was probably the kind of thing the panel were looking for and it was useless to protest, much as I tried. Before I knew it I was pushed into the main hall with the harp thrust into my hands. I was completely on the spot. Small and vulnerable, I sat in the middle of the large hall with a bank of people looking at me in expectancy. One of the faces I recognised as the famous musician and television producer, Tony McMahon. I could feel the blood rise in my cheeks and my hands were sticky with sweat. There was nothing I could do, so I began to sing and play 'Táimse im Chodladh', a beautiful traditional song that I had been practising. While I was playing, Tony McMahon got up out of his seat and started to walk around me. It was so off-putting. I'm sure I must have made loads of mistakes. I didn't want to do this audition anyway, never mind be chosen, so I didn't really care how badly I played. I plucked the final chord and sat waiting, in silence, to be dismissed. 'So what part of Donegal are you from?' he asked. He'd identified my accent and, unlike Michael Hynes at the Strabane Feis, he'd recognised that I was a native Irish-speaker. It was my worst fear.

The panel liked my playing and I was asked to represent the Ursuline Convent Sligo on the television show.

When the day arrived I had to rise early to catch the seven-thirty train to Dublin. Sister Rosario was to accompany me on the three-and-a-half-hour journey. I was nervous. The train was busy and I felt embarrassed and awkward as I heaved the harp around. It only had a soft case so I had to hold it carefully either between my knees or on the seat next to me for the entire journey up to Dublin. Sister Rosario was very excited for me and kept up the chatter for a good hour. After that we sat in silence, she smiling contentedly and I growing more and more anxious at the thought of what lay ahead.

Leaving rural Ireland behind, the train rolled on towards the big city and soon the huge biscuit-tin-shaped tower of Liberty Hall appeared in the grimy window as we pulled over Butt Bridge and into Dublin's Amiens St. Station.

A taxi took us to the television studio. The driver had an amused look on his face as he saw me – a girl in school uniform with a nun and a huge harp-shaped case – struggling to climb into the car. Of course he wanted to know all about where we were going and what we were up to.

'Ach, sure, I love a bit o' the singin' meself,' he said, and proceeded to treat us to a few verses of 'The Curragh of Kildare'. Sister Rosario and I smiled to each other and his warmth made me feel at ease.

We drove through the busy streets in the way that only cab drivers do; before long he was proudly announcing, 'Sure, I told yer I'd get yer here. Right up to the door.' Sister Rosario paid him the fare and I stood in awe, gazing at the television centre. Inside, I was even more in wonderment. There were people everywhere, monitors on the walls and a smartly dressed woman behind the reception desk with a lilting Dublin accent.

'Máire, what are you doing here?' I turned around to see my brother Ciarán, followed closely behind by Pól, Pádraig, Noel and my mother. 'What are *you* doing here?' I returned the question.

There followed much hilarity. It was great to see the family, but we were completely shocked to see each other. It turned out that my uncles and brothers had been chosen to appear on the same programme after winning Slogadh. We couldn't believe that none of us had realised we were to take part in the same show – but communication with the outside world was limited at the Ursuline!

Somehow, being with the family and the general buzz of the television centre, my nerves turned more into excitement. A long day lay ahead, but we were all fascinated to watch the workings of the TV studio. Everyone had to do a rehearsal and the crew seemed to take an age to work out the technicalities of the cameras and lighting. The highlight of the day for me was when we broke for lunch in the canteen. It was a huge place and I wasn't very good at hiding my excitement at spotting various news readers, weather men and television celebrities.

Next it was back to the studio for a final dress rehearsal. Sister Rosario had insisted that I travel in my school uniform, but I'd brought a special dress along with me to wear for the recording. In the final couple of years at school we were allowed to keep some of our own clothes at the convent to wear at the weekend and, thankfully, I'd got a dress there that was a bit special. My mother had had it made for me as a birthday present, but I hadn't yet had an occasion at which I could to wear it. It was a pale green, very fashionable, crochet dress which I thought was fantastic. But before getting into the dress I had to go upstairs to have my hair and make-up done. The convent had granted me special permission to wash my hair the night before, but it was very fine and limp so it took all the hairdresser's expertise and patience to add some body and wave to it, using huge rollers and an unhealthy amount of spray. Meanwhile I could see the 'goings on' in the studio from the little TV monitor. It would be my turn very soon. My stomach flipped and my mouth felt dry.

Down in my dressing-room I had a shock ahead. It was a comfortable little place with padded seats, mirrors around the walls and the smell of perfume and anticipation filling the air. As I wriggled into my dress the words of my song whirled around in my head – random phrases, coming fast and furious, out of control and . . . Oh! The reflection in the mirror glared back at me in horror. My wonderful crochet dress was completely see-through. It had never occurred to me that the holes in the weave were so large that, as it stretched over my curves, it would show

58

off far more than appropriate for a young lady from the Ursuline Convent Sligo. At that moment my mother came in and, in a split second, her face sported the same look of horror, then crumpled into stitches of laughter. That set me giggling. It was a desperate situation, but we could hardly control the wave of nervous, uncontrollable laughter. Just then there came a knock at the door. 'Máire, we're ready for you in five minutes.' It was the production assistant. Mammy and I stared at each other, then, before I knew it, Mammy started to undress. Pulling off her under-slip she thrust it into my hands with a firm instruction to put it on. I didn't have a choice. My dress was short and slim-fitting, while Mammy's slip was a good couple of sizes too big for me all over, so we spent a frantic few minutes trying to tuck it into my underwear so that it didn't show and bulge beneath the dress. A white slip under a green crochet dress – it must have looked ridiculous. Neither of us had the sense to confess my error and ask for the assistance of the wardrobe department so, still struggling to control our giggles, Mammy finally lead me out of the dressing-room towards the studio.

My embarrassment and self-consciousness only added to the nerves and I was thankful to be able to sit down behind the harp where I knew I would be less exposed. It was a frightening thing, sitting there by myself with the cameras looming and the director talking about me as if I wasn't there. The floor manager did her best to keep me calm, while at the same time reacting to the director's instructions in her ear-piece. Could I remember my words? Would I be able to play through without any errors? What about that difficult part in the middle? If I tripped, should I stop or carry on? It was OK for the boys, they were there with their electric guitars, a band, looking cool with their long hair, jeans and frilly satin shirts. I was the nice little Irish girl, with the nervous smile and neatly waved hair, alone with her harp. It didn't sit right with me, and knowing that Ciarán, Pól, Noel and Pádraig were watching only made things worse. The television show presenter was Albert Fry. He was a nice man who took to me and the boys because he loved Donegal Irish, but his introduction of me only fuelled my displeasure . . .

'And now, ladies and gentlemen, this darling girl with her harp, all the way from county Donegal, representing the Ursuline

Convent Sligo, we have Máire Ni Bhraonáin, performing 'Táimse im Chodladh' ('I Am Asleep and Don't Wake Me').'

In a flash it seemed to be over. I was pleased with myself. I had performed well but I was relieved when I could join Mammy to watch the boys do their slot. I thought they were fantastic as they did their Gaelic pop song. In a way I envied them and longed to be with them. I imagined myself stood in front of the mic, looking great in my dress and funky boots, my hair loose and tousled, and long earrings that touched my shoulders. That time was soon to come.

The summer holidays found us all back at the Tavern and, after the television appearance, the boys encouraged me more to get up on the stage and sing with them. The bar took great trade from the tourists and there were always the regulars, many of whom were very encouraging towards us. One was the local police sergeant. He brought his family some Friday and Saturday nights and always came early to make sure he heard us play. One evening he got chatting to my father about a new folk festival competition he'd heard about in Letterkenny.

'Sure, you've a grand group there, Leo. Why don't you enter them?' Daddy just smiled proudly, appreciating the sergeant's enthusiasm, and we just laughed about it, but a few nights later the sergeant came into the bar again, this time with an entry form.

A few weeks went by and the form stayed on the dresser at home, despite regular enquiry from the sergeant as to whether we had sent it in yet. 'Aye, aye, I'll remind them, but I'm not sure that they're that interested,' said Daddy, the day before the last entry date when the sergeant cornered him again.

The next day we were all together in the kitchen. Gog put the form in front of us on the table and said, 'Well, are you going to fill this in or what?' We stared at it for a while.

'Well, look,' said Daddy, 'you'll have to get a move on. You've got fifteen minutes until the postman gets here. Come on, you've got nothing to lose.'

Gog was poised with the pen ready to fill in the details. 'Well, what will we call ourselves?' said Ciarán, staring at the form. Pádraig said, 'What about Clann As Dobhar?' It simply meant 'family from Dore'. We looked at each other. By this time Daddy had run outside to watch for the mail van coming over the hill from Crolly.

'It's a bit complicated, especially for those who don't know Irish,' said Noel.

Now it was Gog's turn. 'Well, why don't you take the "a" and put it with the "d" along with clann and make "Clannad"?'

A moment's silence, with us all looking at each other. Pól was the first to smile. 'That's it then,' I said.

As Gog wrote our new name on the form and completed the details we could hear Daddy's voice outside: 'Hold on there Mick, we'll be with you in a minute, we have an important piece of post.'

That was the birth of Clannad. In many ways it was typical of how we would continue. We didn't really set out to be a proper band. We just loved playing music and things seemed to happen to us, so we went along with the flow, facing each opportunity as it was presented.

So here we were, a band with an entry into one of Ireland's biggest folk festivals, the prize for which was to record a professional album with the Philips record label. Just one problem – we had no songs. It was no good doing the chart music we'd been playing in Leo's and each band in the competition had eight minutes to show what they could do. That meant at least two or three pieces.

'Máire, what can you play on the harp?' asked Ciarán.

'The harp?' I'd never played the harp with the band. In my mind it wasn't very 'cool' and the only instrumental I could play, apart from the religious music I'd learnt at school, was a piece called Brian Boru's March. It was an old tune, composed in commemoration of the Battle of Clontarf in 1014 in which the Irish repelled the Vikings and in doing so lost their gallant leader, Brian Boru. After a little persuasion I picked up the harp and started to play it real slow. Pól began to tap out the beat on the bongos, then Ciarán joined in with long low notes on his electric bass. By the time Pádraig and Noel added some guitar we realised Brian Boru's March was becoming a really atmospheric tune with loads of potential. It sounded good. It felt good. This was the kind of sound that came naturally.

The next obvious piece to use was the traditional Gaelic song the boys had arranged when they won at Slogadh. Noel originally sang the lead vocal, but they suggested, with me joining the band, it was something I should do, so I set about learning the words. It was a good complement to the harp piece and showed that we could have a nice blend when we harmonised.

Our main concern was to present a package that would illuminate different shades and colour in our music, demonstrating the varied influences and capabilities of the band. For this reason we decided we ought to use a more upbeat English song for our third piece. Selecting it, however, proved rather problematic. It was Una McCafferty who finally helped us out. The McCaffertys were very good friends of our family from my ballet days and often came over from Derry to spend part of their summer holidays with us. James McCafferty was a highly respected voice coach and his daughter Una had inherited her father's talent for singing. She had a broad repertoire of songs, most of which were not at all suitable, but she persuaded us to consider one of her favourites, a very rhythmical 'ditty' type song called 'Kitty of Coleraine'.

'Ach, I'm not sure this is for us,' I said when I first heard it. It was very different to the music that came naturally to us, somehow very smart, clean-cut and structured. Still, at least it was in English and arranged in four-part harmony. If nothing else, it would show our versatility. Anyway, it didn't really matter. We were only in this for the fun of it. We'd heard about the prize, but winning and making a professional record didn't even enter our thoughts.

The Letterkenny Folk Festival took place in the town's cinema, over three days. There were so many bands taking part that they had to short-list the acts over both Thursday and Friday, ready for the final that would take place on the Sunday. We performed in the Thursday heats and were absolutely thrilled to be chosen as one of the three acts to go forward to the final. The cinema had been packed out and the audience had given us rapturous applause. What we didn't realise was that in the next few days there was a huge buzz about the band from Gweedore. We just returned home in ignorance and looked forward to returning to Letterkenny in a few days' time.

Sunday morning came around quickly and, after chapel, there was much excitement in the house as we prepared lunch and chatted about how the event might go. I was anxious to get the meal over quickly so I had plenty of time to get my hair done. Aunt Bríd had promised to set it properly for me and I was looking forward to getting ready. I'd got a new, very hippy-styled, dress. It was long and multi-coloured with big wide sleeves, and I thought it was terrific.

The kitchen was lively when Daddy came in with his newspaper.

'Have you seen this?' he asked, laying out the newspaper on the table. The whole back page was filled with a big picture and an article on the McGlynns who would be playing at the festival. They were a family band from Sligo and the newspaper raved about the record deal they'd just signed. According to the paper, they were definite favourites to win at Letterkenny.

'Good for them,' said Mammy.

'Well, guys, that's it then,' said Ciarán.

'Ah now, let's just wait and see. When you get up on that stage there'll be no competition,' my father mused.

'Now Daddy,' I said, 'you know we're not expecting anything. There's some big family bands in this competition. What with the McGlynns and the Sands family from County Down and I hear the Connerys are up from Galway . . .'

'Ach Máire, don't you talk like that. I have a good feeling about this. Wait until they hear my girl sing. You've got your own special way. And if you win, I'll smoke a cigar!'

'You'll do no such thing,' I said, pretending to be cross; 'you've never smoked in your life and you're not starting now. Anyway, it won't be an issue.'

At around six o'clock we all crammed in the car and headed off to Letterkenny. Daddy had to stay behind to play in Leo's so Mammy drove us down there and Una McCafferty came along to support us. We were more excited than nervous, but I was battling with a fear that I might not be able to remember the words to 'Kitty of Coleraine'. Almost all the way to Letterkenny I had everyone singing . . .

*As beautiful Kitty one morning was trippin'*
*With a pitcher of milk from the fair of Coleraine . . .*

There were only six bands in the final and we were third on, so
our time soon came around. The band before us finished to good
applause and we had to move quickly to get our instruments into
place. As I stood fidgeting at the front of the stage, waiting for the
boys to get set up with their electric guitars and amplifiers, I
heard someone on the front row say, 'Oh no, this is going to be
loud.'

'Yeah, but what about the harp,' said the offending woman's
companion; 'this could be really different.' I smiled to myself
and looked out into the sea of blackness.

First we did the traditional Gaelic song. As we breathed
the last note there was a wave of applause. It felt good and
I began to relax and enjoy myself as we moved into the
harp-led instrumental. I loved being there on stage with
the lights blinding my view of the crowd and the boys behind
me. My harp sounded beautiful in the acoustics of the theatre
and for a few moments I was alone, at one with the instrument.
I felt the breath of the audience in the resonance of every
string.

This time the applause was even stronger. I glanced over to
Pádraig and Pól. They were grinning. It had gone well. Now for
the final song. 'Kitty of Coleraine' might have been something of
an anti-climax in my mind, but the audience seemed to enjoy it
and we ended our set to rapturous applause. Perhaps it was
simply that we were a Donegal band, but the crowd certainly
seemed to be with us. It was all over before we knew it. Backstage
we all hugged each other and jumped around in excitement.
'That was great,' enthused Pól. 'Did you hear the crowd? I reckon
that's the best applause yet. We might even stand a chance of
getting a prize.' Even so, I don't think any of us really believed it.
We were just so thrilled to have come so far and got such a good
reaction. That in itself was enough.

The boys hung around backstage chatting with the other bands
but I went straight up to the balcony to find Mammy and Una.
There were no seats left, since all the tickets had been sold, but I
found them standing at the back where they had managed to find

themselves a decent view. Everyone was looking forward to seeing the McGlynns and, as expected, they were excellent. But there were a number of other very similar acts. 'At least your programme was different,' whispered Una, 'and there's nothing else in Irish.' I wasn't sure whether that was a good thing or not. We didn't know what the judging panel was looking for. Our set was good because of its variation, but the prize for winning the competition was to record an album, and who would want to record Gaelic songs in 1970? No one. Then again, one of the three judges was Tony Loughnane, a man whom we knew appreciated the Irish language, even if the others approached it with a certain contempt.

As the time for the prize-giving drew closer, I was happily settled up on the balcony. The Connerys took third place. That was to be expected. They were very popular and had brought quite a following with them up from Galway. Then came a big shock.

'And in second place, you know them, you love them, Sligo's best-loved singing family, it's the McGlynns.'

There was huge applause. 'Only second place,' I thought. My heart started beating heavier than I thought possible. I hardly dared let the thought enter my head, but we had seemed so popular with the audience, and the runners-up prizes had gone to the acts that everyone expected to win. My whole body felt like it was pumping and I stared forward at the stage, gripping Mammy's and Una's hands on each side of me. When the announcement came I was frozen to the spot, overcome with a feeling that I've only ever experienced once or twice in my life – a mixture of disbelief, happiness and a whole flood of emotion rolled into one. I couldn't move, but there, before my eyes, were Ciarán and Pól, Pádraig and Noel walking out onto the stage to claim first prize. My mind was a haze, and I'm not sure whether I ran or flew, but either way I made it to the stage and joined the boys in accepting the prize. Ciarán flung his arms around me. 'I can't believe it, I can't believe it,' he just kept saying. 'What took you so long, Máire?' asked Noel, grinning all over his face. 'Did you not want to come up?'

It was a euphoric night. Everyone wanted to talk to us and there was a great party atmosphere that lead everyone into a nearby hotel. Straight away we called Daddy and told him the good news.

'Hold on there,' he said, 'I'll be right with you.' As soon as he could close the bar he and Uncle Columba and a few other friends travelled down to join our celebration. Everyone wanted to congratulate us and there was a great camaraderie between all the acts. The press were there, taking photographs and asking questions about what we were going to do in the future and when we would be making the record with Philips. Make a record? It was something we'd never even talked about. Our imaginations had hitherto not gone beyond the idea of having a little fun together and doing a couple of gigs alongside our appearances in Daddy's bar! Tony Loughnane introduced us to John Woods, the head of the record company who had been on the judging panel. Although he became a great friend of the family, we later learned that he had needed a lot of persuasion from the other two judges to vote for us that night. He was looking for a great new folk or pop talent for his record label, and would now admit that he had no idea what to do with a Gaelic band whose sound was so diverse. Our act was all very nice on stage, but how on earth would it translate onto a record? I guess he was grateful then that we didn't actually claim our prize until three years later.

I'll never forget Daddy's face as he rushed into the hotel. It was already long gone midnight, but a few hours of great 'craic' lay ahead. So many people knew Daddy from his showband days and he held court at our table, telling tales and reminiscing about the old days well into the early hours. 'Ach, I knew my girl could do it,' he said winking at me. Little did we know that Clannad was here to stay and there would be many more celebrations to come.

Daddy put a cigar in his mouth, but he never lit it.

# Chapter 6

My final year at the Ursuline Convent was 1971. At this time the boys were doing more gigs themselves and they would often invite me along to do the occasional song with them. We'd received a lot of publicity from winning the Letterkenny Festival and there was only one other band doing Gaelic songs at the time, so whenever there was a special event or a Dublin television company making a programme on Irish culture, we would be invited to take part. Ciarán would usually choose a song and do the arrangement ready to send to Pól and myself in Sligo. The day before the television show Mammy would drive Ciarán over to Sligo and then take us all down to Dublin. Mammy only dared drive to the outskirts of the city, but my uncle Columba, who was living in Dublin at the time, would meet us and take over the driving. Pádraig and Noel were also in Dublin by then, training to be radio officers, so in the evening we'd all get together, rehearse the song, perform it the next day at the television studio and then go our separate ways again.

My school was very supportive and I was given a lot of special dispensation when it came to taking days off to do a TV show. I was only really an average student, but when the results came through I was thrilled to pass all my exams, getting especially good grades in art. We had a wonderful graduation day when all the parents came up and each girl was presented with a little silver crested ring. It was a gift I treasured for years, representing a happy time in my life when I was instilled with the values of right and wrong and developed the kind of confidence born out of a discipline of faith and good education.

That summer Clannad received a few invites from further

afield and we found ourselves driving all over Ireland. We had no money, but Gog kept helping us out and many's the day we took off with the double bass strapped to the roof of Daddy's Opel Kadet estate and all of us crammed inside with the other instruments, having the time of our lives.

In September I enrolled in Dublin's Royal Irish Academy of Music. I suppose it was the next obvious step for me. I enjoyed music and it was something I was reasonably good at. I had no particular ambition but I was aware of the lack of music teachers in Donegal and imagined that I might follow in my mother's footsteps. The RIA would equip me for that. I would learn all I could, ready to make a life for myself back home.

Once in Dublin my eyes were opened to more of the world. I was nineteen, but naïve, so it was something of a blessing to be able to move in with my mother's cousin and his family during that first year. They lived out in Rathfarnham, about ten miles from the city centre, so every day I would take the bus, getting off outside a huge Catholic church on Westmoreland Street, beside the RIA. Sometimes I found myself going into the church for a little time of prayer. Occasionally I would attend a mass, but usually I sat in the back of the church whispering a frantic prayer for help. I wasn't a very committed student, and was quite lazy with my piano practice, so with a difficult lesson or a test looming, I would jump off the bus and head for the sanctity of the church in desperation. Strangely enough, there was something about that church. It brought a calm and peace back to my troubled being, and, after spending a few meditative moments there, I always seemed to get through that day's particular trauma relatively unscathed.

Socially I spent time with Pádraig and Noel and we ended up forming a band with another friend from Donegal, Enda McMonagle. Enda was desperately excited about the band and called us 'The Four Leaves'. He even set us up with a manager and a professional photo shoot, but it was something I just couldn't get too enthusiastic about. Enda was heavily into Country and Western music, which didn't really go down too well with the rest of us. After our fourth gig we decided to call it a day. Still, we had a little fun. One of the gigs was out in Bray at the Royal Hotel, where we were due to go on stage at nine-thirty in the evening. There was a good crowd there, but for some reason – probably just our laid-back approach – we were really late. The promoter was frantic and angry with us, so we made up a story that we'd just done a TV show and had been held up at the studio. This sounded impressive, and gave us big credibility when he announced it to the waiting crowd.

There was a thriving grassroots music scene in Dublin. Folk music was becoming more hip and everyone was into Joni Mitchell and the San Francisco flower-power thing. Ciarán was still at home but regularly came down to Dublin where the boys and I found ourselves with a set of regular folk club gigs in The Coffee Kitchen and The Swamp, two gigs that were becoming increasingly popular. We just loved playing and I was amazed when they offered to pay us as well. It seemed strange to me to be paid to do something we loved. Through these gigs we were offered further opportunities to do some of the summer festivals and in May of 1972 we had an invite to go across to Brittany to one of the large European events.

It was a long journey. First the Irish Sea crossing, then the long drive down England's backbone to the south coast where we would get the boat to France. We were so crammed in the car, but I remember the journey seeming like a great adventure. We had experienced life outside Donegal, but still, this felt like the first time we were on our own, setting out as a band with the world at our feet.

We were all relieved to get to Southampton that night. The bed and breakfast was a pokey little place and, much to the amusement of the other guests and displeasure of the landlady, we proceeded to take all the instruments up to our rooms. We could only afford two rooms, so I shared with Ciarán and Pól. Noel and Pádraig had the smaller room which they had to share with the double bass. We were all weary, but no one wanted to go to bed, so we headed out to the cinema.

The next day we took the boat to France. We were ultimately heading for a festival in the south of Brittany, but were breaking the journey to play at a gig in Roscoff. Having little money, we decided the best course of action to solve an accommodation problem would be to hire a tent. As day turned into evening we grew more uncomfortable in the confines of the car and tempers were beginning to fray. The sky grew darker and before we knew it heavy rain was lashing down on us, making it hard to see where we were heading. Driving on the right-hand side of the road didn't help any and we were all yelling instructions at Pádraig – who was at the wheel – trying to make ourselves heard above the driving rain and crashes of thunder. There were a few near misses and plenty of arguments as we each battled to navigate our way around a frightening variety of French maps.

Finally, we reached the campsite. By this time the rain had settled into a miserable drizzle but it was almost pitch black and we had no idea how to put up the tent. I lost my temper, Ciarán lost his temper. Pól told us to calm down and we told him to shut up. We must have looked a ridiculous sight, a bunch of long-haired Irish musicians, all arguing and getting tied up in canvas and guy ropes.

'Well it doesn't help that I can't see the instructions,' Noel protested.

'Right,' I said, trying to take charge of the situation, 'Pádraig, reverse the car around and shine the headlights so we can at least see what we're doing.' In theory it was a good idea. It was a pity, however, that no one remembered the guitar leaning up against the back of the car. Pádraig hit reverse. There was an almighty crunch and a less than tuneful twanging of strings against splintered wood. More arguments. And the rain began to fall heavily again.

Finally one of the other campers took pity on us. Perhaps it was an act of kindness, but most likely he could bear to hear no more of our arguing and cursing. Whatever the reason, we were extremely grateful for his help. Within half an hour the tent was up and we were all beginning to calm down.

The next morning Pól looked rather pale. 'I'll be OK,' he said when I enquired if he was all right. As the hours went by I noticed Pól was unusually quiet and was holding his middle as if in pain. By the time we were due to do our soundcheck it was clear that he was extremely uncomfortable, so we asked the event organisers to help us find a doctor. It turned out that Pól had a nasty stomach bug, but still he was determined to perform with us. Years later we laugh at his recollection of being so drugged up from the medicine the doctor prescribed that he hadn't a clue how, or indeed what, he played that night. Nevertheless, we went down really well and everyone had a great time. We'd expanded our repertoire, and the crowd seemed to love our Gaelic songs.

We all loved the Gaelic language and it would stir a deep passion within us as we moulded the songs of our heritage into atmospheric arrangements. It was important to us to be true to the emotion and intention of the old songs. They had so much richness and the way they were written gave us a strong root into some beautiful melodies. More and more we found artistic expression that captured the rugged landscape of our surroundings, from the vast mountains and sea, to the stoic delicacy of heather and seaweed.

Back home there was a certain scorn from some quarters when we performed in Gaelic, but in Europe our language was just another part of our instrumentation. When we reached the festival in South Brittany we found even greater enthusiasm for our sound. We were surrounded by people from all over Europe, so the language of our songs wasn't even an issue.

The atmosphere of the festival was wonderful and the party mood continued around the clock in the hostel where all the musicians, including us, were staying. We met some wonderful people and the drink flowed as free and colourful as the conversation. One guy caught my attention. He was a handsome, tall French man called Pierre, with dark curly hair, olive skin and deep, dark eyes. He was a guitarist in one of the French bands and I fell for his charm as he improvised songs about the beautiful Irish girl in his dreamy French accent. We flirted with each other and I found a swell of pride to be with him as other girls looked on. On the second evening, Clannad played a great set and my head was ringing with the applause and thrill of receiving a huge encore. When we came off stage Pierre pulled me up in his arms and spun me off my feet. I was on cloud nine. There were loads of bands hanging around backstage and everyone jammed together and sat around talking and drinking into the early hours. Back at the hostel the merry-making continued. It was hot and heavy with the party spirit and, dizzy with too much wine, Pierre and I crept giggling into my room. Before I knew it we were together on the bed and my convent-school promises and pious pledges were forgotten and lost for ever.

The next day I awoke alone. My head was a little fuzzy and it took a few moments for me to relate to where I was. Scanning around in the room, my eyes focused on the pile of clothes strewn across the floor. I remembered the previous evening and couldn't help the half smile that broke across my face. It had been a heady night of passion and, for me at least, that was it – I was in love.

But where was Pierre now?

We were due to leave that day, but I was sure I would find Pierre back at the festival site where the organisers were laying on breakfast for all the bands. Sure enough, there he was, helping himself to coffee. He greeted me with a watery smile and a kiss on the cheek and continued chatting to the guy he was with. A wave of disappointment came over me. I had expected him to throw his arms around me in a huge embrace and introduce me as his girlfriend. It didn't happen. Feeling something of a spare part I went to join my brothers and uncles at a nearby table, all the time keeping Pierre within sight. He continued to talk with his friend and, taking a lump of French bread from a huge trestle table, he headed off to sit down at the other side of the marquee.

There were lots of hangovers but spirits were still high and people stayed around for several hours, eating bread and cheese and putting off the moment of departure. I kept my gaze fixed on Pierre. One time he looked over in my direction and winked. My heart fluttered, but apart from that he didn't show any sign of coming over. Soon it was time to go. We'd become friends with so many people, so the goodbyes took a bit of time. I followed the boys as they headed towards the table where Pierre and his band were sitting. They all shook hands and chatted a little. Pierre took my hand and kissed it quickly. 'Máire, it 'as been lovely to meet you,' he said in his thick French accent. I tried to look him in the face. 'Maybe, you'll come over to Ireland?' I said hopefully. 'Maybe I will,' he said. But with that he moved on to say goodbye to Ciarán, leaving me feeling humiliated and desperately disappointed.

In the car, travelling through France, I went over and over it in my mind. Everything he had said and done. The night before had seemed magical to me but he had taken advantage, and like a fool I had fallen for him and lost myself. My eyes pricked and I reprimanded myself. Still I persuaded myself that it had meant something to him. Perhaps he was just shy in the cold light of day. Perhaps I should have told him I was in love with him and given him a proper invitation to come over to Ireland. But in my heart I knew the truth and I regretted my behaviour. I'd lost myself to a man I hardly knew, and my own weakness surprised me. Mulling things over in my head I tried to justify myself. OK, so what if it was just a one-night stand. What was the big deal anyway? Everybody did it. It was the seventies. We should all love each other, be free in love, where was the harm in that?

Still, a little voice inside churned my spirit. I was annoyed at myself and I just felt stupid. Was this what I was going to be like, jumping into bed after one night with any charmer who paid me a little attention? Guilt and disgust came over me. With it came thoughts of home, of Mammy and Gran and Gog. What if they ever found out? Indeed, how could I ever go to confession and tell the priest of my behaviour? The journey rumbled on and I was a little girl again, being thrown out of the confession box by the angry Father Boyle.

I was nineteen, and painfully naïve. Donegal gave me a long, innocent childhood, but such naivety was also dangerous and I hated myself for being so stupid. When we arrived home I took comfort in the familiar surroundings of my youth. For a few days I awaited the mail van in a romantic fantasy that Pierre might write. The letter never came and I immersed myself in the safe surrounds of a summer in Donegal.

Six weeks later I was feeling strangely different. I had been trying to ignore the sickly feeling in my stomach, but now there was no doubt about it. I had to face the fact that I could be pregnant. I was absolutely devastated. If I didn't think about it, if I ignored it completely, perhaps it would go away. But no, my body told me otherwise. Panic-stricken, I had no idea what to do. My thoughts didn't even go as far as the implications of me actually having a baby. What I feared and focused on most was the potential I had to hurt so many people. What kind of example was I? The eldest of the family, and here I was, only one year out of school and pregnant through a night of silliness at a festival. My youngest sister Brídín was only three years old and I cringed as I watched Mammy taking care of and playing with her. The state I was in just seemed so wrong. My parents would be devastated if they knew. I was so painfully aware of them as they went about their business – Mammy running around trying to prepare music for the choir and Daddy getting dressed ready to go down to the bar. At least the Tavern gave me a little reprieve. I always worked there in the holidays and Daddy usually had me up on stage with him each night for a couple of numbers. When I was busy I could forget the scary reality of my life, but there were times, as I moved from table to table, that I felt everyone knew my secret.

It was my secret and I felt I had no one I could share it with. Meanwhile the days were going by and my problem was only getting bigger. Eventually I confided in a friend (whose name I prefer to withhold). In a way it was a relief to share my burden, but then it made it all the more real. We talked for hours about the options and various scenarios, but I felt there was only one alternative for me. If I had an abortion no one would know, so no one would get hurt. I'd heard stories of Irish girls who had gone off to England for the weekend with their shame and money in a brown paper envelope. Now it was my turn. How had I come to this? My friend got me the name of a clinic in England and I rang from a phone box to make an appointment. Procedure dictated that you had to have two appointments. The first was with a counsellor, then they preferred to give you a little time to be sure that you were going to go ahead with the actual termination. I gave a false name and told the voice on the end of the phone that I would need the appointments on two consecutive days since I was coming from Ireland.

'You do understand that we will require one hundred pounds as you check in,' the voice said.

'Yes, I understand. That won't be a problem.' I put the receiver down.

One hundred pounds, plus the cost of the trip. It would wipe out my savings.

Back in my room I emptied out my money jar onto the bed. My earnings from working in the bar were supposed to help support me through college the next year and I had been saving diligently. I counted out the notes and bits of change with trembling hands. I had just about enough. Within a few days I'd convinced my parents that I was going with my friend to England to meet up with her cousins. It was, of course, only partly true, but they were happy for me to have a short holiday, especially since I had earned a little money for myself and would be staying with someone I knew. I did everything I could to make the story convincing, even booking a weekday appointment at the clinic so that we weren't just going for the weekend, which I thought might be suspicious. It was all part of my paranoia. When the time came to leave, pangs of guilt swept over me as Daddy, and later both Gran and Auntie Bríd, pressed a ten pound note into my hand. 'Have a lovely time,' they had each said. I came dangerously near to breaking down in front of them.

A couple of days later my friend and I were on the ferry to England. I had never been so lonely in my life. I felt that everyone knew what I was doing, as if all the passengers on the boat could see the money in my pocket and the scrappy piece of paper with the address of the clinic in Birmingham. I watched happy families, children and parents. That's how it is meant to be – happy faces and special family outings, like when we went to the seaside at Bundoran. I persuaded myself not to think about what I was doing, and tried to concentrate on the good time we'd have later in London when we'd meet my friend's cousins and go shopping. Whatever was happening in my body was a mistake that had to be dealt with, something that wasn't meant to be there, something that had to be taken away. It would never come to anything. The day after tomorrow it would be gone and forgotten. The ferry lurched on the Irish Sea. I felt sick to the core.

## Chapter 7

I knew I had to be strong to get through the counselling. I had to prove to them that I was sure of my decision, that I knew what I was doing, that I would have no regrets and that it was all right to go ahead with the termination. How can anyone be sure of such things? Of course I didn't know what I was doing, but I was trapped. As far as I was concerned this was my only option, the only way to right my mistake, the only way to prevent anyone else getting hurt. I convinced myself that, in two days' time, it would all be over. I had no idea of the consequences of this decision or how long it would live with me, nor did I recognise how it might set the course of my life in the next few years. Still, I gritted my teeth, set my face and spoke calmly to the lady in front of me.

She was an older woman, with a white coat, hair to match, steel-rimmed glasses and a matter-of-fact manner. In a way I was relieved that she wasn't too friendly. She was efficient, which was all that was required, and I was thankful. As far as I was concerned this whole event called for a culling of emotion. I was to become anonymous, both to the people around me and to my inner self. Máire Brennan of Donegal would return when this was all over. After we talked she examined me. Even then, as I stared up at the ceiling, I thought 'Maybe I'm not', and longed for her to announce that I'd made a mistake, that I wasn't pregnant after all. She must have met hundreds of girls like me. I don't really remember much about our conversation, apart from her talking about preventing another pregnancy and giving me some contraceptive pills.

'All right Miss Walsh,' she said solemnly, 'you need to be at this address by nine-thirty in the morning.'

My mind was still pretty numb when I greeted my friend at the café where we'd arranged to meet. She ordered tea for me and I sat gazing out through the window at the world going by. I was grateful for my friend being there. I didn't want to talk, but at least she could look after the mechanics of the trip. 'Come on,' she said after a while, 'Let's go check into the bed and breakfast.'

My hand quivered slightly as I stumbled to write my fictitious name. The landlady surveyed us both. She knew what I was up to, I was sure. She'd probably seen it many times over – two nervous Irish girls on a one-night stay in a budget B&B in Birmingham. It was hardly on the usual tourist trail. She handed us a large wooden tag with a tiny key on the end and told us breakfast would be served from eight o'clock.

We whiled away the day as best we could, speaking nothing of the reason for our journey, but chatting lightly about the shops we would find in London in the next couple of days. In the evening we went to see a movie. That night sleep did not come easily but I eventually fell into troubled slumber with dreams jumbled with scenes from the stupidly romantic film we had just seen. Unlike the movie, there was no slushy romantic ending and I awoke many times with a jolt, my body aching and damp with sweat.

The next morning I was faced with a plate of bacon, egg, sausage and tomato – the full English breakfast. We ate together quietly, my friend struggling to make light conversation before she left to take the train down to London. She was meeting her cousins ahead of time and, if all went to plan, they would meet me off the same Intercity the next day. I didn't want her to come with me to the clinic. This was a part of my life that no one would share. That way it didn't really exist.

The clinic was a large forbidding private house with a gravel drive. Inside a group of women sat on red plastic chairs gazing at the whitewashed walls. It was smarter than the counselling offices of the previous day, but to me it had an acrid smell of disinfectant and fear. A cheery young girl greeted me at the desk. She was pretty, with a warm, friendly smile. It was a comfort, but I was careful not to lose my composure as I signed in with my false name and handed her the envelope containing the cash. It was all so surreal. I have no real recollection of the time or order of events, and my memory is just snapshots of detail. I was shown to the 'Rose room'. Pale pink walls and worn carpet housed just two beds, one already taken. The other girl didn't acknowledge my presence when I entered the room and we both sat speechless, staring at the floor.

A few moments later a doctor and nurse broke the spell of silence as they came laughing together into the room. 'Now, Martina Walsh,' the doctor smiled at me. 'Isn't that a nice name.' It took a second to compose myself and I'm sure my eyes must have betrayed my shock and horror. What did he mean about the name? Did he know it wasn't my own? Was he really just being nice? No, calm down, you're just being paranoid, I told myself. The doctor continued in the same friendly manner, going through a set of questions and scribbling notes. 'OK, that's all,' he said, springing up from the bed. 'Don't you worry, it will all be over soon. Now, you had nothing to eat or drink this morning, so we're ready to go.' This jolted me out of my daze.

'Nothing to eat?' I stuttered. 'Well yes, I had breakfast. Bacon and egg and . . .' Both the doctor and nurse stared at me in horror.

'You ate breakfast?' The question was repeated in sheer disbelief.

'Yes. Was I not supposed to?' I asked weakly.

'Well, we can't possibly do the operation, you'll be dangerously sick if we give you an anaesthetic on a full stomach.'

I felt stupid and naïve. I couldn't remember anyone telling me not to eat, and this was my first experience of hospitals or anaesthetics or any such thing. How was I to know? The pair disappeared to consult outside the room.

'It's OK,' said the nurse on her return; 'if you stay here, we'll see if we can fit you in at the end of the day. Hopefully by then that breakfast will have gone through your system.'

I was moved to a larger room where six beds awaited their afternoon check-ins. It was still early and I had to wait there by myself all day. Still, I was grateful that no one else was around and I took the bed in the far corner, near the window. Through the venetian blind I could see the morning sun warming the street below, but it avoided the window's gaze and the ward remained a chill, steely white. I pulled my cardigan tighter and tucked my feet underneath me, saving them from the cold, clean pool of a floor.

My mind's eye watched, as though looking in on some kind of nightmare, detached from the body that sat holding itself on the bed. Gradually the day wore on and each bed was filled with its sorrowful charge. Time was beyond me. Part of me longed for the nurses to come and take me away. But mostly I feared the passing of the hours that would bring the time closer. I had a newspaper and magazines, which my eyes read, but my mind did not register. Around mid afternoon a ray of sunlight filtered through the window. It picked out the particles in the air and fleetingly turned the corners of my mouth in a transient moment of peace and comfort. Would the same sun be shining in Donegal? I checked myself abruptly and banished the thought. Such mind wanderings were dangerous. I had to concentrate on focusing on my nothingness.

A girl stirred in the bed opposite. She had been brought back on a trolley half an hour before, still groggy with the anaesthetic. I could hear her whimpering and before long her whimpers turned into sobs which she muffled under the sheets. I didn't know what to do. If I went to her I risked my own composure. I didn't want to talk to anyone. One of the orderlies had tried to chat to me when I first went to the ward. She asked me what I did and I told her that I worked in a bank. I felt terribly lonely in this strange place in a foreign country, but in a way I was relieved there was no one Irish there. It helped keep home at bay. The girl's sobs were turning into deep tortured wails which she was failing to subdue in the white cotton. At that moment it hit me. All day and for the past few weeks I had persuaded myself that this was a necessary evil. I had made a mistake and it was up to me to deal with it with minimum fuss. But what I was about to do was . . .

'It's your time now, Miss Walsh,' said a nurse as a porter brought a wheelchair to my bedside and told me to get into the white gown. Moments later I lost myself to the needle-induced haze.

I awoke, back on the ward with a pounding head and lurching stomach. I was terribly sick and longed for the numbness of sleep. It was dark and quiet on the ward, except for the restless stirring of other haunted dreams. Eventually, I too quietly cried myself to sleep.

The next morning I set my mind that there would be no more tears. As the train slowed down into Euston station I concentrated on looking out for my friend with thoughts of the big city and wonderings about what the day might have in store. What needed to be done was done. I had walked out of the clinic resolving to leave the nightmare of the last few weeks within its walls. The only reminder would be the packet of pills in my bag and the needle bruise on my hand.

'Oh, what did they do to you?' asked my friend in horror as she met me and spotted the ugly mark. 'It's just from the needle,' I whispered; 'they couldn't get a vein in my arm.'

'Goodness knows what the others will think you've been up to,' she said. But I didn't understand what she meant.

Somehow, meeting people helped relieve the guilt of all the lies. I had told my family I was going to London to meet friends. And sure enough, here I was, in London, meeting friends.

Back in Donegal I picked up the reins of my life and resolved to lay the experience to rest. It wasn't easy. My mind kept flashing back to that dreadful ward and I kept expecting someone to stumble across something that would unveil my secret. Only one week later, a very real horror caught up with me. I was serving in Daddy's bar which, as usual in the summer, was filled with tourists and strangers. At one time a woman stopped me and started chatting. The conversation was light and friendly. Then she said something that really stopped me in my tracks.

'Y'know you really remind me of someone,' she said. 'Oh really?' I laughed. Then she said the name. In that moment the room spun around then dived into silent slow motion. I didn't hear the first name, but the surname the woman mouthed was 'Walsh'. I stared at her and began to shake as time held its breath.

'You couldn't be related could you?' Her question brought me to my senses.

'No, no, I don't know anyone of that name,' I said flustered and hurried off to the back room of the bar. Thankfully there was no one there and I stood clinging onto the table to steady myself. Who was this woman? Was this just one big coincidence, or did she know me? Had she seen me in England and recognised me? I was haunted and traumatised. When Daddy asked me to get up and sing with him I refused, making an excuse and leaving the bar as early as I could.

A few days later I took myself up to the monastery where I used to go with my grandmother. It was an awful time. The priest reacted bitterly when I confessed that I'd had an abortion. He refused to give me absolution. I was angry, but more at myself than the priest. He had acted in the only way I should have expected. I realised my cheek. In one moment I had asked for forgiveness for the abortion and in another I told him about the contraceptives. He advised that I should strongly reconsider my intentions for my life and sexual behaviour. In my mind I wrote him, the church and God off as being 'old-fashioned'. Didn't they understand that the pill would prevent the necessity for so many abortions?

That was the last time I went to confession and I didn't take communion until many years later. In my heart I didn't feel pure enough and couldn't expect that God would forgive me for what I had done. My mother was aware that I had stopped going to communion, but I guess she thought it was tied up with my attitude towards confession. She too remembered the hurts of my childhood and knew that I had always found it difficult, but had more sense than to push me. She also had the wisdom to trust that I would resolve my issues of faith alone with God.

It will always hurt to look back on this period in my life. It was just one mistake and a few days in a lifetime, but it will live with me for ever. My naivety told me I could keep it a secret and one day it would disappear from my memory. But a secret like that burns you up. When it came to the time when I dearly wanted a family, I was haunted by scenes from that awful day in the clinic. I didn't deserve a child. How could I even imagine myself as a mother after what I had done? In the years that followed, I hardened my heart, gritted my teeth and got on with life. Little did I know that I was building a hard wall around a fragile shell that one day would need to be broken.

# Chapter 8

In September 1972 I returned to Dublin to begin my second year at the Royal Irish Academy. I'd made loads of friends in my first year and although I'd been happy living with the McFaddens in Rathfarnham, I was eager to get my own place nearer to both the college and Dublin's thriving social scene. I took a little flat on Palmerston Road in the Rathmines area where there were lots of other students. Now I could live my own life and do my own thing. I loved it. Ciarán also moved up to the city that year, so Clannad played many gigs around Dublin's pubs and coffee bars, with Pól joining us whenever he could get away from Sligo. The Coffee Kitchen and The Swamp remained our favourite haunts and we'd often meet there, whether or not we were playing a gig ourselves. Even if you turned up on your own, you could be sure to bump into someone you knew and there was always a good band on.

One evening I was out with Ciarán, Pádraig, Noel and my friend Maria. The place was in great spirits, noisy and crammed with students, and we stayed for a couple of drinks while we waited for the dance over the road to get going. A group of lads were propping up the bar and I noticed that one of them kept looking over at me. He was good-looking and one time I smiled at him before quickly turning back to talk with Maria. From the corner of my eye I could see him still staring and when we later got up to leave he caught my arm as we passed by the bar.

'You going over the Mount Pleasant?' he said, in a light west-country accent.

'Yes.'

'Well, do you think I could have the first dance with you when we get in there?'

I looked at him. His face was warm, handsome and friendly. 'Yeah, maybe,' I said and quickly walked off to catch up with the others. Maria squealed when I told her. 'He's lovely,' she said. 'Are you gonna look out for him?' 'Yeah, I'll see. Notice he didn't offer to pay me in though!'

I danced with Bernard most of the night. He was charming and came from Mayo but was living in Dublin for his work. He was a couple of years older than me and had his own car. It wasn't the best-looking thing on four wheels, but for a twenty-year-old girl from Donegal, it added to his appeal. He too had found many friends in Dublin and there was always a party somewhere. We found ourselves seeing each other regularly and became close friends. Bernard could get on with anyone and I was pleased that Ciarán and my uncles liked him. Of course news got back to the family and there was lots of fuss and excitement from the girls when I eventually took him home. He was great with the younger ones and my parents warmed to him instantly. In many ways he was my first real boyfriend. I'd had a 'childhood sweetheart' back home, a local boy who spent many hours up at our house. We'd grown up together and when I came home from school in the holidays we would meet up to go to the dances and he would be my 'boyfriend'. It was a lovely, innocent relationship, but it had fizzled out over the years I had lived away from home. Now Bernard had come along and it was my first experience of 'going steady'.

At the beginning of 1973 Clannad were asked to perform a song in the National Song Contest. This is a fairly big deal in Ireland, with the winner going forward to the Eurovision Song Contest. There were ten bands of many different styles from all over Ireland and we considered it an honour to be asked to perform. Our entry into the contest resulted in a large amount of national publicity and it was this that caught the attention of the Philips record company. Three years had gone by since we had won the Letterkenny Folk Festival and we'd not yet claimed the prize of making a record on the Philips label. They'd probably been happy enough that we had not pushed the issue, but now, with all the extra publicity, they considered it a more viable time to get us into the studio.

We might have predicted the result of the contest. We came second to last. It was the same old story. We were chosen for the contest because they knew we would perform a Gaelic song. The one we chose was written by Mick Hanly, called 'An Pháirc' ('The Field'). It was a beautiful song that we all loved and we performed it well. But when it came to the judging, as expected, we got loud applause and big marks from the regions of Donegal and Galway, but very low marks from all the other regions who didn't appreciate our Irish-language song. It didn't bother us unduly. We were starting to get used to it by then and it was more important to us to stay true to what we wanted to do with our music.

The making of the album, however, was great fun. We recorded and mixed it in just two days and it was a huge thrill for us to be in the studio – the kind of experience we'd only read about. Most of the pieces were our own arrangements of traditional Gaelic songs, with a slightly funkier edge born through the influence of some of the jazz records Ciarán had been listening to. John Curran, the producer whom the record company had chosen for us, was also a complete 'jazz head' and a great saxophone player. He loved what we were doing with our arrangements of the traditional folk pieces and brought in a friend of his, Johnny Wadham, on percussion. Johnny's reputation went before him and we were totally in awe of one of Ireland's finest jazz drummers.

Working with John Curran was wonderful. I'll never forget first meeting him. He came to see us in Dublin and we all met in my little bedsit. Mammy was also up to visit and as she and John sat on the bed, the five of us had to line up in front of them and sing a few lines of music so John could get a feel for our voices.

Who could have imagined that a few months later we'd have been holding a piece of vinyl in our hands? It was our very first record, simply called *Clannad*. It felt good.

Bernard was really excited for me. We were getting on well and enjoying life but the months were passing quickly and I was due to leave college in a couple of weeks. It was looking hopeful that I might be able to get a job back home and, although I would miss my city life, something in me was yearning for

The Slieve Foy Dance Band in the mid-1950s. From left to right: Rosemarie (Daddy's sister), Gran Harden, Johnnie (Jennie) Gallagher, Patsy Fagan, Daddy, Mammy and Lala (Daddy's brother).

Slieve Foy in the 1960s. From left to right: Danny Ward, Lala Harden, Charlie McCole, Daddy, Paddy Joe O'Donnell, Rosemarie O'Donnell and Mammy.

Daddy, Mammy and me.

Mammy and me before we left Dublin to go and live in Donegal, 1953.

The Duggan family. From left to right:
Pádraig, Eoin, me, Gog, Noel, Bríd and Columba.

My first choir led by Gran Duggan at Dore school. My mother saw too many Shirley Temple movies – that's me in the front!

Mammy with Pól, Ciarán and me outside my grandparents' house in Dore.

Spending our holidays in Dublin in 1959.  Daddy holding Deirdre
with Pól, me and Ciarán sitting in front.

Family members in Donegal,1959.  Back row, from left to right:
Bríd (Mammy's sister), Daddy and Mammy; second row, from left to right:
Pádraig, me, Ciarán, Pól and Noel, with Deirdre sitting in front.

Gog's class of 1961. I'm in the second row, second
from the right, beside my friends.

With Gran Harden after she came
back from America.

Daddy and me on the day of my first
Holy Communion.

Daddy's band in Scotland in the mid-1960s.
Back row, from left to right: Columba Duggan, Lala Harden, Daddy,
and Michael Morgan. Front row, from left to right: Francie Diver,
me (in my Irish dancing costume) and Bobby Doherty.

A trophy for the singing family. Back row, from left to right:
Daddy, me (I was singing and dancing at the Feis), Pól, Ciarán and Mammy;
front row, from left to right: Deirdre, Eithne and Leon.

The Irish Pantomime. I was principal girl and Noel Duggan was principal boy, with Gweedore actors, singers and dancers.

Pádraig, Enda McMonagle, Noel and me in our group with the ridiculous name, The Four Leaves, 1972. We lasted just three months.

Clannad at the launch of our third album, *Dúlamán*, 1976.

Clannad in concert in Germany in 1977, with Davy Arthur on the Bordhrán.

Donegal's mountain and sea air. Bernard and I rarely talked about the future. We didn't really have any plans – except maybe somewhere in the back of our minds – but after a romantic evening at the beginning of June he asked me to marry him. I was surprised, but delighted. Fancy me becoming engaged! I liked the idea and Bernard was thrilled when I said 'Yes'. The next day we went into town and chose a ring. It was a single diamond, costing sixty pounds. That was an awful lot of money to me, but Bernard was earning and he wanted it to be special. My parents seemed happy enough at the news and we arranged for Bernard's family to go down to Donegal for a few days' holiday so they could all meet. It was a lovely time and I knew Bernard's parents approved of his choice of fiancée. Everyone got on well together and I felt very much at ease about the whole thing. Of course, with Daddy's bar there was an easy social scene for our guests to fit into and I was happy enough to get up on stage with Daddy to show my future in-laws the true Brennan hospitality. Still, there was little talk of a wedding. It probably never really sunk in that this would be the next step. Anyway, with me not earning yet it would be a long time before we could save enough to get married. We were just enjoying the fuss around our engagement.

As the term ended we parted company, looking forward to the odd weekend when Bernard would come down to Donegal. He had to remain in Dublin for his work and I could not afford to stay there myself. At least if I went home I could earn some money in the bar until I found myself a teaching job.

My twenty-first birthday fell on 4 August 1973 and we had planned that Bernard and a group of other friends – largely musicians whom I hung around with at The Swamp or The Coffee Kitchen – would come down to celebrate with me. Bernard brought his car so we went out driving on one of my favourite routes towards Errigal, Donegal's highest mountain. It's a beautiful area – the mighty mountain governing the landscape, casting its stern eye across the Dunlewey Lake. As we pulled up in the car I pointed out Dunlewey House, only just visible through the trees over the other side of the lake. You often hear local people telling of the curse on the house. The story goes that three peasant families lost their homes in order that this mansion could be built and one of the peasant women cursed that no children would ever live there. Sure enough the two twins born to the builder's wife were dead at birth. The story had always made me shiver and the place held something of a fear and fascination long into my adult life.

'Come on,' said Bernard, 'let's go drive over to the house.'

'Oh no, I don't think so,' I said nervously. The folklore stories of my childhood were full of spirits and ghosts that haunted the house and all the locals could tell you about the notorious Major Cooper who owned the place at that time. I'd never actually encountered him myself (nor, I am sure, had many of those who spoke of him) but he was supposedly a crazy-eyed man with a huge curly moustache who was liable to chase you with his gun. My protestation fell on deaf ears. Bernard had already started the car and begun to drive down past the burnt-out church and along the tree-shaded long narrow road towards the house. Meanwhile my ears were full of the taunts and teasings of my friends and I was forced to join in nervously with their camaraderie.

As we approached the driveway I could feel the hair standing up on the back of my neck. Part of me was shaky with excitement and curiosity to see the house that had haunted my childhood dreams. The other part of me wanted to turn around and go home. We drove on further and then, pulling up just beyond its view, left the car to walk the last few hundred yards up to the house. We were all chatting, but something about the place made us whisper and, though we probably wouldn't admit it, I suspect each one of us had that slightly knotted feeling in the stomach. All at once Maria grabbed hold of my arm, making me jump.

'Máire, look.' She pointed towards one of the gables. We all looked up. There, in the little window at the top of the house, we could see a woman dressed in a white gown. She was waving and beckoning to us.

'Let's get out of here,' said Maria with a tremble in her voice.

With that we all turned and bolted back to the car. Leaping in, Bernard spun the car around and sped back down the driveway. We were all laughing and breathless.

'But she was beckoning to us,' protested Bernard, when we

regained our composure. 'Why did we run? Let's go back and see her.'

'No way,' I said, 'we're not going back there. It was too weird.'

'Yeah, what if she's some kind of lunatic locked up in the attic,' said Maria. But again, our protestations proved futile.

'Come on,' challenged one of the other lads, 'we'll drive back up there, then walk around the house. What's the worst that can happen? They can only tell us to leave.'

Again, intrigue goaded our excitement and we headed back towards the house. Maria gripped my arm and looked straight ahead, as if afraid to be the first to see anyone or anything. It was a hot August day, but still her fingers chilled my skin. As we made our way to the back of the house we were stopped in our tracks and caught our breath. It was so amazing. We were met with a huge working courtyard. It was obviously a place where animals were often kept, and probably prepared for slaughter. At the far side stood an imposing bell tower and sun rays bounced off big axes that regimented the courtyard, momentarily blinding our sight. As we squinted back at the house, a woman emerged from the back door. She was wearing an overall and rubber gloves and had a cloth in her hand.

'Can I help you?' she asked, in a familiar local accent.

We were all a little taken aback and looked at one other. 'Oh, sorry, we didn't mean to intrude,' said Bernard. 'We were just intrigued by the house. You see, it's Máire's birthday,' he said, gesturing towards me. 'She's always been intrigued by this house and we thought today would be a nice day to bring her for a closer look.' The woman was looking at me suspiciously. 'It was us who insisted,' said Bernard awkwardly; 'Máire said we shouldn't really come, it's just that the place seemed so interesting.' The woman looked us all up and down and half smiled. 'Well, I'm sure it wouldn't do any harm for you to drive once around the estate. I can't let you into the house because there's no one else here at the moment. The family aren't in residence just now.'

None of us felt brave enough to protest that we'd seen someone in the window. The mystery woman was obviously a family secret that the loyal housekeeper intended to keep that way.

'Thank you very much,' I said, reassuring her with my Donegal Irish. 'We didn't mean to trouble you.'

It was all very strange, and we spoke no more of it until we got back to the main road.

A year or so later I went to my cousin Biddy Doohan's bar for lunch. She lived near to the school in Falcarragh where I had, by then, taken on a teaching job and I would often pass an hour with her and the family. The bar could be busy and they also did bed and breakfast so Biddy was grateful to sit down for a spot of lunch and a chat after all the morning chores were done and the beds made up for the new guests. Mrs Leary, who rented a room in the house and helped out with the work, would also sometimes join us in a cup of tea. This particular day we got chatting and it turned out that Mrs Leary used to be a housekeeper up at the house in Dunlewey. She started to tell me a story about when she first went there how she used to find it strange that things were being moved around. There was one room in particular – the pool room – where she would often find that there were a couple of swords laid out on the pool table. The first time she thought nothing much of it and, giving them a quick dust, she mounted them back on the wall where they belonged. The very next day the same thing happened. Then again, a few days later, there were the swords on the pool table, yet no one was staying in the house at the time. It was strange, yet it didn't concern her too much. It was probably one of the other staff messing about. Then one day she came in from shopping and unloaded all her parcels in the kitchen while chatting to the two kitchen staff. 'What's that parcel there?' asked one of the women when most of the shopping had been put away. It was perfectly wrapped in brown paper.

'I don't know,' said Mrs Leary, 'it's not something I bought.'

The other women looked at each other. 'It wasn't here before,' they insisted. 'We've just cleaned this kitchen from top to toe and there was definitely no parcel on the table before you came in and we sat down for this cup of tea.' When they unwrapped the parcel they found it was a very old tea box, completely empty.

'How funny,' exclaimed Mrs Leary. 'What an odd thing to wrap up, and where on earth has it come from?'

The two women looked at each other knowingly and went on

to tell Mrs Leary that there was a ghost in the house, the Green Lady. She was a mischievous ghost who meant no harm, but did strange things around the residence.

As Mrs Leary recounted the story to me I sat in wonder, remembering the figure at the window on my twenty-first birthday. Could she have been the Green Lady? When I told Mrs Leary my tale she said that the window I seemed to be describing would have been that very pool room where she kept finding the misplaced swords.

It was all very strange. Years later I would return to the house at Dunlewey, this time with an official invite. The house was bought by the Guinness family and it was here that we filmed the video for 'In A Lifetime', the 1986 duet with Bono. Even then, as I was allowed freely to roam the house and grounds I felt a strange kind of eeriness, as if someone was watching, perhaps smiling and ready to make mischief. Who knows what went on in that house. Today a little boat sails on Dunlewey Lake and the guide charms the tourists with the stories of the Green Lady. Irish folklore is full of these kinds of tales – leprechauns, ghosts, fairies and pixies – but what happened on my twenty-first birthday is a mystery that only the house will ever know.

# Chapter 9

It was strange saying goodbye to my fiancé after my twenty-first birthday. We'd had a great time, but with so many people around we'd hardly spent any time alone together. Funnily enough I realised that this hadn't been too much of a problem for me. Indeed, when I thought about it, I recognised that I'd not really missed Bernard much at all that summer. He had become a great friend and he was lovely to be with when I was living in Dublin, but my college life was over and he – along with various other people I used to see and things I used to enjoy doing – was becoming less and less part of me. I was happy living back in Gweedore, working in the bar and spending time with the family. Brídín was running around the place like any crazy five-year-old and I think Mammy appreciated having me there as an extra pair of hands. I was also very excited to have an interview lined up for a teaching job at the boys' school in Falcarragh. It struck me how silly it was for me to be looking for a job in Donegal. If Bernard and I were to plan for a future together shouldn't I be ready to give up everything to be near him in Dublin? Although I harboured a little dream that I could perhaps do some music teaching, I wasn't confident enough in my ability to imagine I could get a job in Dublin, where school life was very different to the country. But then surely I could put my dream on hold and get some bar work so we could at least be together? I taunted myself with the various pros and cons of going back to Dublin with Bernard but, no matter how much I tried to convince myself otherwise, I had to admit to my overwhelming desire to remain at home in Gweedore. Still, I pushed such thoughts to the back of my mind. Bernard and I had no plans to see each other until

Clannad went up to Dublin for the Irish Music Awards ceremony in a couple of months' time. Perhaps I would feel differently by then.

The job interview was to take place in Letterkenny and Mammy drove me down there, chatting all the way about how she loved teaching and how proud she was that I might follow in her footsteps. We arrived in plenty of time and decided to go into a local café for a sandwich and cup of tea.

Sitting in the interview I found myself struggling to concentrate. My head felt fuzzy and there was a slight cramping in my stomach. Strange that a little nervousness should affect me so badly. I had been looking forward to the interview and was generally relaxed and calm.

Driving home in the car I felt increasingly sick and the nausea only grew worse as I rushed about getting ready to go down to work in the bar. I'd barely been there twenty minutes when I found myself leaning against the wall overcome by a pain in my stomach and sweating profusely. The next thing I knew, Daddy was calling my name: 'Máire, Máire, wake up, what is it?' There was a nasty taste of blood in my mouth and as I regained my focus I realised I had collapsed on the floor and was surrounded by a crowd of anxious-looking faces. I was taken to the hospital in Dungloe and treated for serious food poisoning. I was upset and shocked at knocking one of my teeth out with the fall and felt as if I was going to die with the pain in my stomach. It barely subsided all night and the pain-killers, given by the nurses, didn't seem to have any effect.

The next day, however, I felt much brighter, although desperately weak. Mammy and Daddy came to see me in the afternoon, then to my great surprise, who should walk in but my old childhood sweetheart. The hospital in Dungloe is a very small place with only three or four different wards and a strong community feel, so generally if people are visiting they check the register to see if there is anyone else they know receiving treatment whom they might call in on. Sure enough, my childhood sweetheart had been visiting a friend in the hospital and discovered my name on the list. We'd not seen each other in ages and it was lovely to chat and catch up with the news. A couple of hours soon went by as we filled each other in on the news of the last few years and reminisced about old times. I told him about the Royal Academy and meeting Bernard and my engagement, and some of the things the band had been up to in Dublin. We'd always found it easy to chat and laugh together and as he left I realised how much I had missed his friendship.

Laying there alone, I went back over some of the conversation, smiling to myself at some of the stories and memories they brought. Somehow it made me ponder more about what I wanted for my life. Thoughts of Bernard niggled at my mind and I began to face up to the realisation that the relationship wasn't going to go any further.

In November Clannad headed up to Dublin to perform two songs at an Irish Music Awards ceremony. There was an air of excitement about the evening. The ceremony was held at the prestigious RDS concert hall and it was great to be in a proper theatre with a large stage and a full house. I was nervous, but it wasn't entirely to do with the concert. Bernard had been thrilled to see me, but I couldn't return the warmth of his embrace. It was a difficult thing to do, but after the show I gave him back my engagement ring and told him that I didn't think I could marry him. He looked desperately sad and didn't say much. I babbled on about the time not being right and being too young, willing him to say something. Maybe I expected him to be angry. But he wasn't. He just walked away quietly, and that was that.

By then I was a couple of months into my teaching career. I had been employed to teach music at the boys' school in Falcarragh, and it soon became more than just a job. I loved my life there and was happy to put all my energy into developing good and unusual lessons for my charges. I got on very well with the priests who ran the school and, still being young myself, the boys seemed to think I was cool. Beyond my set lessons, I found myself getting involved in many aspects of school life, going to football matches with the boys and staying late for extra music lessons and activities. I was committed to opening their eyes to the wonder of music and passionate about its ability to bring out something creative in the most regimented boy's mind. The music lessons I had been sent to as a child were valuable, but I also recognised how limited that kind of teaching can be to the development of musical imagination. So many people learn to play an instrument according to a strict classical regime which does little to develop the natural musical ear. I saw it as my mission to free my pupils from this kind of approach, releasing their minds to their own music appreciation and creativity. Teachers passing by my classroom may have raised the odd eyebrow as they heard everything from Bach to the Beatles and Led Zeppelin being played. We used all sorts of association games as I tried to get them to understand the importance of music in painting pictures and setting atmospheres. I'd play the '*William Tell* Overture' and, of course, they'd recognise the 'Lone Ranger'. Then I'd give them some kind of classical piece that might be used in a movie and get them to write the scene as the music unfolded. Young boys have wild imaginations and I could sense their excitement as their eyes were opened with each musical nuance. They came from a generation where music wasn't important in school, so they had no preconceived ideas about music lessons and I know my classes were highly anticipated.

One day I was teaching them about some of the instruments of the orchestra. We were concentrating on the string section – the cellos, double bass, violins and violas – when one little boy at the front piped up, 'Oh Miss, is that what's out in the shed?' I was mystified.

After the lesson, young Sammy took me and a bunch of other curious boys around the back of the school and down the path to the huge old barn that people rarely bothered going near. The boys pulled at the door and as it creaked open, sending up a cloud of dust, my eyes were met with hidden treasure. There were two old cellos and a couple of double basses. They'd been left there years ago when the school used to have an orchestra and here they were just abandoned, thrown in the hay. They had clearly been beautiful instruments, but were now covered in thick cobwebs and being eaten by the rats and woodworm. That evening I told Ciarán about the find and he was so excited to see them that he came the very next day to pick me up from school so that he might take a look. One cello and a bass were way beyond repair, but with a couple of bob donation to the school and a promise to tune all the pianos, Ciarán persuaded the headmaster to let him have the other two instruments. He took them off to Derek Nelson, a restorer in Dublin, and still today

Ciarán is the proud owner of the revived double bass. It has a beautiful, rich tone and has travelled the world with Clannad as a treasured friend.

It was a happy time in my life. Since visiting me in hospital something had rekindled with my childhood sweetheart and we began to meet up regularly again. We shared so much in common and had many a laugh reminiscing about our childhood days when we used to do the pantomimes together. He always took a lead role back in those days and could still charm an audience even now. He was popular and my mother and sisters adored him. It was a nice, easy relationship and he'd often pick me up after work to go for a drive or walk on the beach, or sometimes to the cinema. Life was, indeed, good.

My return to Donegal had also fuelled my passion for the traditional music of the area. There were so many wonderful poems and stories put to music, many of them laments over a lost love. That 'love' usually referred to Ireland itself. In the years when you weren't allowed to be proud to be Irish, to sing of its beauty was strictly forbidden. So people used to encrypt these sentiments using girls' names to refer to their beloved country. Popular songs such as 'Róisín Dubh' and 'Cáit ní Dhuibhir' were none other than songs about Ireland.

The boys, especially Ciarán, shared my passion and we were all hungry to hear more of the songs from our heritage, researching their origins and later working new musical arrangements around the melodies. We'd often head off with a reel-to-reel tape recorder and a half pack of Guinness (depending on who we were visiting) to speak to the older people of the area. Most of them are now long gone but it is to these people that we owe Clannad's beginnings. Sometimes we'd sit for hours as our wise friends delighted in sharing stories and songs from their childhood. They'd usually begin by carefully relating the origin of the song – what part of Ireland it came from and its purpose or message. Then they'd give us the words, followed finally by the melody. We have tape upon tape of world-worn voices singing out proudly in Gaelic tongue. Some of them were just too 'traditional' for my voice to interpret, but many of the songs were reworked as we gave them the Clannad treatment, trying to recreate the moods and pictures of the stories using instrumentation. Still many of the locals who heard us when we played in the bar shunned our commitment to our Irish culture, but we continued collecting the songs that were later to fuel the interest of a far wider community.

In the summer holidays we made the most of the Irish festivals and it was exciting to find that we had a small following. Other European festivals beckoned, but our most exciting offer came from a couple of German agents who were putting together a complete tour the following year. They had been over in Ireland on holiday and, having come across our first album, had deliberately lengthened their stay in Donegal, awaiting our return from a little festival in France so they might share their idea. It was to be a twenty-one-date tour, featuring seven or eight Irish acts and covering the whole of Germany. We, of course, were flattered to be considered and knew that it might be the beginning of something bigger for the band. Pádraig and Noel were still in Dublin, but we knew that by the time the tour came around they would have completed their exams and would perhaps be able to take some time out before fully committing to life at sea. I loved teaching, but I was overwhelmed by excitement at the thought of going on tour with Clannad. Thankfully the tour would fall quite near the end of the term and I thought I'd be able to persuade the school to let me take the time out if my mother offered to cover my classes.

Before the year was out we were approached by the Gael-Linn record label about the possibility of recording another album. They were only a small organisation, but had a certain underground credibility in Ireland and were committed to supporting anything that promoted the Gaelic language. At that time a large plastic company, Wavin Pipes, had approached the label with a request for a custom-made album that they could use as Christmas gifts. Gael-Linn had immediately thought Clannad might be able to offer something suitable. The timing was perfect for us as we already had a stack of new songs and were eager for any opportunity that would get us back in the studio.

The producer that Gael-Linn recommended was Donal Lunny who had a huge reputation in the Irish music scene. His imprint could usually be found on the music I most loved – from the Emmet Spiceland to Planxty and Moving Hearts – so I was especially thrilled at the opportunity to meet and work with him. He was brilliant and really knew how to bring out the best in our arrangements of traditional music. We were delighted with the result and called the project, simply, *Clannad II.*

April 1975 and the German tour came around before we knew it so I left my students to my mother's charge and headed off, not then imagining that my teaching days might be coming to an end for good. It was the start of a new adventure. There was a brilliant atmosphere on tour with all the other musicians and we loved the lifestyle. Each show was three hours of music and after a few nights we had worked our way up to become the headline act. We'd do a show and the buzz would keep us up most of the night laughing, talking and jamming with other musicians and any local hangers-on. There were many long journeys and after twenty dates we were exhausted but, as we say in Ireland, it was a great 'craic'. The final evening took us to the Philharmonic Hall in Berlin. There was a tremendous vibe in the place and when we got up to play it was reminiscent of that night in Letterkenny five years ago. I felt free on stage, moving to the music. There was a surreal connection between us, as the music floated and played off against each other. It was, of course, the result of rehearsal and fine-tuning, but that night everything gelled together in an almost spiritual way, as if we were fulfilling some kind of destiny.

Our final piece – 'Nil se'n lá' ('It's Not Yet the Daytime') – was a song that is still very dear to us. We'd discovered this version through an old lady who lived on Tory Island. Traditionally, it was a drinking song and we'd taken the spirit of the song and arranged it into a more jazzy six-minute-long piece that worked up into a mighty crescendo. (The song has remained with Clannad over the years and has developed along with us, still being a favourite to perform in concert today.)

As we played our final chord the audience went wild and we received a standing ovation. It felt more than good. In our dressing-room afterwards the beer flowed and we were high with the excitement of our performance and the reaction of the crowd. In a moment we all looked at each other. We'd hardly discussed the subject before, but we were all thinking the same thing.

'So,' I said, 'will we go professional?'

The look on everyone's faces told me it was unanimous and

Ciarán said, 'Well, I suppose we could try it for a while.' We were all grinning from ear to ear.

'So that's goodbye for now to the boats then,' said Pádraig to Noel.

'Yeah, and no more teaching for me,' I said with a touch of sorrow, but the excitement of what might lie ahead quashed any inkling of regret.

So began Clannad's professional life, but still we had no real illusions. We would try it for a season. If ever we were to play music seriously, the time was now, before life became more complicated. We knew that we would not be able to make a living in Ireland playing the kind of music we wanted to do, but the past few months had proved that we could earn ourselves a committed following in Europe. We had two albums to sell, so maybe, just maybe, we could make a go of things.

We were terribly naïve. There was no proper record deal, no manager, very little professional equipment and we didn't even have our own means of transport. At the very least we needed to buy a PA system and a van. Thankfully Gog, supportive as ever, offered to lend us the money for equipment, and what we lacked in wisdom we compensated for in pure gall and cheek. The boys nominated me to make a call to a friend of my father's who was a banker in Northern Ireland. He often came over to the bar on a weekend and we knew he loved to hear us play. So the plan was simple – as a bank manager he had money, and money was what we needed to buy a van. In my naivety I was quite taken aback when he asked me to outline our business plan. What business plan? All we needed was money for a van. It had never occurred to me that he would need to know more detail about it – what condition it was in, how long it would last, how we planned to make the repayments on the loan . . . Whether he really believed in us, or whether he simply couldn't refuse our cheek, we will never know, but within a few days we had the money we needed and soon became the proud owners of a blue transit van.

Meanwhile, I also landed us a manager. 'Celtic rock' had become the 'big thing' in Ireland and a band called Horslips were riding the crest of the wave. We'd heard they were on tour and were absolutely thrilled when our return from Germany was met with an invite to support them on their date at the Dublin

Stadium. It was a fantastic show and we knew there was a real buzz about us, but the surprise was to come a couple of days later when I bumped into Horslips' drummer, Eamon Carr. He'd just bought a newspaper and we walked along together as he flicked through to see if there was a review of the gig.

'Get a load of this,' said Eamon, as he stood still so that I could see the paper properly. 'Somebody certainly likes you!' There was a whole page review of the concert, written by a local journalist, Fachna O Kelly. I was a bit embarrassed to say the least as I realised that, rather than concentrating on Horslips, most of the feature was given over to a rave review about Clannad – with thanks to Horslips for introducing this new band to a wider audience.

A few days later I got in touch with Fachna to thank him for the article and the conversation turned around to our need for a manager. We had a gig scheduled in Buncrana, back in Donegal, and he promised to come down to see us and talk further. When Fachna turned up he also had a friend with him, Nicky Ryan, who was something of a sound engineer. We had a great evening together and became excited by Fachna's and Nicky's enthusiasm for what we were doing. Nicky seemed to know a lot about the kind of equipment we were going to need to be a self-sufficient band and was amazed when we told him of our grandfather's offer of financial help. Gog was wonderful in that way. There was no interest on the loan and no pressure to pay it back within a certain time. He was just happy to see us chasing our dream. By the end of the evening we had resolved that Fachna would become our manager and that Nicky, having helped us buy the equipment we needed, would join us as our sound engineer.

It was a good move. Fachna had many contacts in the music business and, over a period of around six months, he really helped us broaden our audience. By November that year he'd booked us on our first solo tour of Germany. We took off in the transit, with both Fachna and Nicky, and had the time of our lives. The budget was tight so we were staying in people's flats, sleeping on floors wherever anyone would put us up, or bunking down together in the cheapest motels we could find. We met loads of people, many of whom followed us back to Donegal the next summer. (In fact Mammy and Daddy still shudder at the memory of dozens of European hippy-types who frequently camped in their garden and ate them out of house and home.) The venues were mostly small clubs and cafés but we usually got a good reception and we were happy to work hard, doing twenty-five or more dates in the space of a month.

After Christmas it was back again to Europe. This time France, but by then things were not running so smoothly. Fachna had organised the tour, but was often nowhere to be seen. We could rarely get hold of him and no one knew what was going on. That was when it emerged that things were hotting up for him with the Boomtown Rats. He and Bob Geldof had been friends for years and Fachna had watched the Rats develop a huge underground following. When the time was right he officially took over as their manager, just as they were offered a big record deal. We couldn't be angry with him. In fact we were almost proud. Before us he was just a journalist, now he was managing the hottest band in Ireland. He later went on to manage various other people including Sinead O'Connor and a whole host of other success stories. Meanwhile, we stumbled through the French tour and decided that Nicky Ryan – already travelling with us as our sound engineer – should take over more of Fachna's role, becoming the spokesman for the band.

Before his departure Fachna had been negotiating with the Gael-Linn label for us to do another album. We had been working on new material all the time and were excited at the thought of going back into the studio. This time Gael-Linn came up with an advance of six hundred pounds. At the time it seemed like a huge amount of money. Today it would barely get you a day in a studio. With a little finance behind us, Nicky wanted us to record in a new state-of-the-art studio he had heard about in Wales. We loved the idea. Of course, being a sound engineer, he was like a child in a sweet shop when we took a ten-day residence in Rockfield Studio, and for us it felt as though we had really joined the ranks of the 'professional band'. Rockfield was in a beautiful setting and it certainly helped the creative juices flow as we lived and worked together full-time. There was lots of experimentation, including putting the harp on top of the grand piano to see how it would alter the sound. It didn't. A lot of effort was put into elaborate harmony arrangements and it was the first time we really experimented with our voices as instruments. There were lots of 'oohs' and 'aaaghs' as the vocals were arranged to create atmosphere and capture the ambience of the original songs. Ten days later we had a finished master, and we were thrilled with our work. The resulting album was *Dúlamán*. It was largely made up of Gaelic songs, taking the title from one of our favourite folklore songs about two dulaman (seaweed) merchants, one of whom is trying to win the hand of the other's beautiful daughter.

We were working hard and loving being part of a professional band. It was all so new and exciting and I soon realised that my interest at home was becoming less intense. I barely had any time to invest in my relationship and though I was terribly fond of this man who had been my childhood sweetheart, I was increasingly distracted by my work and knew that our relationship would not stand the strain of my continual absence from home. It was the end of an era. We were both disappointed in a way, but parted on good terms and several years later Mammy shed a little tear as she played the organ at his wedding.

Another love had passed me by. Still, I was only just in my twenties. I had the whole world at my feet, and an innate passion for music and travel ran richly in my veins.

## Chapter 10

It turned out that 1976 was a busy year. We were delighted to be invited back on the 'Irish Music' tour of Germany again in the spring and, having spent much of the year doing as many live shows as possible, we finished up back among our German friends for our second solo tour before Christmas. We were still based at home and barely scraping a living together, but we were living a dream. We'd made many friends in Germany and they held great parties. I soon realised that people tended to assume that, being Irish, we had an innate penchant for the drink. Every night after a show we'd be taken on a tour of the local bars, then it would be back to someone's flat for more drinking. People would produce instruments so there'd often be a session going and the chatting, laughter and general partying would go on deep into the early hours. I'd never really indulged in drinking, even when working in Daddy's bar, but somehow it just became part of life on tour. I'd usually drink German beer or lager and sometimes vodka, but at four o'clock in the morning you'd drink anything that was going. We were all singing, and thought we were enjoying ourselves. Of course the next morning we'd wake with thumping heads and say, 'Never again'. But we always did. Another show meant a new town and new friends with more drinking.

We also developed another habit. I'd never smoked as a teenager. I knew some of the girls at school did it, and later in my father's bar the air used to be thick with nicotine fumes, but we'd grown up in a cigarette-free household and admired our parents' stance against it. Then again, life on tour was different. We were musicians and that's what musicians did. It was in Germany that we were also introduced to cannabis. It seemed quite widely available, though I was shocked when I was first offered it. The first time I tried it, I hated it. But it was 'cool', so I persevered. That's the worst thing about young people with drugs, drink and sex. It becomes the 'thing to do'. It was all part of 'having a good time'. More and more we found ourselves surrounded by people who indulged and supplied us, and the odd joint every now and again helped us wind down after a show.

Despite all the partying, life on the road in those days was pretty rough. There's not a lot of glamour in a clapped-out transit van in the middle of winter. This particular year we were only a few dates away from the end of our pre-Christmas tour when we had a rather hairy experience on the autobahn. Our beloved van had done us proud, clocking up hundreds of miles in the summer, but it was now in need of urgent repair and maintenance and we were all willing it to survive the final leg of the tour. The clutch had started giving us trouble in Berlin and by the time we reached our gig in Frankfurt it had completely given up on us. The next day we were due to head back north towards Hanover but having no time to get the clutch professionally fixed, we did a makeshift repair with the aid of a wire coat-hanger. We were both mad and very stupid. It was a death trap. Our cousin Colm Gillespie was our driver for the tour and I sat in the front passenger seat, with Pól in between us both operating the clutch with the coat-hanger used as a hand control. Germany's autobahns are renowned for their lack of speed limits and only a few miles out of Frankfurt we found ourselves surrounded by vehicles, all doing over eighty miles an hour, with a huge juggernaut rapidly gaining ground in the rear-view mirror.

'Erm . . . Colm,' came Ciarán's voice from the back of the van, 'I don't know what's going on, but this juggernaut seems to be getting very close up behind us.'

'I know, I know, the clutch seems to be jammed, I can't get a gear,' came a rather frantic reply. I noticed Colm had begun to sweat profusely as Pól pulled and writhed with the coat-hanger in a more than distressed manner.

'It's not working, it must have become detached or stuck or something,' said Pól in a frenzied tone. I turned around and could see the front of the lorry looming large behind. Within seconds it would be bearing down on us.

'Pull off, pull off!' screamed Pól, but there was nowhere to go. Frantically I fixed my eyes on the road. The lay-by widened ahead. 'There, there!' I shouted. Then came the horn blast. A long, loud bellow. In a second we had spun off the road into the grit of the lay-by. The van jolted around and the air was filled with the smell of burning rubber and dust. Colm wrestled with the wheel to get control before we finally ground to a halt. Everyone sat for a moment in stunned silence holding our breath. I am sure that if not for Colm's rally-driver skill, being able to manoeuvre the van quickly off the road, we would not have escaped so lightly.

We only had five more gigs left to do, but they were all up north, out past Hanover. We were only a few miles outside Frankfurt with another one hundred and sixty or so miles ahead, but it was late in the afternoon and our van was completely, as the Germans would say, 'Kaput'.

The two mechanics who came to rescue us looked none too impressed as they towed our wreckage into the garage. Germans in general have huge respect for their motor vehicles and this pair looked at us in horror and disbelief when we begged them to try anything they could to get our rotting lump of metal on the road again. It had been sub zero temperatures for the majority of the tour and we joked that the van was probably held together by no more than ice, both inside and out. That is, ice and the boxes of records that we hid in the van door linings. We weren't really supposed to take them abroad, but hey, we had to earn a living somehow.

After much pleading and persuasion the mechanics agreed to help us. We only needed a few more days. If we could just get back to Hamburg after the final couple of shows we would be all right. From there it was the ferry to Harwich and then home. Time was ticking by and we knew that there was no way the van would be ready to get us to the show that night. But, born into the tradition of my father's showband, there was never any thought of cancelling. The show must go on! There was only one option. We would have to hire a van to get us up north and come back for ours later. It was a depressing scene. We could only get a van big enough to carry the gear and so had to rent a car for us to travel in, knowing all the time that this was going to completely eat away the money we had earned on the tour so far. Then there was another problem. One by one the boys realised that they didn't have their driving licences with them. I had not even taken my test at that time, so we found ourselves with only one driver for two vehicles.

'What about Brad,' whispered Pól to me. 'You talk to him Máire, he really likes you, see if he's got a licence.' Brad was a 'friend' we'd picked up on our travels. He was an American travelling in Germany and was hitching a ride for some of the final leg of our tour.

'Yeah, come on Máire, use your charm,' encouraged Ciarán. 'You know he's sweet on you.' I did and I didn't much care for the idea. Thankfully, however, Brad twigged to the situation himself. Yes, he did have a driving licence with him, and yes, he was willing to drive us until Colm could return to Frankfurt in a few days and pick up our own van.

It was after nine-thirty in the evening when we finally rolled up at the club. We should have been there at eight o'clock. Thankfully everyone was really good to us. At least the venue, being a club, meant that the bulk of people had hung around, happy to drink and chat while they waited for us to show up. As the boys set about putting up the gear I struggled to get changed in the van. It was freezing cold, my hair was tangled and lifeless and my hands were too frozen to put my make-up on properly. I was exhausted and still reeling from the shock on the autobahn. The last thing I was fit for was going on stage. Still, we knew that having spent most of our earnings on vehicle hire and repairs, these last five gigs would be the only source of profit from the entire tour. 'We'll laugh about this one day,' I told myself.

A few days later we were reunited with our own van and finally made our way back to Hamburg, where our good friend Sita accommodated us for the night after we had played our final concert. It had been a great tour, but now our attention was turned back towards Ireland.

Saying goodbye to Sita, we set off the next day to the ferry port, thankful to be heading home for Christmas with the rest of the family. The van was shaking badly and seemed to have very little power.

'Come on, baby, come on,' Colm coaxed. But it was no good.

We were still about twenty miles from the ferry port, when our heap of rotting metal gave in again and the boat sailed across the Channel leaving us on foreign soil. Deep depression set in, especially when we finally relented and made our way back to Sita's house.

'I want to go home,' said Pól in a painful wail.

'You think the rest of us don't,' snapped Ciarán.

'Shut up, will you,' I said. The last thing we needed was an argument. In my mind I was trying to make the best of our dire situation. Perhaps it comes from being the eldest in the family, or the only girl in the band, but in my head I was plotting: 'Well I could get a turkey and some spuds and perhaps we could all have Christmas dinner round at Sita's house.' I swallowed hard. I wanted to be home too. More than anything I wanted to sit at Mammy's table, surrounded by the wittering of my sisters and everyone making merry in the traditional Brennan Christmas.

We spent the rest of the day wondering what to do about our sorry plight and growing increasingly miserable. Then Colm disappeared to phone his brother, Joe, who lived in Manchester, England. The plan was to try to persuade Joe to drive his jeep down to Harwich and tow us back. It was a huge favour to ask anyone, especially so close to Christmas. The journey was over four hundred miles and the weather in England was atrocious at that time. Colm returned with a smile on his face. The deal was done. We should arrange to have the van towed onto the ferry the next morning.

Sita waved us off again and we set our minds on the long journey home. We were too embarrassed to stay with the van, so once we'd seen Colm fix it to the back of the tow we walked onto the ferry as foot passengers. It was a long, arduous sea crossing and – after nearly twenty hours at sea – when we arrived in England it was dark with winter and distressingly cold. I was exhausted, both physically and emotionally, and if I hadn't been so numb with cold I might have burst into tears at any point. Colm's brother Joe met us from the ferry and fixed our van with all the gear to the back of his vehicle. Colm volunteered to steer the tow. At that point the boys announced that it would be easier and quicker to get the train up to Manchester.

'Come on,' said Ciarán, poking me to attention. I was so drowsy and miserable that I couldn't bear to move.

'No, I'm gonna go up in the van; I'll just lie down here,' I said, climbing into the back of the vehicle where I lay on the floor and pulled a pile of coats over me in an attempt to warm my aching limbs. A bit of an argument ensued as the boys tried to persuade me to go with them, but I was stiff with cold, almost delirious with exhaustion and nothing was going to get me to shift. There I stayed for the next eight or nine hours, feeling more miserable than anyone can imagine.

When we finally reached Manchester I had to endure a lot of stick from the boys. They had been there for hours and, after eating a hearty meal, they were happily drinking beer by the fire. I couldn't be bothered to rise to their jibes. Let them carry on, they'll soon get tired. Joe and his wife Anne were wonderful to us, providing mattresses, sleeping bags and blankets and even moving their children into the same room so that I could have a proper bed.

The next morning we all felt brighter. We were delighted to be finally within reach of home. It was Christmas Eve and, putting all her personal arrangements aside, Anne did a couple of runs with us in her car to the airport. We abandoned the van and the gear in Manchester. We could deal with that later. Telephoning ahead, we arranged for a driver from home to pick us up from Belfast airport and take us to Donegal. Flying was something of a novelty to us and we had no idea that we were supposed to get to the airport at least an hour before take-off. In those days security in Belfast was extra tight and the airport staff couldn't believe how slack and laid-back we were, just making our way to the gate five minutes before the plane was due to leave.

It was wonderful to be back in Donegal and before making our way to Gweedore we asked the driver to stop in Letterkenny so we could do some last-minute Christmas shopping. We didn't have much money left after the vehicle hire, repairs and flights, but I'd kept something back to buy a few Christmas presents for the family. Digital watches were all the rage and I knew that Daddy would love one. I was right – he wore that watch every day for years. He was delighted with the gift, but ironically, before the Christmas week was over, I had to borrow the equivalent money from him until I could earn it back in tips in the bar!

Our parents were wonderful to us and when most would have ordered their offspring at our age to go out and get 'proper jobs', they were nothing but encouraging of our artistic ambition. Still, we had to think of some way to earn money. The tour had left us penniless and there wouldn't be any more major gigs until next summer. Nicky was living in Dublin and kept things ticking over for us with club gigs, but even then it cost us to get up there. It was then that we hit upon the idea of a schools' tour. We sat down one day and wrote to a variety of schools all over Ireland, offering Clannad's services. We convinced them that our visits could be a worthy addition to their cultural education. We'd sing our Gaelic songs and talk about our roots, charging each pupil twenty pence at the door. If we ended up playing to six hundred pupils in a school, it was a respectable wage. For me, it was lovely to be back in school, seeing the children's faces light up. Sometimes the teachers would greet us woefully, telling us how there had been little response to the advertising of our coming. After a few concerts this didn't concern us. We soon learned that when the children saw us arrive – a young band, with long hair, cool clothes, amplifiers and guitars – they would flock to see what was going on. We rarely played to small crowds and the feedback from the kids was great. Still today I meet people who remember us playing at their school and we won many fans who have stayed loyal over the years.

We loved being out and about on Ireland's highways and byways, but in the mid to late seventies there was increasing nervousness in the communities. We'd grown up in the wake of political and cultural tension. It was part of Ireland's history, but things were becoming more frightening and threatening as the years went by. Donegal was a Catholic Republican stronghold, but in my years growing up it had never really been a personal issue. Through the Feises I had made many friends from different walks of life, Protestant and Catholic alike. My only recognition of the troubles came when we heard of the marches in Derry and had to cancel a couple of ballet classes and visits to the McCaffertys' just to be on the safe side. Still, it all seemed very distant from our ordinary lives. The harsh reality of sectarianism hit me, however, when Clannad were playing at a concert at Queens University, Belfast. There were many people I knew there, but when I saw them after the concert they walked straight past me. I was shocked and confused and followed one of the girls to find out what the problem was. 'I'm sorry Máire, I can't really talk to you anymore,' she said, before she hurried away. It was only then that I recognised her as a 'Protestant', rather than a 'friend'. Until then her religion carried no consequence for two girls who shared much in common.

For years we had imagined we were safe from the violence. We never really talked about politics and were appalled by the terrors of fighting, no matter what the cause. It had little to do with us. We were simply a band from Donegal, with no political agenda. Our interest was purely in the art, music and cultural history of Ireland. But over the last few years more civilians had been killed. The introduction of internment in 1971 had everyone feeling nervous. It basically meant that anyone from Northern Ireland could be pulled in, or even shot at, if there was the slightest amount of suspicion that they might be carrying weapons or have any involvement in the IRA. It was something the boys, in particular, had to be wary of and a group of young men travelling around the countryside in a dodgy-looking transit always had to remain alert. In 1975 there was an atrocity that really shook us and made us realise our own vulnerability. It was the killing of the Miami Showband. They were simply a Dublin-based showband, who, like us, travelled the length and breadth of the country as entertainers, but became the target for a bomb plant by the UVF. The intention was to get the musicians unwittingly to carry the bomb across the border into the Republic where it would detonate, thus proving that Nationalists were involved in transporting explosives. It all went wrong, and caused the deaths of both the band members and terrorists. The incident motivated a response from the IRA who planted a bomb in a pub on Belfast's Shankill Road. That was the beginning of a pub-bombing season, and no one could be safe.

I suppose, in a way, we got used to the checkpoints. The ones at the border were usually OK. It was the unofficial ones we most feared, especially at night. You'd hear stories of motorists being stopped along a road in the middle of nowhere. You never knew whether they were genuine. It was a case of taking pot luck that they were official. If you didn't stop they'd shoot you anyway. We tried to avoid travelling at night if at all possible. We had to be careful to plan our tours so that we could stay overnight with friends and travel to the next place in daylight. Thankfully all the road blocks we encountered turned out to be genuine. That wasn't the case for everyone.

Going home invariably involved passing through one of the country's largest checkpoints. Donegal is part of the Republic, but physically it is very much in the 'north' of Ireland, so unless you want to spend hours going around on the coast road, you have to make your journey through the borders of Northern Ireland to get there. The checkpoint at Aughnacloy was a very familiar sight to us, but there were times when I could feel the hair stand up on the back of my neck as we approached it. We'd see the snipers in the fields around the point, and knew that we were also being watched from the huge lookout towers. Depending on what was going on, there would usually be around six soldiers at the actual checkpoint and they were guaranteed to stop us, especially if it was a nice day and the roads were quiet. Some were fine, searching us quickly and letting us go, but mostly we could expect to be detained for a couple of hours. When that happened we'd be taken off the road and into the barracks. I hated that. It always ran through my mind that anything could happen to us here and no one would know. There were also certain regiments that we were more fearful of. Some were notorious for their anti-Irish attitude and there were individuals who used the authority of an army uniform to vent their own racist convictions. They assumed that all the Irish hated the British and did their best to intimidate us.

Still, it wasn't always bad. Some of the soldiers were really nice and genuinely interested in what we were doing. They had to search us – that was their job – but they would love to hear about our travels, especially in Germany where they had friends in barracks. One time we even met a soldier who had been at one of our concerts in Bielefeld. He recognised us almost instantly and we enjoyed a friendly half-hour passing the time of day while his colleagues carried out their business.

\* \* \*

For too many years the people of Northern Ireland have lived with the threat of violence and terrorism. Too many mothers have cried over dead children and too many worlds have been torn apart. From a God-fearing heartland come atrocities to vent the sorrow of the heavens, all in the name of man-made religion, none of it in the wake of love and true justice.

# *Chapter 11*

Towards the end of 1977 I found myself gravitating more towards Dublin again. We were spending more time there as a band, often bunking down on the floor in the flat Nicky – who was increasingly taking on the management of the band – shared with his girlfriend Roma. We were still paying back the money we had borrowed and being in Dublin meant it was easy to get the ferry across to Europe where we had much better earning potential. After gaining a respectable following in Germany we set our minds on exploring other European territories and Nicky arranged some dates in Austria, Holland, Switzerland and Belgium. We had a wonderful time over there and the Swiss dates provided the setting for a live recording we put together and released as *Clannad in Concert*. The touring was still very basic, although we made friends in Switzerland who owned a hostel that became our base for the time we were over there. Their hospitality was wonderful and we had the place to ourselves which was a great bonus. It meant that on our days off we could relax, rehearse more and also do some of the necessary 'fixing' to the recorded material.

It was around that time that I began to think about taking on a flat in Dublin. Nicky and Roma were good to us, but it wasn't ideal to keep staying with them. Besides, I was the eldest of the family and it was about time I stood on my own two feet. Thoughts of this kind passed through my mind throughout the following year, but in the autumn of 1978 something happened that convinced me I needed my own space. One night I went along with Nicky down to the Baggot Inn, a bar in Dublin, to see his friend Pat, who was playing a gig with his blues band. It was a great gig and I was instantly enthralled by Pat's guitar playing. I had never seen anyone play so well and he had an intriguing manner about him, so obviously absorbed in his music. Nicky introduced us after the show and I'm sure we both realised that there was a certain attraction between us. He had wavy blonde hair and was unassumingly good-looking with an endearing shyness about him. Pat knew that Nicky had been working with Clannad, so we talked a lot about music. As the evening wore on, an electricity developed between us and we flirted outrageously with one another. In the early hours of the morning he came back to Nicky's flat with me.

In the next few days we were desperate to see each other again, but I was supposed to be going back to Donegal. I left for home with my mind made up to find a flat in the city. I had grown out of my life in Donegal and reasoned with myself that I was bigger than the 'small-town mentality' would allow me to be. I wanted my freedom. I wanted to socialise and, yes, if I met a guy I wanted to spend the night with, that was my choice. I had changed a lot in the last few years. The band was starting to give me a certain confidence. I liked being on stage and I liked the attention afterwards, particularly the male attention.

Clannad was earning some money in Europe, but it wasn't a great living and I had never been very conscientious about saving, so I couldn't afford to be too choosy in looking for a flat. I took a tiny bedsit in a large house in Windsor Road, Rathmines, not far from where I had spent my student days. It was owned by another musician who spent most of his time abroad so he had no problem letting it to me. Barely more than a 'box' room, it just had a single bed in one corner. In the other corner was a little place to hang clothes, and the tiny kitchenette had a sliding door on the end which hid a toilet and a rather morose-looking shower. Still, it was a place of my own and it signified my freedom.

On my second night there I was lying in bed reading when I felt something itching on my shoulder. It was a little earwig. I flicked it away, shuddered and continued with my book. A few moments later, another itch, this time on my leg. I threw the bedclothes back and in complete horror flung myself into the opposite corner of the room, clasping my hands over my mouth to stifle a scream. The bed was a mass of earwigs.

There was no one to come to my rescue and I knew I had to pull myself together. Pulling the bed away from the wall I could see the source of the offending visitors. The bed was placed against an outside wall in which the creatures had made a nest. The plaster was in poor repair and it had been easy for them to burrow their way through in pursuit of warmth. I killed as many as I could and stuffed the hole with cotton wool. Cleaning off the mattress, I dragged it onto the floor in the opposite corner and tried to settle down again for the night – not before plugging my ears with cotton wool, so that the earwigs couldn't get through and eat my brain. (Maybe that was just a bad childhood story the boys had teased me with, but I wasn't taking any chances!)

The next day I had the landlord spray the place down and thankfully that was the last of my uninvited-guest problem. Looking back now, it was a miserable little place for what I paid for it, and the rent didn't come easily. On more than a couple of occasions I'd find myself sponging off friends, having spent my rent money down the pub. Sometimes it was Gran Duggan who helped me out of trouble. I hated to ask, but when she came up to stay she would invariably leave me a few extra bob. I loved her visits. We had always been very close and enjoyed some special times together. She probably worried for me and I so much wanted to show her how grown-up I had become and how strong I could be – but making money in the music business could be so hard!

My flat was also the source of little holidays for the younger members of the family. I loved treating my brothers and sisters and we'd go off to the zoo and the museums. Then I'd take them out to eat or we'd catch a movie before all cramming together to sleep in my little room. If we separated out the bed and the mattress we could just about all get a decent space to sleep (though after hearing the story of my first night they would never settle until their ears were stuffed with cotton wool, just in case).

Pat and I were seeing a lot of each other by then, but he rarely came by when my family were around. He introduced me to a wider, more sophisticated – or so I thought – social life. He was a few years older than me and was very well respected among other Dublin musicians. Some nights we'd be out seeing a band and going to their parties, but our social life was largely in the pubs and, unwittingly, I was becoming quite a heavy drinker. I rarely got what you might call properly drunk, but we were out most nights, so the drinking was regular if nothing else.

Musically, Clannad was continuing to explore new sounds through a couple of keyboards we invested in – a Novatron and a Wurlitzer. Even though in the studio we were experimenting with drums, electric guitars and keyboards, our live show still consisted of acoustic instruments – mandola, flute, whistle, double bass, acoustic guitars and harp.

It was 1979 and our younger sister, Eithne, was finishing school. She had become a very accomplished pianist and was keen to pursue a music career so it seemed a very natural progression that she should join the band. We had the keyboard player we needed and, being a member of the family, her voice blended very well with our sound. We also had a string of summer festivals arranged and it was lovely for me to have another girl on the road.

Also that summer we set to work on our next album, *Crann úll*. We couldn't get financial backing at home, but a German company came up with the funds and set us up in a wonderful studio over there owned by a well-known engineer/producer called Connie Plank. The day before we were to start the recording, Nicky, still then our sound engineer, was taken seriously ill with facial palsy and had to be flown home and hospitalised. We continued the work without him, but although the studio's replacement engineer was very good, there was no way he could be as familiar with our sound and I have always felt that we never quite captured the full potential of the songs. Still, it remains a special album to me for other reasons. One of the songs we recorded was 'Bunan Buí', drawn from a favourite poem of my grandfather. We couldn't have known then, but it was one of the last pieces of music Gog got to hear before he died. His death came as such a shock to all the family and the community at large. In November of that year he had been sent up to Dublin for an operation from which he never recovered. I will not forget following the hearse back down to Gweedore. It was a sombre day and the end of an era in so many ways. They say you can judge the popularity of a man by how many people attend his funeral. I don't remember much about the service – I was beside myself with grief – but I do remember you could barely get into the church for people.

I stayed in the 'earwig' flat for a year, then moved on to another place at the north side of the city, nearer to where Pat came from. Although Pat spent a lot of time with me, he never really moved out of his mother's house. Sometimes it would annoy me that he didn't seem terribly committed to our relationship. I thought we were in love, and yet there were times when I felt very lonely. That year was the first time I stayed away from home at Christmas – something I found especially difficult with Gog's death being so recent. Part of me was pleased that Pat wanted me to spend the holiday with him, but another part of me longed to follow the others home. When Christmas Eve came Pat was playing a gig so I went along and hung around with his friends. That night he dropped me off at my flat and went on home. I lay there watching TV by myself as the Christmas bells rang out across the city. Christmas morning I awoke to my loneliness. Pat was due to pick me up at lunch time to take me over to his mum's house for dinner, but that morning I was completely at a loss. There were Christmas carols on the TV, and in my head I pictured the scene at home – everyone running round in high spirits, dashing to get ready to go to church . . . That was it. That was what I needed to do. There was a Catholic church just down the road and if I got myself together quickly I could just about make it for the start of the mass.

The church was heaving with people, all bright-faced and alive with Christmas cheer. I wandered in, alone, and found a seat at the back. Listening to the priest and aware of the happy families around me, I went through the motion of the mass. It was when it came to singing the carols that I really lost myself and had to pull my coat up around my chin so the tears could fall silently into its depths. Oh, how I longed to be home.

By lunch time I had regained my composure. We enjoyed a hearty Christmas dinner with Pat's family and I pushed the loneliness of the morning aside. It was easy with a few 'Christmas drinks' inside me. Pat knew nothing of my feelings. I guess I wanted so much for him to show some kind of passion and commitment to me, but he was the same as usual. In the last few months there had developed something of a distance between us.

We still shared many a laugh together, but we were bickering more. On the odd occasion, things got very intense between us. We were both drinking too much and our tempers would clash. Sometimes Pat would storm out of the flat and I would end up running down the street after him, begging him to come back. I would panic. I didn't want to lose him. What if he really meant to leave me? But a few days later he'd come around or I would make sure I bumped into him in a bar where I knew he was playing and everything would be all right again. This kind of scene continued over the next couple of years, although at the time I barely recognised what was happening. I suppose I was too close to the situation to be able to stand back and realise how emotionally cruel we could be with each other. Somehow things just drifted along and neither of us had the inclination to stand back and really consider the relationship we were stumbling along with.

It didn't help that Pat had always been less than encouraging when it came to what I was about musically. It seemed that the more I was doing with Clannad, the more it interfered with the relationship. Even though Pat played on our *Fuaim* album he could be very condescending about Clannad. He was a blues man and the way he spoke, the blues was the be all and end all of music. I found myself being absorbed into his way of thinking. Sure, I loved the blues – B. B. King was a big hero to me too – but whereas I had always been proud of our music, I began to feel slightly embarrassed about it. I also felt personally very undermined as a vocalist. I would never be able to sing like Bonnie Rait or Aretha Franklin or any of the 'big' vocalists Pat loved. There was no way I could compete. It seemed as though everything I did was an irritation to him. The most hurtful thing was that he didn't seem to understand or have much respect for the closeness I felt towards my family. He was polite enough if he met them, but if I had any of them to stay he rarely hung around. He only ever went down to Donegal once to meet my family, and that was because he had a gig nearby. They, of course, never really said anything to me, but I sensed that they were worried about my relationship. This deepened the ever-increasing hole in my heart. I was extremely close to my family, but I was seeing them so little, and sometimes didn't even feel I could talk about them in Pat's presence. I was torn. I had believed that Pat was my future and had justified to myself the distance I had created from my family, but now I was missing them more and more.

Inevitably it affected the way I was with the band and the boys began to wonder what was going on. I know it must have seemed that I wasn't as interested in the music. It just wasn't that important to me anymore. I was having serious doubts about my future with them, but it was all mixed up with the way I was feeling in general. Though I didn't realise it at the time, I had spent the last few years drifting into something of a no man's land and was fast losing my confidence and, in a way, my identity.

Things became really difficult towards the end of the summer of 1981, as we put the final cuts down for *Fuaim*. It was a great album. All the time we were developing the harmonies and melodies and really enjoying the music that was emerging from the basis of the old songs. Synthesisers were becoming all the rage and the band took on fresh creative impetus. We were experimenting more using the wealth of new sounds available to us, playing around with the blending of harmony and a more layered effect. Gran Duggan came up to help us with some of the Gaelic songs and translations and was staying in my flat. Pat hardly came near and the only time I saw him was when he came into the studio to lay down his guitar parts. I think Gran sensed my increasing unhappiness and she tried to encourage me to spend a little time with my parents when I could next get away from the studio. A few weeks later, with *Fuaim* almost complete, I took her advice. Mammy and Daddy had never been on a foreign holiday before, but I bought them a package tour to Tenerife and they were delighted when I offered to accompany them. Gran was right, I did need to get away for a while.

As it turned out, the whole thing was all rather last minute. The album was finished musically, but we had done nothing about artwork, photography or cover design, so the day before I left for my holiday I was frantically running around trying to get something arranged. Eventually we came across a photographer who seemed to specialise in portraits. He probably only came to my attention because his name was also Brennan. Within a few hours I'd assembled the band at his studio. It was a rather farcical situation. We had this old chair that we thought would look really cool and the photographer set us up in a family portrait type pose. I don't think he'd ever photographed a band before, and it was all very heavily 'constructed'. We had no change of clothes or scenery. He took one roll of film and the whole thing was over within an hour.

I went away and enjoyed a wonderfully refreshing holiday with my parents. But back home there was heartbreak only a couple of weeks ahead.

I don't know the detail of the incident, but by some mistake and misinformation my Gran Duggan's house became the target for an army raid. In years gone by our family, like most Catholics, had sympathies with Sinn Fein and at one time some of our relatives were jailed for possession of arms. Since then the house has always been a point of call for the authorities if there is any suspicion of trouble in the area. In my grandfather's day the house was raided on a number of occasions. They never found anything. Certainly my grandfather had his political ideals – there weren't many Irish people at that time who didn't adhere to the principles of Sinn Fein's fight for a more 'free' Ireland – but he would never condone any kind of terrorist activity.

Now my grandmother and Aunt Bríd were in the house alone when the ten or twelve army men and police stormed in. They barged through the house and up into the attic, leaving my grandmother gasping for breath in shock and horror.

The raid deeply distressed and shook the family and my grandmother never really recovered. Within the week she had a heart attack and my last memory of her is in a hospital bed. Her face managed a smile when she saw me and as she tried to wipe away the tears from my cheeks she told me not to worry. 'I don't think I can hold on much longer Máire,' she said. I knew what she was telling me. Her heart had broken when Gog died and she wanted to go to him. She was so peaceful and certain about the way ahead, but I knew her passing would be hard on everyone. Gran Duggan was a saintly woman, known to many in the parish for her kindness, patience and generosity, and loved by her family, at the very least, for just being Gran.

Gran Duggan died in December and I stayed in Donegal to see the year out. Christmas was a more sombre affair that year. Mammy and Aunt Bríd took their mother's death very badly. I spoke to Pat a few times on the phone, but he didn't come down for the funeral.

As 1982 dawned my heart was heavy and there were many uncertainties in my life.

# Chapter 12

'Get a load of this beauty,' said Nicky as he threw open the door to our new van. We all gaped in awe. It was fantastic. A large white van, really professional looking, with 'Clannad' written on the side. It was customised especially for us, with comfortable seats and space in the back for all the equipment. At last, we could tour in comfort.

'I just hope this tour goes well or we'll be paying off the loan for ever,' I muttered to Ciarán.

The tour was the longest yet, taking in Holland, Germany and Switzerland, and we knew that at the end of it we would still have little money for ourselves. It was all being sent back to pay for the van and some new equipment we had got together. The only way to bring things back on an even keel would be to do an Irish tour when we eventually returned home. That would see us through to the summer festivals, by which time we should be seeing a little return for the months of hard touring.

I was still struggling to come to terms with my 'on–off' relationship and began to face the fact that I didn't know where I stood with Pat. I had let things drift, but it worried me that after four years, I didn't know what kind of future we might have together. Pat was busy doing his gigs and I had my own music so we'd often be going in a different direction, and we'd fall out over the silliest of things. Still, it seemed to me that Pat was comfortable enough with the situation, that he didn't really need the relationship to develop beyond where we were. I, on the other hand, knew that ultimately I wanted more. I wanted marriage and a proper commitment, but I was now beginning to feel confused about my life with Pat.

There was also a lot happening in other areas of my life. Even around my brothers, I could feel lonely, so I appreciated having Eithne on the road with us, but towards the end of the European tour there was a lot of tension between us all. We were exhausted, having been on the road too long, and were beginning to get on one another's nerves. It didn't help that I had a terrible temper that flared all too easily. Playing in a family band has many advantages, but it can often mean that when the going gets tough you take it out on each other with a liberty that only family can tolerate. I suppose it had always been difficult for Eithne. We loved what she brought to the band, but I know it was hard for her to infiltrate our years as a tightly knit nucleus. Musically, Ciarán and Pól had always been the creative force, and Noel, Pádraig and myself had then worked our own expression around them. It was a good formula that worked well. Inevitably, when Eithne joined us full time, she found it hard. She hadn't been part of the original song-collecting days and consequently didn't share our enthusiasm for the old songs. I suppose she always felt little more than a 'guest musician'. As sisters we had always been close and talked about everything together, so I was sorry when band business caused a strain between us. One day, just after the tour, Eithne announced that she had decided to leave Clannad. She was going to pursue a solo career with Nicky Ryan as her manager. (Later she changed her name to the easier-to-read phonetic spelling, 'Enya'.)

In the long term it turned out to be a good decision. I missed her, but I'm sure the apprenticeship with Clannad helped Eithne develop her own sound and afforded her strong contacts in the music business. She is talented and ambitious and, in the years that followed, the family was delighted to watch the success that came her way.

Still, her premature departure from Clannad left us with a hole to fill. We had the Irish tour coming up – not to mention the summer festivals that would take us out to Europe again – with no keyboard player and no manager. By that time some of our material relied on the keyboard and synthesiser, so the pressure was on to find a replacement. I called up a good friend, Tríona Ní Dhonaill, whom we knew from Clannad's early days. She was living in North Carolina, USA, at the time, but to our relief she was delighted to get the next plane out and join us ready for the tour. Her father came from Ranafast, near Gweedore, and she and her brothers and sister used to spend the summers there, forming a family band that sang in Gaelic. She was a wonderful vocalist, keyboard and harpsichord player and fitted into the band immediately. She also slotted into my social life rather too well. We were nearly dangerous together. Tríona liked a couple of drinks and all too often the two of us could be found knocking back Bloody Marys in the bar when we should have been in sound-checks. We had a ball together. At the same time we also hooked up with a guy named Dave Kavanagh who helped us out on the Irish tour, not then knowing that he was later to become our next manager.

It was a heady time and, though I probably didn't realise it then, I was on an emotional rollercoaster. Pat and I were still 'together', but there was little tenderness between us and I knew he hated me being away on tour. We could be quite bitter and very manipulative towards each other and I had become deeply suspicious that he was seeing other women. Then, like a bolt out of the blue, at one of the festivals in Europe, I fell madly and passionately in love (or so I thought) with someone else. It was stupid really, but at the time I thought I had met a man who could love me the way I wanted to be loved and help me find some direction to my life. Not that I felt a great loss of direction. That was perhaps my trouble – I didn't really feel anything. I was just going along with the flow, not particularly miserable, but not particularly happy either. I would stand on stage and perform, but I didn't really appreciate that I, myself, was any good. I was performing the music, but in my mind I was only able to do it because Ciarán and Pól were there to help me develop my harp and vocal parts. Yes, I enjoyed being on stage. It gave me a kick and infused my body with an adrenalin rush that I loved, but I never attributed any of the band's success to my own talent or ability.

Roly, a gentle-faced bass player from LA, gave me the boost I thought I needed. He was travelling around Europe with a friend, playing many of the same festivals as us and, finding ourselves together on more than one occasion, we took a wild fancy to each other. At the end of a passionate and indulgent two days we were all but promising ourselves to each other for life. It was hard to say goodbye, but in the cold light of reality I had to put it down as just another fling. I had enjoyed myself, but I couldn't help feeling a little guilty. Since the early days of my relationship with Pat I had remained faithful to him, despite his continual paranoid suspicions and innuendoes about me. Now I had done exactly what he feared. Still, I reasoned, maybe he deserved it. Roly had brought some excitement back into my life, if only for a couple of days.

Back in Ireland things remained cool with Pat. I should have probably called off the relationship. Roly was very much on my mind, but I kept pushing thoughts of him away. Surely it was nothing more than a brief fling – a little interlude that boosted my confidence and made me feel like a woman again? Again I let things drift for a while, but it all became rather complicated one August night when I was feeling particularly lost and alone. It was my birthday and I was out at one of Dublin's bars with Pat. We had a lot to drink and were both very quiet and introverted, sitting together, smoking and watching other people in the bar. On the way home I told Pat that I wanted to ring a friend. It was stupid really. I was going to ring Roly in LA. How I ever imagined that Pat would not suss out what was going on, I just don't know. As far as he was concerned, I was making a local call, but the whole street must have heard me pushing coin after coin into the box and talking at the top of my voice so that I could be heard on the international call. Roly was taken by surprise, but obviously delighted to hear from me.

'Hi,' I said, hearing his sensuously sweet American drawl. 'It's my birthday, and I just wanted to say hello.' We chatted briefly, but by this time Pat was opening the door to the telephone box and demanding to know who I was speaking to. It became difficult and Roly knew there was something wrong.

'Máire, Máire, are you OK, what's going on there?' He could obviously hear the scuffling and deep tones of Pat's voice.

'I'm fine, really, I just wanted to say "Hi"; I'll have to go now, I'll call you later.' With that I managed to prise Pat's grasping hands away before he could grab the receiver. Roly must have been left holding the phone in bewilderment, wondering what on earth was happening. In the meantime Pat and I embarked on an almighty row in the middle of the street. He accused me of having an affair and called me every name under the sun. At first I stupidly tried to deny it, but eventually confessed that he was right. Perhaps I had wanted him to find out. I don't know what was going through my head. I was careless and confused. I knew then that this meant the end of our relationship.

Despite our lack of earnings on the tour and a rather serious-looking album cover, the *Fuaim* project was to start Clannad on a path to another level of success. We'd only just settled back in Dublin when we received a call from a producer at Yorkshire Television. They were completing a three-part series for television adapted from a Gerald Seymour fiction thriller based in Northern Ireland. Seymour himself had heard *Fuaim* and suggested that one of our songs might be a suitable soundtrack to the programmes. It was a very atmospheric tune, with harmonies and synthesiser. But it was a Scottish Gaelic piece, and as such we believed it was wholly unsuitable for use in a film about the troubles in Northern Ireland. The producer was initially disappointed, but thrilled when we suggested we might write a piece of music especially for the series. Within no time the producer, the director and Gerald Seymour himself made plans to fly out to Dublin to show us the film. We had no idea what to expect, never having come across Seymour's work before. For all we knew it was just another dramatised documentary about Ireland and its politics. But after sitting through three hours, we were all completely taken with it. We'd always been slightly wary of getting involved in any kind of political propaganda. Our mission, rather, was to reveal more of the good things in Ireland's culture – its beauty, art, music and poetry. But as the film drew to a close we were completely compelled by it. It was a movie that showed that nobody wins in the end. No side wins in war, because there are so many people killed and lives destroyed. It set a quietness among us, a reflection and, I suppose, an awareness of how fragile we are. Here was the war, on our doorstep, and day by day families would grieve over a loved one, lost to terrorism and a cause that no one seemed to understand any more.

A few days later we went off to Pól's house in Wicklow, just south of Dublin, to see what we could come up with. Ciarán brought along one of Gog's old books of Proverbs. 'Listen to this,' he said, and read aloud,

> *Imtheochaidh sior 's siar*
> *A dtáinig ariamh An ghealach is an ghrian . . .*

It basically translated as 'Everything that is and was will cease to be . . . everything is meaningless, the sun and the moon, youth and beauty, everything will pass'. The tone and sentiment of the proverb was very much in keeping with the *Harry's Game* message. We started working on a melody and put together a demo based around this theme. It was really very simple. We just harmonised slowly and arranged it as a kind of lament. It only took a couple of hours and we were pleased with the result, but didn't consider that it was anything particularly special. I don't think we realised that what had come so naturally in those few hours was the result of our years of experimenting and working with the music of our heritage. It was sent off to Yorkshire Television and the very next day they were on the phone. They loved it.

The television team suggested we work with a guy called Richard Dodd for the recording. This was exciting. Dodd had engineered some major bands, including 10CC, and was renowned for his intricate workings with vocal harmony. As the weather started to turn and the autumn leaves lay thick underfoot, we booked two days in Dublin's Windmill Studios. There was an electric atmosphere as Ciarán sat at the Prophet Five synthesiser, with me standing opposite him in the recording booth. The others were in the control room looking on as Ciarán, with each chord and the nod of his head, led me into my vocal. We chose to work in a very 'live', free style, using no click track. This seemed to add to the drama and tension of the piece and it felt as though everyone held their breath with me at the opening of each phrase. As we spent time building around it and layering our voices, we each began to sense that this was something unique and quite special. The air tingled as we sat in silence after the first full playback. I remember looking expectantly at the faces of the people who had come over from the TV production team. They didn't need to say much. Their faces expressed a certain awe, and within a few minutes Gerald Seymour broke the spell of silence with a slow applause and everyone laughed and hugged each other.

From there it all got terribly exciting. The talk was of approaching record companies to see if our 'theme' could be released as a single. We could barely believe what we were hearing. We weren't the kind of band that produced singles and got radio play. Besides, this was a song in Gaelic! Still, we were riding the crest of the wave and knew that what we had just created was something special. What we didn't realise was exactly the turning-point this would become. We had created the 'Clannad sound' – a sound that would be imitated by others for years to come. It had developed down the years as we had spent time working with the richness of our musical and cultural heritage. We had not been distracted by pressure to write our own material and instead had honed a sound that captured emotion and imagery, allowing us a freedom to blend, experiment and discover new depths from the music and art of ages past. Without us really realising, this sound had grown from within and was now ready to take us to new heights. We had no idea what lay ahead, but we had certainly become more excited about our seeming ability to write and create new songs using the sound that had emerged from our very souls.

In the middle of all this excitement I was also trying to balance the complications of my personal life. Pat was barely off the scene when Roly came over to see me and the relationship resumed with even greater intensity. The boys, of course, wondered what was going on. I had a smile on my face again and a spring in my step, but I imagine my brothers were surprised at the sudden appearance of a new man in my life. I daren't tell them of our plans – especially in the wake of potential big things for the band – but everything was moving very quickly and within a few days of Roly's visit we had agreed that after what had now become our annual German pre-Christmas tour, I would fly out to America. There I would meet his family and we would head down to Mexico and get married. We even bought two matching Irish claddagh rings that we were going to use as our wedding rings. I was swept up in the excitement of it all. I barely knew this guy and here I was, promising to make a new life with him, away from my family and all that I held dear. I was chasing some kind of romantic dream and daren't think too much about the consequences or what lay ahead. The rush thrilled me. Then one day I picked up the phone to a familiar voice. It was Pat. He sounded low and all but begged me to meet him in one of our old haunts. I had to go. Roly offered to come with me, but I didn't think that would be very tactful.

Pat and I shared an hour together. He was calm, quiet and genuinely affectionate towards me. We talked about old times and the relationship we had enjoyed together. Most of it focused on the early days. Then came the shock. Pat told me that he wanted us to get married. In all the years we had been together, I had perhaps longed for him to show this kind of commitment, but now I was just terribly confused. I had been trying to come to terms with our separation and had been swept up in a new and passionate romance. The timing was all wrong and I left Pat sitting in the bar while I wandered home the long way, trying to get my head together.

There was so much clutter and confusion in my mind. We were potentially on the brink of a break in our career but I was harbouring secret plans to escape to America, and I had two men wanting to marry me. I wasn't sure about anything any more.

In a way it was a relief to be able to head off with the band. Germany had been good to us over the years and we had many friends there. Roly went home to America and we kept in touch by telephone, speaking to one another every second day. We still talked about our plans to get married, but as the days went by the doubts were beginning to push through from the back of my mind and pour oil on the fire of my confusion.

In the meantime the 'Theme from Harry's Game' was touted around some of the major record companies and RCA (who later became part of the BMG group) rose to the challenge. It was a brave move for the label. Did they really imagine they could profit any commercial success from a Gaelic song, wholly unlike anything else that kept the chart music business going? The radio plugger who took on the project was a Scottish guy called Jimmy who became a huge ambassador for us. The story goes that he took the single to Noel Edmonds – who, at that time, had a Sunday morning show on Radio 1 – and wouldn't leave his studio until it had been played. After only one listen, Noel was convinced and agreed to play the track that week on his show. It was only two minutes in length, so he played it twice during his time on air and the switchboard reportedly lit up with requests to know more about the song. The next morning it was top of the play list on Terry Wogan's breakfast show. There began the rollercoaster ride. The *Harry's Game* film was broadcast over the next three nights and by Wednesday the sales of the single had rocketed.

Bono tells a story that he nearly went off the road when he heard it on his car radio. He had to pull up and listen to it properly. It was so unusual and, of course, Bono recognised that the singing was in Gaelic. We were very flattered when U2 later used it to open and close their show and also in their concert video filmed at Red Rock.

Over in Germany, we were frantic to know what was going on. Dave, our manager, was ringing us daily at first, then, by the end of the week, we were getting almost hourly updates from him. The song seemed to spread like wildfire. One night we were watching a football game in the hotel TV room and we could hear in the background that they were playing our song at half-time. We were tense with excitement, especially when Dave informed us that, with the way the sales were going, we would need to fly back to London to do *Top of the Pops* in the next few days. We knew it would mean cancelling two of the German shows, but *Top of the Pops* would be the biggest thing we could hope to do. It might even mean a proper record deal on the horizon, which was something we'd never even dared to dream about. Filled with excitement and disbelief, we were ringing home at any opportunity we could get, desperate to share our excitement with our family. At that time, though, you couldn't dial direct, so we had to go through an operator and ask for 'Bunbeg two-seven'. It would often take up to four hours to get through and by the time the operator got back to us we'd had to leave for the hall.

As we waited to hear the details of our necessary return home we received a call that caused much amusement. Having played our song for two or three days, Radio 1 suddenly stopped playing it. An urgent message came through that we were to provide a translation of the song. It had occurred to one of the controllers that we might be singing something very offensive or politically too sensitive. As soon as they'd seen our translation the 'Theme from Harry's Game' was all over the airwaves again.

On the plane bound for London we were all in something of a daze. The German promoters had been very understanding at us having to postpone a couple of the gigs and we had arranged to reschedule them, promising we would return to Germany before the year was out. It was a very important place for us. We couldn't forget that while there had always been a certain derision from our own people for our use of Gaelic, Germany had welcomed us with open arms and made it possible for us to pursue our lives as professional musicians.

We weren't used to the luxury of air travel but all of a sudden we were on a very different ticket. All expenses would be paid, and when we were met at the airport by a driver and limousine – complete with bottle of champagne – we knew that things were really on the up. There was nothing 'cool' about us. The novelty of the limo was too much and we ran around like children, taking pictures of ourselves with the car to send back to the family.

The day continued in the world of the surreal and indulgent. We were driven to the Kensington Hilton and I was appointed my own stylist who met me with a case full of clothes to try out ready for the show. I was even more excited when I heard the outfit we chose together was mine to keep! The boys wandered around the hotel feeling like lords. There was a tennis tournament at the Royal Albert Hall and many of the stars were staying at the Hilton, so my brothers and uncles could be found propping up the bar alongside some of their sporting heroes. We couldn't help but laugh among ourselves. Here we were, a family band from a sleepy parish in Donegal, living the high life and being treated like celebrities.

With *Top of the Pops* recorded and a short round of publicity appointments under our belt, we headed back to Germany. It was the beginning of December and I knew that Roly was expecting me to join him in America as soon as the tour came to an end. But more and more I longed to be in Donegal for Christmas, and all of a sudden my career was becoming exciting to me again. The thrill of 'Harry's Game' had brought the family close together in celebration of our success and I couldn't wait to see Mammy and Daddy and Aunt Bríd. Poor Roly. He would be so hurt and he had been so good to me. It was a hard decision, but I sat down and wrote him a letter. At that time David Essex had a song in the charts called 'A Winter's Tale' and every time I heard it I thought it related to us. I used the song to explain to Roly that I realised I had been swept up in a romantic cloud. We had enjoyed a wonderful and very special time together, but it was all a fantasy. My reality could never be with him in a foreign land.

Years later I met Roly again and am pleased to find that we have been able to remain friends. He had been very hurt by the whole episode and told me he had frantically scoured the stores looking for the David Essex song. It was never released in America.

We flew straight from Germany back to Dublin and were immediately caught up in a swell of publicity. With the success of 'Harry's Game' we had become like national heroes and every show and newspaper wanted to speak to us. We were desperate to get home to Donegal, but still, there was something very exciting about this new life of pop stardom. We kept being asked what it was like to achieve such 'overnight' success, which was hilarious to us, since we had been a professional band for around seven years by then. Of course Gay Byrne on *The Late Late Show* knew the truth about us and was very proud to lay claim to our history and the nights performing in Daddy's bar. It was Ireland's most popular television show and we had a prime-time slot. It felt as though the entire nation was cheering us on.

I was on a total adrenalin-induced high when I received a call at the TV studios. It was Pat. He'd just seen the show, and again begged me to go over and meet him. The boys were ready to party, but somehow Pat still had a kind of hold on me and I left them to their merry-making and set out across town to meet him. When I got to the bar Pat was terribly drunk. It was embarrassing to see him like that through my own quite sober eyes. We could barely have a conversation and eventually I took him back to where he was living. He wouldn't let me leave, but after an hour or so he fell asleep and I sneaked out.

The next day Clannad headed home for Christmas. Thankfully the excitement of 'Harry's Game' and our imminent homecoming occasionally broke through the confusion that still possessed my heart and mind. I had too many secrets and had hurt too many people. Pat was desperate to get back with me, but we had a lot of history to deal with and I was still smarting from my lost passion across the Atlantic. Life was complicated and difficult and I felt a distinct lack of control. I had little imagination for what might lie ahead for me; all I knew now was that I was longing to be home. The boys were in good spirits and anticipation of our homecoming ran high. As the wheels of the van clocked off the miles I set my mind towards Donegal. Soon we would be home, and what a Christmas it would be.

# Chapter 13

To enter the British charts at number five with a Gaelic song was really something. We had never set out to prove anything, but we couldn't help the swell of pride we felt in being the first band to bring the Irish language to the pop scene. The success also meant that all of a sudden there were major record companies knocking on our door wanting to sign contracts for albums. It was all a huge novelty for us and we were very naïve to the workings of the industry. Still, RCA had taken a risk with the 'Harry's Game' single and we felt that they at least understood a little about us. We signed a five-album deal and, in the early part of 1983, set about putting together the songs that would appear on our first truly professional album, *Magical Ring*.

After my break-up with Pat, my brother Ciarán and I decided to rent a little terrace house together in Clontarf on Dublin's north side. Noel also stayed there on and off and the house became something of a base for band business. The small front room was set up with the keyboards, guitars and amplifiers and it was there that we found ourselves crowded together, looking at each other and saying, 'Right, now where do we begin?' The 'Theme from Harry's Game' was our first 'real' song. Up until then we had dabbled with writing, but our previous albums were largely made up of new arrangements of traditional songs. Now a huge challenge lay before us. We spent hours playing around with riffs and different ideas, with the weeks passing quickly. We weren't used to working under any kind of time pressure, but now there were record executives in the picture we had constant visits from the A & R men looking for demos. RCA wanted to release the album in the late spring and it soon became clear that we would not have enough of our own original material. We were still playing around with our collection of traditional songs, so eventually we persuaded them to let us use half original and half traditional material. They were fine about it, but in turn persuaded us to record a song by Jim Rafferty. We knew of Jim's brother, Gerry, through his huge hit, 'Baker Street', and the song RCA presented to us was quite pleasant. It wasn't at all 'Clannad', but we were inexperienced and starting down a new and exciting path, so we went along with their ideas.

Meanwhile I found myself seeing Pat again on a social basis. We had spoken a few times over Christmas but I had remained cool towards him. Now it seemed that every time I went out in town, he was there and I realised I was enjoying his companionship. Singing all day with the boys could be quite intense and I was glad for a little distraction. I was never part of the writing process anyway – that was Ciarán's and Pól's job, and it never even crossed my mind that I could be capable of doing anything myself. I really looked up to my brothers and I guess I was too much in awe of their musical ability to offer anything myself. Somehow, as the weeks went by, Pat and I drifted back into a relationship and again he 'half' moved in with me. At first it was good, but in no time we found ourselves embroiled in the old regime of bickering and rowing, and all too easily I would lose my temper. Pat still appeared quite resentful towards my work, and Clannad's new success did little to change his attitude. If anything, he was even more disparaging and almost scornful of our record deal. It didn't help that I had to be away for a couple of weeks to begin the recording of *Magical Ring*. RCA booked us into a studio in London where our A & R manager, Shawn Greenfield, could keep an eye on how things were going. It was exciting to be there but we were beginning to realise life was starting to be very different and there were demands on us that we had not experienced before. They put us in a really nice hotel near the studio and basically organised everything for us – from meals to stylists and photo shoots. But it was also a time when we had some great news. The 'Theme from Harry's Game' had been nominated for both an Ivor Novello and a BAFTA Award. I'll never forget that day when Dave, our manager, came over to tell us the news. We were too excited to work and lost the day in boozy celebration.

Both award ceremonies were in March that year and by the time they came around we had completed the recording of *Magical Ring*. We were really excited and high with the relief and sense of achievement of having just finished our first truly professional album. Tickets were limited for the awards, so Pat was unable to accompany me. In fact, only Ciarán, Pól, Dave and myself were able to go. The Ivor Novello Awards were first. I spent the whole evening in an awe-filled daze. We were surrounded by celebrities. Phil Collins, the members of Queen, and Annie Lennox and Dave Stewart from Eurythmics were all seated near by. Lulu was on the table just in front and I remember clearly, as they announced, 'Clannad, for the "Theme from Harry's Game" ', hearing her turn to her partner and say, 'Oh, I love this song'.

We were simply astounded to win and I will never forget that mighty adrenalin rush. When it came to the BAFTAs we found ourselves surrounded by even bigger stars from stage and screen. Perhaps after winning the Ivor Novello we were a little more cocky. It certainly seemed that everybody loved the song. When the list of nominees was read out, the whole crowd seemed to be behind Clannad. Still, we had a lot to learn and disappointment was soon to come. The award was presented to Patrick Gowers. Of course, we clapped politely, but we'd really been brought down a peg or two, especially after everyone around us seemed to think we would have been the more obvious winner. Even Patrick came over at the end of the evening and all but apologised. He also thought that we should have been walking away with the award. Still, it didn't do to take those things too seriously. It was enough that we had got this far and we were thrilled to ride the crest of the wave.

Back home tensions ran high between Pat and me. During the time we had drifted back together we had never really discussed my affair or our break-up and his subsequent proposal, but one morning Pat brought up the subject of marriage again. It was cold in the house and my head hurt from a night of heavy drinking. Hauling myself out of bed I pulled on jeans and a big sweater and made for the tiny kitchen. The remains of the previous night cluttered the surfaces. There was a disturbing array of half-drunk beer tins, an empty bottle of vodka, and congealing food that clung to dirty dishes in the sink. I hated the mess. We were out of milk. I was desperate for both a cup of tea and an escape from the house. Pat came down after me.

'So are we going to talk about it?'

'I told you, Pat, now just isn't the time.' I was irritated and flustered.

'Máire, I told you, I want us to get married. Why can't we talk about it, why is it never the right time?'

His monologue got more heated, but this time I didn't want to answer back. I couldn't face getting into an argument. Grabbing my coat, I forced my feet into my shoes and went out into the street. I walked fast and determined towards the bus stop. I wasn't really sure where I was heading, but I knew I had to get away from the house, from Pat's pleading, and the thoughts that bombarded my brain and tortured my mind.

There was no one else at the bus stop. 'Please God let a bus come along before anyone sees me.' On the other side of the road a young mum held the hand of a pretty little girl who was trying to count the cracks in the paving stones as she walked along. She caught my attention for a moment. She was beautiful, innocent and ignorant of the pains of the world around her. Without being fully aware, I found myself counting the years since that dreadful time in the clinic, wondering what might have been. Before I had time to check myself, Pat drew up in the car.

'Come on Máire, get in.'

'No, Pat, leave it, I just want to . . .'

Pat wore that sad sorry look I had seen so often. I gave in. Yet again I was going along with things. Yet again I was totally confused.

We drove into town. It was still early, but we went to The Ambassador and started to drink. The alcohol helped numb my tension and soon Pat and I were chatting and laughing together as though the morning's trauma had never happened. It was easier to brush it aside rather than deal with it. Pat knew how to make me laugh, but inside there was a crushed spirit crying. The afternoon wore on and merged into evening. Dublin's streets were cold, but the warmth of the bar made my head swim. We'd been there too long, but I didn't want to go back to the house.

'Let's go to the cinema,' Pat suggested, sensing my growing restlessness. There wasn't much on, but anyway I didn't care, so we ended up buying tickets to see *E.T.* There we sat in a theatre crowded with families and the smell of popcorn and ice-cream. Its sweetness was a comfort. It reminded me of our holidays in Bundoran. For a couple of hours we lost ourselves to an alien world, then went out and drank some more.

I had barely eaten, and from early in the day I had been drinking brandy and port. My head was muddled, but all the time I battled to reason with myself. I knew Pat wasn't going to give up this time, but how could I possibly make up my mind to marry him? Clannad had just signed a deal for five albums and the band was the most important thing in my life. He had never been supportive towards me when it came to my music and I knew I would find it even more difficult to balance the two if the band's career really took off. His lack of warmth towards my family bothered me more than I cared to admit and I knew that if I married him I would be split down the middle and torn between two loves. He'd always said it wasn't my family he wanted to marry, but in my heart I knew that – especially being the eldest – I always wanted to be able to be there for my family. I have always believed that when you get married, your partner has to take priority in your life above your parents and siblings, but it worried me that in this relationship I had already drifted too far from those I loved so much. I hated the turmoil of it all and even the port and brandy wouldn't make this one go away. One way or another I had to face up to things and make a decision. Why was I so afraid of getting married? I did care for Pat and we'd been together a long time. Maybe this is it, I reasoned, maybe this really is as good as it gets. Perhaps I had an over romanticised view of what a relationship should be. Why not just go for it? After all, I would be thirty years old in August. Maybe things would get better if we were married. There were so many 'What ifs' and 'maybes', but I was getting to the stage where I was past caring. I looked at Pat's sad face, his chin propped in his hand with a curl of cigarette smoke rising up through his fringe. The other hand gently caressed the pint of Guinness which took the weight of his stare. He looked tired and his eyes, like mine, were red from the drink. He felt my gaze, but didn't look at me.

'Máire, what about it. Will we take the plunge?'

It was time to give in. I took a gulp from my glass and replied, 'Well, why not.'

Pat was thrilled at my response and we ordered another round of drinks to celebrate. In those moments my spirits lifted. I had made a decision which, in itself, was something of an achievement for me. Pat was a good guy, we knew each other well and, on the whole, we were friends. Yes, we would get married. Why not indeed!

I suppose it was a strange thing, but after that night we didn't really talk of any wedding plans. I didn't even tell anyone about it. Clannad was the focus of my energy. The Ivor Novello Award and BAFTA nomination set us up for a lot more publicity and RCA were anxious to release a follow-up single as soon as possible. Our choice would have been 'New Grange', an arrangement of one of our older songs, but the record company insisted that the second single should be the Jimmy Rafferty song, 'I See Red'. To us it proved how little they understood the Clannad sound and we were frustrated when, as we might have predicted, the single was something of a flop. Eventually 'New Grange' was released, but by that time it felt as though we had lost something of the momentum that 'Harry's Game' had afforded us.

As the lead singer I found myself the centre of attention in terms of media interest in the band and was travelling back and forth to London on a regular basis to do interviews and promotions. Although we still had little personal finance, there seemed to be a lot more record company money available and travel became significantly more comfortable and appealing.

One day in the early summer Pat stopped me in my tracks by raising the subject of our wedding. It was something I had barely thought about in the last few months. Still, I remained resigned to the idea and we discussed the possibility of an August wedding. Both our birthdays were in August and by that time my brother Ciarán and his girlfriend Lynda had announced that they would be getting married in October. Perhaps subconsciously I, being the eldest, wanted to be married before any of the others, and if

I was to marry Pat at all, it might as well be sooner rather than later.

Neither of us wanted to make a big deal about the ceremony and resolved to book the wedding in a small church in town where we would hopefully be married by Father Frankie, a priest and friend I knew from Donegal. To this day I don't know how we had the gall to have a church wedding. It meant little to us. Neither of us had been near a church in years, except for christenings, weddings and funerals, but that's just the way it was. Everyone got married in church. Other than that, we wanted to break with convention. We were almost scornful of all the fuss made about weddings and decided that ours would be a very casual affair with only a couple of witnesses.

We weren't even going to tell our families. I suppose this in itself should have been a warning to me. Here I was, the first daughter of a large and wonderful family, and I didn't even want them to share in what is supposed to be one of the happiest days of a family's life. I knew Mammy and Daddy would be worried. They barely knew Pat. They'd met him a couple of times in Dublin, but he'd only been to our home in Donegal once in all the years we'd been seeing each other. Eventually I told my sister Deirdre of our plans. We had a terrible row. She couldn't believe that I would not tell our parents. 'OK, if you want a quiet affair, forget the rest of us,' she had said, 'but you can't get married and not invite Mammy and Daddy.'

I was stubborn and angry at her reaction, but eventually conceded that she was right. A few days later I phoned home. It was easier to do it on the telephone, that way I couldn't see their faces.

'Well, that's lovely, darling,' said my mother's voice after a moment's stunned silence. She was trying to be nice, but I could hear the anxiety in her voice. She knew me too well.

'We don't want a big fuss, Mammy, but you and Daddy can come up if you want.' I suppose it was hardly the best invitation to a daughter's wedding.

All of a sudden there seemed to be a lot to arrange in a very short time. I had to collect my baptism certificate from the local church. I smiled to myself in surprise as I read the wording and detail about my birth. I hadn't realised before, but it seemed that my parents had taken me for baptism at the church near the Royal Irish Academy – the very church where I had sought guidance, comfort and refuge in my student days. I knew there was something special about that place.

Father Frankie was a lovely priest who had been to school with my uncles. He tried to talk to us both about marriage, my work and what our future together might hold. I suppose there was a lot of wisdom in his words, but I'm sure he must have detected something of our apathy to the church. We were pleasant and polite, but told ourselves there was no way he knew about people like us. Our lives were so removed from anything he could experience or imagine, so how could he possibly understand? Funny, though, how something he said touched a nerve in me. I watched Pat's face as Father Frankie tried to talk to him about me and my career. He warned Pat that he should be prepared to handle my career and the possibility of higher profile and fame. It was Pat's reaction that rang an alarm bell. He just laughed, in that scornful manner he had when he referred to my music. 'Ach, don't you worry, Father, I'll sort her out,' he had said. I laughed back with him, but I was hurt and angry. Still, I pushed my anxiety aside. Surely things would be better when we were married.

Pat and I went together to choose a dress that would do for the occasion. I didn't want anything too fussy or 'bridelike'. We were a 'cool' couple and there was no room for a fairy-tale gown. Indeed, the dress took very little choosing. We went straight to Marian Gales in Dublin and I picked out a pretty looking ivory dress that came down off the shoulders. It had orange trim and I thought I could put some matching flowers in my hair. I tried it on. Pat liked it and I knew I looked good.

The third of August soon came around. Pat and I woke up together and I lay for a while thinking about the day ahead. The last couple of weeks had been a struggle. I had tried to push thoughts of the wedding out of my mind, as if in denial that it would actually happen. But I kept my anxieties inside, convincing myself that it was just natural pre-wedding blues. Surely everyone had them?

It would be nice to see my parents and I looked forward to the hooley we would have later that night. Still, I couldn't think too much about the actual wedding or my future with Pat. There was little consideration of the significance of the ceremony or the idea that I would be making this decision for life. This was the start of my new family, but, as always, I was just going with the flow, telling myself everything would sort itself out.

At about midday, Mammy and Daddy arrived at the house to get ready. I suppose it was a little strange. They did their best to make conversation with Pat and Daddy was his usual jovial self, but they barely knew their son-in-law to be, so the conversation was very trivial. Just before one o'clock we all set off together for the church. We were to pick up Pat's mother and Auntie on the way and introduce them to my parents. There was a warm and excited welcome at the house. Pat's sisters had gathered there to wave us off and wish us well. We allowed them to pin flowers in our lapels before setting off to get married, with Mammy and Daddy following behind in their car. I don't recall much of what Pat and I talked about on the way to the church, but I remember wondering what the conversation was like in my parents' car.

We were met at the church by Father Frankie, Mairéad Kennedy, who was my bridesmaid, her husband Damian and Pat's best man Noel with his wife Olivia. It was a very small wedding party, but that was the way we wanted it – no big deal, no fuss.

Father Frankie led us into the vestry for a short confession so that we could take communion. Of course it meant little to me, but everyone took communion at their wedding, it was the Irish Catholic way. Still, in my younger years, the ritual had been quite sacred and special to me and now I felt a pang of guilt and, I suppose, irritation, at our irreverence. Sure, we went through a confession, but I hardly felt worthy to be partaking of the body of Christ. We should probably have gone to a registry office to get married. It would have been more honest that way. After all, we didn't intend setting foot in a church again, apart from weddings, funerals, baptisms and the like.

Father Frankie led a pleasant service for us. Pat's best man played the accordion and, after communion, he sang a Beatles song. It was a sweet little church and the service held a certain charm. The sunlight filtered in on us through the stained glass and Father Frankie's warmth and joviality helped us feel relaxed.

I was especially pleased that I had invited my parents. I supposed it was a special day after all – it's just that I had this chill of confusion inside . . .

I was keen to leave the service behind and get on with the day. We'd arranged that the small wedding party would have a meal in a hotel in Howth. Following the dinner we would move to the room upstairs where we'd invited some of our friends and family for a hoedown. The drink flowed and the room was lively with chatter, dancing and laughter. Now I was OK. I could relax and enjoy a drink. I might have caught the odd anxious glance from my mother, but with a drink in my hand and a song to sing, I engrossed myself in the party. It didn't end at closing time. A host of friends came back to our house and the merry-making continued until the wee hours of the morning.

The next day Pat and I drove off on our honeymoon. We both loved the countryside, so we'd decided to take ten days travelling around Ireland. It was a good week. We were away from anything to do with our life in Dublin and we got on well. I was beginning to reassure myself that this would be the beginning of a new, very positive chapter of my life. However, it didn't take long to shatter my illusion. On our way home we called in to see some old friends of Pat's. They were a lovely family with teenage children and the house was busy with us and some other friends they'd invited around. The kids were excited to meet me and wanted to know all about Clannad and especially what it was like to appear on *Top of the Pops*. I suppose I was flattered by the attention and thrilled that they appreciated our music, but I could sense a certain tension about Pat and tried to make light of the whole thing. As the evening wore on Pat grew more and more quiet and seemed irritated by me. I tried to be friendly, coaxing him into the conversation, but I knew that he was in a sulk. I didn't understand exactly why, but suspected it was something to do with the attention I was getting and the talk about my music.

By the end of the honeymoon, reality had reared its ugly head. I had been naïve to imagine that things would be different. Pat was still resentful of my career and instead of confronting our problems before we got married, I had brushed them under the carpet in the hope that they would go away. Now I felt that I couldn't even broach the subject with him. I began to fear about what the months ahead would have in store. Best not to think too much. Clannad were only one record into a five-album contract and we had a schedule of touring and interviews that would probably keep me busy for the best part of a year. If only I had been brave enough to confront my doubts before now.

Once again I felt that I had been naïve and stupid. I had let events control me, going along with what someone else wanted. I wasn't strong enough to know my own mind and suffered by trying to span the various roles that everyone else had for me. I was thirty years old and my life was not my own. When I looked behind me I saw a catalogue of personal disaster and failure. But to look ahead was too frightening. In fact it never really occurred to me to do so. What would be would just have to be.

# Chapter 14

Pat and I had barely returned from honeymoon when it was time for me to go on the road again with the band. We had a long European tour ahead of us and everyone was looking forward to it. With the record company behind us we had better tour support and the success of 'Harry's Game' had caused a groundswell in our fanbase. In many ways we were raring to go, but I was deeply troubled at the thought of another long separation from Pat so early in our married life. I had gone into the marriage thinking I could address and dispel the fog of uncertainty when I got there, but this was no way to start a salvaging operation.

It was an eight-week tour and I only saw Pat for a brief two days when we flew home for Ciarán's and Lynda's wedding. The wedding had been planned for quite some time, so when they realised it would fall in the middle of the tour they resolved to return home, get married, then 'honeymoon' on the road. That was fine by the rest of us. We all got on well with Lynda and she had become like another sister to me. She was Australian and had met Ciarán several years ago at one of the Irish festivals. Within a few weeks she had arrived down in Donegal and Ciarán and she really clicked.

It was to be a fairly big family wedding, with all the brothers and sisters. Only my young brother Leon couldn't make it. He, along with our friend John McFadden, was driving for Clannad at the time and, as we took a flight home to Dublin, he had to drive the van on to Austria for the next leg of the tour. It was a great day, full of autumn colour and all the family were very proud. There were loads of musicians so we enjoyed a fantastic party afterwards. Then the next day it was back to Dublin airport bound for Austria, this time with Lynda in tow. We were all in high spirits until we got to the airport, whereupon Ciarán discovered his passport had expired. There was no way of getting another one that day, but equally, we simply had to get back out to the European gigs. After much debate we decided to risk it. I remember feeling hot and panicky as we all went through the gate together. Thankfully, on this occasion, the officials didn't check the detail on the passports very carefully and we all went through without a problem. I think we all breathed a sigh of relief, not daring to think about what might have been.

With a successful tour under our belts we arrived home to even more excitement. Dave, our manager, had a proposition on the table for us that was more than interesting. It came from Paul Knight, a London television producer who was working on a new adaptation of the English folklore legend Robin Hood. It was to be called *Robin of Sherwood*. Paul and his team had already been using tracks from our *Magical Ring* album to view the preliminary film rushes and invited us to write a full soundtrack. It was a huge project. There would be thirteen episodes to write for, plus an accompanying album. We had no idea how much work it would be, or how much it would take out of us, but we were thrilled to rise to the challenge. (As it happened, the first thirteen episodes were so successful that very quickly the team had to set to work on another series. By then the lead actor Michael Praed was contracted to another job so Jason Connery stepped into his shoes and we found ourselves working on another thirteen episodes worth of music.)

We did some early work at home, but the film and record companies were keen for us to be in close proximity to them in London. After Christmas they set us up in a studio in Soho and rented a very smart house for us in Berkeley Square, just off Oxford Street. Living in London was fantastic at first. We were right in the thick of it all and I had a wonderful room to myself in the house. But the novelty soon wore off. There are many excellent studios in country settings that would have been far more conducive to the creativity needed on such a project, but booking us a place had been left very late so we ended up in the middle of the city. In some ways it was a great studio – certainly for the technical side of things – but with no windows or natural light and nothing to gaze at apart from the gear, it was actually quite stifling. It was accessed off the street through a heavy iron door that was permanently locked. If you wanted to go outside, even for a moment, you had to go through a huge rigmarole of getting the security guy with the keys. Then you'd stand for ages outside, waiting for him to respond to the buzzer so you could be let back in. Inside there was nowhere comfortable to relax. There was a tiny kitchen, but the cooker had only one ring and the whole place was very ill equipped; it was impossible to organise any kind of decent meal. Consequently we were all desperate to get out as much as possible, and of course, once out, we dragged our feet about going back. We'd sit in the pub for hours at lunch time, and our evening meal – usually in a pizza or pasta place – would normally be extended by a further visit to a local drinking house. Inevitably we ended up drinking heavily and, with little 'healthy' food, I found myself piling on the pounds. I regularly drank a couple of pints or a couple of vodkas at each session, and felt absolutely no effect. I also became very lazy and would spend hours lounging in my room, watching television. I was always late to the studio, even though it was just around the corner, but there were times when I was so bored, I had little incentive to get there. It wasn't too bad for Ciarán and Pól. They were involved in all the writing, but it never occurred to me that I could get involved in any of the arrangements and many hours would pass before I was even needed to do a vocal. The Fairlight keyboard had just come in and there was a lot of new recording technology that the boys wanted to play with. Again, that only meant more waiting around for me. I had little interest in learning anything about it.

We must have made things really difficult for Tony Clark, the producer. He had a schedule to keep to, but we were all so laid-back. We were naively unaware that ultimately we would end up paying the costs, and didn't really think of it as being 'our money' that we were spending. In our minds, we had months ahead to get ourselves together. Even so, there were times when we felt the pressure and it didn't do much for internal relations. It was the first full project on which we needed to write all original pieces. Pól was quite highly driven and anxious to work through things, but Ciarán was always more laid-back. They were compelled to work together, but their individual approaches led to several heated discussions, with poor Tony trying to keep the project together and maintain peace in the band. It didn't help that there was a constant flow of people coming into the studio. At times when we should have been writing and recording, we were having to accommodate both the TV and record company people who would 'drop by' to hear demos of what we'd done so far – that could be so time-consuming.

We spent the best part of six months on the project. I talked to Pat every other night on the phone and he came over to see me a few times, but it was always a little awkward. Ironically – after all the days of waiting around with nothing to do – it always seemed that when Pat was over I was needed in the studio to do some vocals. He would come along with me, but I was extra conscious and nervous of myself when he was around. It was always in jest but I don't think he realised how his constant teasing wore me down. That was just his way, to criticise and make fun. I found myself making excuses all round – juggling my priorities between Pat and the band. I was always caught in the middle in what felt like a no-win situation.

Still, for all the difficulties, *Robin of Sherwood* was a wonderful project to be involved with and we made many friends among the actors, film crew and production team, particularly with Paul Knight himself. We were invited out on location which was very exciting and really helped us with the creative process. We'd always arranged our music with a 'visual sense' so we worked quite naturally when it came to creating music for the different scenes, images and atmospheres of the film. We wrote 'themes' for each of the key characters – Maid Marian, Will Scarlett and Hern the Hunter. One of the most fascinating pieces to put together was for a battle scene and I will never forget the boys experimenting with different percussive notes and strange rhythms to a time code. At one stage they even used a fork on the piano strings to capture a certain sound! Another favourite was a dance scene. It had already been filmed by the time we got around to writing and it was a challenge to write the music in with the visual timing. Then of course there was the all-important theme tune which everybody loved.

*Robin of Sherwood* was a long – sometimes arduous, sometimes thrilling – piece to put together and I think we were all relieved when it came to an end, yet very proud of our work. I was particularly thrilled to be able to put my name on one of the songs, 'Ancient Forest'. I'd contributed some of the words and it felt wonderful to be part of the writing process for the first time. Still, it was nothing to write home about!

The summer fed my laziness. I hung around the house a lot and went out around Dublin's bars in the evenings. Pat often had gigs and I liked going along to support him, but of course it usually meant that I sat for hours knocking back the vodkas. I tried to concentrate on making a nice home life for us, all the time conscious of how little I was getting back to Donegal. I especially missed my sisters, who were my best friends, but reasoned that my priority now was to Pat and making up for the time we had spent apart since our marriage. At least we were now getting on a little better together and enjoying a few evenings at home. We'd have a couple of drinks and stay up late watching television, laughing and chatting as we did in the early days. I tried to cook more and eat healthily, ever conscious of my escalating weight and the perils of take-away food. I didn't look good. My skin was sallow and there were dark rings under my eyes. If I did promotional work, the make-up artists could sort that out and I could hide my expanding waistline under dark, flowing shirts, but it didn't help my self-image. Gone were my carefree days where I enjoyed being the popular girl at school. Even with Clannad's success, my confidence had been gradually, and fatally, eroded. Pat wasn't one for flattery and I rarely got any words of encouragement from the boys. I was just one of the family – 'Máire, who sings'. I suppose as far as they were concerned I didn't need any praise or encouragement about my voice. It had always been there and it served a purpose, so I never considered that there was anything good or special about it. Though I probably didn't realise it at the time, my self-esteem had plummeted and inside I was dreadfully lonely. It was easy to drink and smoke a joint. It helped me forget all that and meant I didn't have to think too deeply about anything. I should have been excited and on top of the world with the way my career was going, or thinking about starting a family of my own, but no, my future didn't get beyond the next couple of hours in a day.

When *Robin of Sherwood* came out it was a huge success. Everyone loved the series and there was a huge buzz about the music. The soundtrack album sold really well, but, irony of ironies, Clannad were actually criticised by certain fans for not using any Gaelic. Things had come full circle. In the early days we were ridiculed for the use of our native tongue; now we were getting complaints that we had recorded an entire album in English. It was quite ridiculous. Anyway, how could it make sense to use Gaelic on an album based on a story from English folklore?

The project cast the band into a much broader limelight and there were great days as Michael Praed and I went off around the country promoting the series and its music. It seemed as though every television and radio station wanted to meet us and there were endless interviews and promotional appointments that kept us on the road. This did nothing for my marriage. It wasn't that Pat wanted me to be a housewife or anything, but I had realised that things were a lot calmer between us when he knew that I was either at home or by his side. There was a lack of trust, and rather than being pleased for my success and the opportunities that lay before me, Pat only saw it as something that would come between us. It didn't help that there were rumours going around about myself and Michael Praed. He was the 'hot and happening' actor of the time and we had become good friends, but there was never any hint of anything romantic between us. He was very committed to his girlfriend. However, like many people caught up in the showbiz circus, we became victims to press speculations and scandal-mongering.

After another Christmas in Dublin Clannad started to rehearse for a major UK tour and during that time we heard that we had been nominated for a BAFTA award. We were just as excited, if not more so, than when we had received the nomination for 'Harry's Game' several years ago. People had gone Robin of Sherwood crazy and our music was being played everywhere.

When the night of the awards came around we were all in very high spirits. Ciarán, Pól and I were sharing a large round table with Paul Knight and some of the gang. The boys were all in tuxedos and I had tried to dress up for the occasion. We still had very little personal money and I didn't want to splash out on a new gown that I'd never wear again so I decided to pull out an outfit I'd picked up a couple of years ago in a sale in Germany. It would just have to do. It was a bright yellow shirt-style dress and I wore a thick orange belt around my waist. I had false nails in the same shade of yellow and wore leggings and a pair of sandals. I cringe now to think what I must have looked like among all the other guests – the 'beautiful people' – actors and actresses, models and general celebrities, all in their designer gear and glitzy hair-dos. Still, when Ronnie Scott made the announcement that Clannad had won the award for 'Best Soundtrack', I couldn't have cared less what I looked like. The moment was simply breathtaking. I followed Ciarán and Pól onto the stage and stood there, grinning inanely in my yellow glory, as Pól made the acceptance speech.

Champagne flowed and we chatted and laughed our way through the rest of the evening – to the point where we were getting angry looks and eventually a telling-off from the table next to us because they couldn't hear Charlton Heston do his speech. Later we joined the line-up with Heston, Jane Seymour, Roger Daltry and other stars from stage and screen to be presented to Princess Anne. It was a fantastic evening and after the ceremony we all took off to Tramps nightclub where we danced and made big plans across the table with the BAFTA standing in the middle – a proud icon to our success. The next morning the film company sent over bottles of champagne which we sipped over breakfast in the hotel room as we giggled at our pictures in the newspapers.

Without doubt Clannad had now achieved another level of success and when the next tour came around our own van had been replaced by a luxury tour bus and we had a juggernaut to carry the equipment. There was also a ridiculous number of people at our beck and call. We had one of the best tour managers in the business – Phil McDonnell, fresh from working with Van Morrison – a whole team of sound and lighting engineers, caterers and my own personal stylist. It was a quite outrageous and hugely expensive operation. We had no idea how badly our money was being handled.

We also seemed to be attracting different types of people and found ourselves at larger-scale parties. It was at one of these parties that I was first offered cocaine. I was quite taken aback. I was just having a perfectly normal chat with this guy from a record company when he dropped the merits of the drug into the conversation and told me I really ought to try it. Smoking dope was one thing, but cocaine really worried me. I knew it was addictive.

'Ach, go on,' he said; 'just have a little line, it won't hurt you.'

I was hesitant, but I watched what he did and then followed. He smiled at me and we both waited for a reaction. I remember turning around and saying, 'That did nothing for me'. But I didn't stop talking all night!

It soon became a habit I indulged in, albeit on an occasional basis. Dope and cocaine were always available through the crowd I now mixed with and I found that it could sometimes help me when the work got tough. Looking back, it's hard to understand why it did not become more of an addiction. For some reason it didn't get a grip on me the way it does with so many others. Perhaps it had something to do with Mammy and Daddy back home on their knees praying, as they always had, for the protection of their children.

While that 1985 tour was a huge success for our professional profile, my home life was beginning seriously to fragment. I was the only girl on the road with thirty other people and I knew that didn't sit well with Pat. Trust had always been an issue, and of course, in his mind, it wouldn't be the first time I'd let him down. When we returned home things were decidedly strained. Then, in what seemed like no time, the boys began work on our next album and I found myself leaving Pat again to go off to Switzerland. It dawned on me then that I really was putting the band before my marriage, but I felt helpless to change anything. Pól was living out in Switzerland by then with his girlfriend, Christine, and had found a studio where he wanted us to begin the new project. The material was wonderful, some of the best Pól and Ciarán have ever written together, but it did not come together as quickly as we had expected, so when time ran out in Switzerland we reconvened the recording at Ridge Farm studios in Horsham, near London. It was a beautiful setting and we worked there until the summer when we returned home to complete the writing and final mixes on the album – *Macalla* (meaning 'echo') – in Dublin's Windmill Lane studios.

We were still in the final stages when Dave announced that we were booked to play six nights at Dublin's Olympia Theatre. It was a lovely venue and we were expected to sell out, but the promoter was keen for us to do a promotional press reception that would ensure maximum ticket sales.

A reception was arranged and I was faced with the usual bank of journalists among the cheese and biscuits. I didn't mind doing this kind of thing. Every artist relies on the press for their career and we were always happy enough to talk to them about our music. There again, to court the press can lead to immense suffering and we were aware that our increased profile brought a more virulent preoccupation with the details of our personal lives. Over the years I have learnt to be on my guard but, as any artist will testify, you are completely powerless if a writer has a certain agenda. There have been many damaging articles that have hurt my family deeply – stories about our relationships, particularly between myself and Enya. We resolved in the early days not to talk about our private lives but, especially in Enya's case, this has often led to more intrigue and false speculation. For an artist, it is the unfortunate consequence of being in the public eye, but what makes me really angry is the way the family inevitably bears the suffering.

I answered a round of good questions about the forthcoming dates and the new album we had been working on. A woman journalist then asked me what it was like to work with Michael Praed and went on to ask whether I had any plans to start a family. In themselves, these were fair, reasonable questions that I was happy to answer, but the next morning when Ciarán handed me the newspaper in the studio I was horrified at the angle of her piece. It was full of insinuation about romantic connections between myself and Michael and reported that I had no plans to start a family yet with my husband.

I knew there would be trouble when I got home. Things were strained enough between Pat and me and, although he prided himself in not believing anything the papers said, I suspected that this could be the final straw. I was right. Pat was furious. I suppose he had every right to be. From his point of view it looked as though I had been talking about decisions I had made about our future and our family life without involving him.

I had not wanted to go home that evening and it was late when I finally left the studio. Pat had been working on the other side of town and I met him in our doorway, immediately noticing the crumpled newspaper in his hand. We had both been drinking and a nasty row soon ensued. If only that journalist had realised the consequence of her scandal-mongering report. It was the episode that finally opened up the crack in our marriage and smashed its fragile form to smithereens. During our years together we had swept so much under the carpet and done little to build on the crumbling foundations of the relationship. In the eighteen months of the marriage I had been away for weeks at a time and there was very little trust between us or respect for one another. We argued bitterly throughout the night and by daybreak I knew that this really was the end of the marriage. Pat was still asleep when Murty, our driver, arrived to take me to the studio. I packed a suitcase with as many of my personal belongings as I could scrape together and left the house, fearing that this was most certainly for the last time.

The next stop was Ciarán's house. I was awfully upset by the time we arrived there and Ciarán and Lynda were horrified to see the state I was in. They assured me that I could stay there until I got myself together. I felt numb inside and wanted nothing more than to go to bed and hide for ever. But I had to face the studio; there were still vocals to be done. I was to lay down the lead track on a song called 'Almost Seems too Late to Turn'. It was painfully pertinent and, with Pól in the control room, I sang the song with all the hurt burning within me and tears brimming over from my eyes. It was done in just a couple of takes and that's what ended up on the album.

My misery was intense. The last thing I had wanted was a failed marriage, but I had gone into it with such naivety, ignoring all the early warning signs and not strong enough to listen to my better instincts. Everything I touched seemed to be a complete and utter failure. What had my family – and even Pat for that matter – done to deserve this? I came from a wonderful home, but all I kept doing was letting them down. The younger members of the family had always looked to me as an example and now I felt so ashamed to have to resign myself to a broken marriage. Perhaps I would never be happy. I didn't deserve to be after all the stupid things I had done in my life. What more tragedy would tomorrow bring?

It was just as well that I had no idea of the days ahead or the rollercoaster ride I was about to embark upon.

# Chapter 15

Despite the uncertainties in my personal life I was still able to recognise that, as a band, we were 'really happening'. The writing was better than ever and I loved some of the material the boys were bringing to the table. In the final stages of writing for the *Macalla* album they had been playing around with a beautifully atmospheric backing track that we all realised could be something special. The struggle was in working out the melody line and putting words to the piece.

'OK, let's call it a day,' said Ciarán. It was late in the evening, we'd been down at Windmill Lane studios all day and we were tired and ready to relax. Maybe we'd get fresh inspiration for the piece tomorrow.

As usual there were many familiar faces in The Dockers. At that time of the evening it was generally full of musicians and actors winding down from their work in the area's plethora of studios, film companies and advertising agencies. The members of U2 could often be spotted in there when they were home and the wall around Windmill Lane studios was a graffiti shrine to the band who, at that time, were playing football stadiums around the world. We'd often met up and hung out with them before. Dublin is a small place, with only three-quarters of a million people, and the musicians all tend to gravitate towards each other. Traditional musicians mix with the rock, pop and folk bands and there's generally a great vibe with each other. I think it comes from the days when we all used to do the festivals. In the seventies, no matter who you were, you would go to a festival and stay there for the duration, mixing with and supporting the other acts. There would be none of this 'turn up, do your gig and go home', the way it often is today.

U2 had used the 'Theme from Harry's Game' for their 'Red Rock' concert video they recorded in the US and we appreciated the respect and the friendship that had developed between us. This particular evening, we found the boys relaxing in the bar and got chatting to them about how our record was going and their upcoming big Dublin gig.

Bono was really interested in what we were up to and by the end of the evening we thought it would be a great idea to try something together on this backing track we had.

Two days later I found myself, microphone in hand, sitting opposite him, singing old songs and enjoying swapping stories. Then Ciarán played the backing track. Bono started improvising over it. He was incredible to work with because he was so relaxed and carefree about the way he sang. He wasn't afraid of trying anything, no matter what it might have sounded like. I was fascinated by his confidence and as we finished the session we all recognised there could be the makings of an incredible-sounding song.

That night there was an almighty thunderstorm and when we met together again everyone was full of lyrics about thunder and lightning. The song came together naturally. Bono sang one of the best melody lines I think I've heard and Pól guided me with my vocals. It was just one of those magical things. We called the song 'In a Lifetime'.

Not since 'Harry's Game' had we felt that kind of excitement about one song. We knew it was special and of course RCA couldn't believe it when we took them the recording, complete with Bono's awesome contribution. It was the obvious single to launch the *Macalla* album and opened up a whole new audience for us. I'm sure many young people came to our concerts just in case Bono showed up to sing that track. We have never actually performed it live together – as yet!

Bono's involvement also gave us a bit more power to call the shots with the record company. When we talked about doing a video, there was one obvious place, Donegal. We had a wonderful director called Meirt Davis, who had previously done some work with U2. He loved the track and the film was beautifully shot. It perfectly captured the feel of the song – moody and atmospheric, but its filming was filled with much hilarity and really helped lift the darkness in my soul.

The song was about 'a lifetime – from the cradle to the old', and Bono had this idea to use a hearse. He actually went out and bought one in Dublin and got a friend, Charlie Whisker, to drive it down to Donegal. Charlie had the most amazing face – very long, stark and clean-shaven. His hair was cropped close and hidden underneath a top hat; he looked completely at home behind the wheel of the funeral car. So there we all were in this cavalcade coming down from Dublin, led by the hearse. It was a five-hour drive and of course we had to go through the borders of Northern Ireland. As we drove out passed Monaghan and approached the Aughnacloy checkpoint Bono got in the back of the hearse and lay with his arms crossed over his chest where the coffin would be. We were in tears with laughing so much as we watched the shocked reaction of the soldiers from the car behind. They didn't know what was going on. They soon recognised that it might be Bono, but what was he doing? He was lying there, stock still, with his long hair, dark shades and deadpan expression. It was hilarious.

'Well, what have we got here then?' said a young soldier as we pulled to a halt.

'We're just going down to do a bit of filming,' says Charlie.

'And what's he doing in the back?'

'Oh, he's just getting used to the feel of it.'

By this time there was a lot of sniggering among the other soldiers who were fairly confident that it was, indeed, their rock hero.

'So he's not dead then?' offers one.

'No, he's not dead', says Charlie.

'In that case, can I have his autograph please?'

At this point Bono rose from his slumber, obliged with the autograph and the soldiers waved us through.

Once in Donegal there was more fun. The weather down there is wild at the best of times, but the film crew had turned up with wind and rain machines to make sure they could create the atmosphere. We had authentic grey skies and spent most of our time frozen to the bone. There was a great atmosphere and we involved some of the locals in the video whom we bussed around with us. This, of course, assured a ready supply of hot tea and sandwiches and we all convened to Daddy's pub in the evenings. Word had got around the area of what we were up to so the place was packed. I had a great time pulling pints alongside Bono and Adam Clayton, who had come up for the craic. The boys fell in love with the place and its culture and Bono had me phonetically teach him a Gaelic song whenever we had a spare moment in between shots.

At this time the family must have had their suspicions, but I didn't tell them exactly what had happened between me and Pat. It was only at the end of the summer that I confided in them about the split. For now I was glad to be home, and proud to bring something of our success back to the local area. In my life of darkness, the earthiness of the surroundings and the humour of good friends kept me going.

When I left Pat I had stayed with Ciarán and Lynda for a few weeks and then found myself a two-bedroom flat in the hope that my sister Deirdre would join me when she started college in Dublin in September. The album was complete and the 'In A Lifetime' video was 'in the can'. Now it was a case of waiting for the release dates and everyone was happy to have a little time out before starting rehearsals for the *Macalla* tour at the beginning of the next year. But 'time on my hands' was a dangerous thing for me.

Perhaps it would have been safer to have remained busy and focused on something, but as it was, I was left to my own devices, and my own near downfall. I was hurting badly from the failure of my marriage, but in the pursuit of distraction I became something of a party girl. It was a time when I didn't allow myself to think too much. I spent my days in bed or lounging around the flat watching television and smoking dope. Then in the evening I would go out to a couple of Dublin bars. They soon became regular haunts for me. There was always someone to share a drink or a line of coke with and I would inevitably end up leaving a club as dawn came up with a bunch of strangers I called 'friends'. To the outside world I was having a great time. I was fun to be with and spending more money than I should, but I didn't care, I was out to impress. Nobody could see inside.

I had little self-respect and found myself becoming quite

promiscuous. Perhaps there was something in the power of being able to 'pull' men. It made me feel strong and in control. It was as though I felt I had something to prove. I avoided looking at myself in the mirror too closely. I was now eating less, because of my habits, and consequently losing weight, but I still hated the way I looked.

I'd often bump into my brother Leon who would get angry when he saw my behaviour. He was also making the most of the club scene, but would always be looking out for me. As brother and sister we were very close and there were many parallels in our lives. Somehow I could share with him some of the trauma of that time. Still, there were times when we had to turn a blind eye to each other's behaviour. 'Oh Máire,' he would say as he saw me leaving with some man I'd got chatting to. 'Not him, you can do better than that, come home with me.' Sometimes he'd talk me round, but I usually ended up telling him to mind his own business.

To my great relief Deirdre moved in with me in September 1985. Despite a wild social life, I was desperately lonely and it was wonderful to have my sister around. She was very supportive and I know she was very scared for me. Looking back I realise that it was probably the true friendship of Deirdre and my brother Leon that saved me from myself.

*Macalla* was released in the late autumn to strong critical acclaim and we found ourselves back in the *Top of the Pops* studio performing the single, 'In a Lifetime'. It had huge airplay and hit the top twenty chart immediately. 'Almost Seems too Late to Turn' was the follow-up single. It was a song that carried so much pain for me, but I was happy that we were able to donate it as a Children in Need song, performing it live on the show hosted by Terry Wogan.

Yet again, however, I found the press on my back. 'In a Lifetime' was a high-profile project and by that time they had got wind of my separation from Pat and implied that there had been more than just music-making between myself and Bono. It was absolutely ridiculous. The truth was that Bono and his wife Ali were very supportive through this very difficult time. Talking for hours, Bono often tried to persuade me to use my distracted emotions to write music and encouraged me to keep a diary and write down my thoughts. I suppose it made a lot of sense, but I didn't have the heart for it then.

I didn't have the heart for anything. I was simply cold inside. My life was passing me by. To an outsider it might have looked glamorous, exciting and successful, but every morning I would wake with the same sinking feeling and spend the day blocking out the truth of my misery. I had failed in love and, I believed, failed my family – the most precious thing in my life. My only direction and structure came through the events and bookings of the band and it was only on stage that I felt truly alive.

# Chapter 16

With the success of the *Macalla* album Clannad began to work towards the tour. It was to be the biggest, most elaborate production yet (probably far more than we could afford) and we needed a place where we could rehearse and set up the equipment properly. Woodtown Manor fitted the bill. It was a huge house in the Dublin hills, owned by one of the Guinness family. Pól and his girlfriend moved in and, when we returned from the tour in the early spring, Deirdre and I also gave up the flat and took residence in Woodtown's grandeur.

The tour was a huge success. No longer were our crowds simply made up of people who appreciated folk and traditional music. We attracted a new type of fan and I remember one particular night looking down along one row and seeing a granny at one end and a young fella wearing an AC/DC T-shirt at the other. There were our loyal supporters who were into contemporary folk or Celtic music, then *Robin of Sherwood* attracted a wider audience and the hit with Bono gave us big credibility with the rock crowd. Our record company were keen for us to start work on another album. They suggested that this time we might consider using an American producer – a move that should help guarantee Stateside success. Inevitably this meant that we would have to spend more money, but it was an exciting time for the band and we ensconced ourselves in Woodtown Manor – investing in some state-of-the-art recording gear – and began writing.

Meanwhile I became more lethargic than ever. Sometimes I didn't leave the house for days at a time. I made my room as self-contained as possible and would come down only when I was needed in the studio. Pól and Ciarán were writing, and still it never occurred to me that I could be of any creative input myself. I suppose I became more distant from the boys at this time. No one bothered me in my room and it was out of bounds for everyone except Deirdre. I'd look forward to her coming home. She would come up to my room and we'd chat for hours. She was my confidant and she had to put up with a lot. If I wanted to go out I'd meet her from college. She'd be there with her bicycle and work things. She was doing a lot of etching at the time and her fingernails would be black with ink. She was always pleased to see me outside the college gate, but I know her heart often sank. She knew what the night would turn into.

'Come on, I'll take you for dinner,' I'd say.

'Ach, Máire, let me go home first, look at the state of me. Can't we just cook something at home.'

'No, come on, let's go out, I'm starving and you need to let your hair down.'

So we'd go eat, I'd buy a few bottles of wine or champagne and then I'd insist she come with me to a club. Poor Deirdre, she nearly always came, I suspect more to keep an eye on me than anything. Her bicycle would end up chained outside the night club and her rucksack in the cloakroom. We always met loads of people. They were 'good-time friends' – many who, unknown to my sister, could supply me a line of coke – but I'm sure Deirdre saw through the facade. She knew too well that she was one of my very few real friends in Dublin and I love her for the way she stuck by me. In the early hours of the morning we'd make our way home. The bicycle would be loaded in the back of a taxi and we'd go off up the hill to Woodtown, Deirdre knowing that in a few hours' time she'd have to get up for college again.

Those were the good nights. There'd be others when I'd be taking a stranger home.

Thomas Bevins, the butler, came with Woodtown Manor. He was a lovely, well-built, jolly man in his late fifties, with silver hair and a big smile. He lived down the road, but every day he would come up and do the chores in the house and generally look after the place. He was a huge fan of Daniel O'Donnell and you'd hear him singing country songs at the top of his voice above the noise of the hoover. Thomas had been there for years and had seen many comings and goings. In his time the house had been host to a multitude of musicians, writers, actors, film-makers and all manner of public persona. I'm sure he could have made a comfortable retirement for himself selling his stories to the tabloids, but no, Thomas was a friend to all, and the soul of discretion. He minded his own business and turned a blind eye to whatever was going on. It was always warm when he was in the house and I loved to sit and drink tea with him, just passing the time of day. Many a time he'd see a stranger leaving my bedroom. He'd just make the tea and say, 'Will I call a taxi now, Máire?'

As the car went off down the hill I'd look at him over the steaming brew. 'Oh, Thomas, what am I doing?'

'I don't know,' he'd say in his firm but cheery manner.

'I don't think that guy is for me.'

'I don't think so Máire,' he'd say, and hand me a piece of toast. He'd never pass judgement or make comment unless I spoke about it, and that meant a lot to me.

Just before Christmas 1986 I discovered I was pregnant. For days I wandered around in a shroud of disbelief, numb with shock. I told no one, not even Deirdre. I needed time to think and work out what to do, but Christmas was fast approaching and everyone was preparing to go home. Pól and his girlfriend, Christine, had already left for Switzerland where they were spending Christmas with her family, and the rest of us were due to set off for Donegal in the next few days. I had missed out on so many family get-togethers over the last few years, and I knew that Mammy was especially excited at the knowledge that I was planning to be there.

It was a difficult time. Once again I found myself separated from my family by a huge secret. Sure enough, there were all the usual festivities. I tried to join in, but my heart was heavy. I was surrounded by the people I loved most in the world, but I was lonely. I was lonely, and wanted to be alone. After Christmas I told the family I was meeting friends in Dublin for New Year and headed back to Woodtown Manor by myself.

The house was empty apart from Pól's and Christine's dog, MoGrá. Thomas was still coming in every day to give him a walk, feed him and generally keep an eye on things. He was surprised to find me back so soon. We shared half-an-hour together, but even Thomas' company was too much for me. I was glad when he left me alone with only MoGrá to distract my attention.

I lived a very melancholy week, but I needed to be alone to review my situation. I should have been assessing my life, taking stock, making plans, deciding what to do. But in truth, I was still just existing from moment to moment. I wasn't really thinking at all. Somehow I was just numb and my mind sought peace in a haze of nothingness. Each day I'd walk down the hill, a mile and a half to the nearest shops. I'd buy milk and a newspaper, then go to the bar for a glass of Guinness. I cut out my other drinking because of the pregnancy, although in the months before Christmas I had been drinking more than ever in my life and generally abusing my body. Any damage was probably already done. MoGrá would sit at my feet. He was a good-natured, obedient dog. He'd look at me with love and loyalty and bring a little light into my day. Out we'd go into the cold and wander back up the hill. The air was crisp with winter and the sky a watery blue. Sometimes a thin ray of sunlight would break through the clouds, resting on the naked branches of the trees that lined the road. It was quiet in that area. People were at home with their families or in the city bars with friends. A family was out walking. A little girl, in a new bright red coat with blonde ringlets popping out from under her hat, pushed a dolly in her pram. Her parents held hands and the brother rode along on a small bicycle. Obviously a Christmas present, he wobbled about trying to keep his balance with Daddy's steady hand, ready to save him from a fall.

'Happy New Year,' they called from across the other side of the road. It shocked me for a few seconds.

'Thank you, the same to you,' I called back, surprised even to hear the familiar sound of my own voice.

Of course, it was New Year's Eve. I had almost forgotten. The days had gone by in such a haze, and for all my hours in front of the television I had hardly registered what day it was. I spent New Year alone in Woodtown Manor. I watched the revelry in the count-down to midnight on the television and fell asleep. A new year had begun and I had a life inside me that one way or another was going to change everything. I had made that one decision. I was going to keep this baby. Other than that, my mind was nowhere. I didn't think of the consequences: what it might mean for my career, how the band would react, how my parents would react, where we would live, how I would support the child . . . None of these things really played on my mind, just the all-consuming numbness where my soul took refuge.

By the end of January I decided I would go down to Donegal and tell my parents. I sat on the bus for the five- or six-hour journey. It was possibly the longest journey of my life and at that time I wouldn't have cared if it had never ended. I knew Mammy and Daddy would stand by me and respect my decision, but still, I was nervous. More than anything I knew how hurt and worried they would be. I pulled my coat around me as the bus jolted along and the landscape opened out into rural Ireland. I was ashamed of myself. There I was, thirty-two years of age, with a broken marriage and pregnant with an illegitimate child. My life was a sham.

Mammy and Daddy, as expected, were shaken by my news. Mammy put her arms around me and cried a little. Daddy looked at me tenderly and said, 'If it makes you happy, I will be happy for you.' Though they tried not to show it I know they must both have been extremely worried for me. Over the last twelve months I had become painfully thin. I didn't really eat and the mirror betrayed my unhealthy lifestyle in the sallow complexion and dark-ringed eyes that stared back at me.

I could not ask for two greater parents. Yes, they were a little overwhelmed by the situation – it wasn't the circumstances they'd have chosen to welcome their first grandchild – but they were strong for me and promised to do anything they could to help. They were glad that I felt strong enough to face up to the responsibility, still not knowing that I had walked this path once before.

I stayed a week in Donegal and then returned to Woodtown to continue work on the new album. The band were in fevered excitement. There'd been a shortlist of American producers drawn up and top of the list was Greg Ladanyi. He'd worked with the likes of Don Henly, Jackson Brown and Fleetwood Mac, so when word came through that he was on his way over to meet with us, the boys were beside themselves. It would be a big move for us, a new direction. The demos were coming together quite well, though things were a little strained between Ciarán and Pól because of their different approaches when it came to the writing. I remember one evening questioning the direction we might take with this American producer. Sure, we admired his work, but it was so far removed from the 'Clannad sound'. Maybe we shouldn't be so wildly enthusiastic about the whole thing. It might not be that great a move.

Pól was particularly stirred up by my misgivings. 'What do you mean?' he said in exasperation. 'This guy is the best of the best, he's going to make you famous, what's wrong with you Máire?'

Pól's anger was probably justified. He loved the band and yearned for us to make it big in America. What he saw in me was complete apathy. I suppose I had little visible enthusiasm for the songs and couldn't see any further than that afternoon's work. Greg was coming over at the end of February – so what?

My sleep was often broken with troubled dreams, but one particular night I awoke in the early hours with cramping pains in the pit of my stomach. They subsided and I slept on again, but later in the day I started to bleed. Panicked, I rang my mother. I didn't know what it meant or what to do. I was crying on the phone to her and she began to cry too. 'I'm sorry, Máire,' she said, 'but it doesn't sound too good.' She had given birth to nine children and had never experienced this kind of thing. 'Don't panic,' she tried to tell me, 'but you must go to the doctor.'

The doctor was kind and sympathetic, but after an examination he had to tell me there was no sign of life. I had lost my baby.

My world finally fell apart. All those months, even years of pretending, all the hurt caught up with me. I went into my room and cried until I thought my heart would break. The boys were worried for me. They'd heard me crying on the phone to Mammy and now I'd come in and disappeared to my room for hours. I ignored their knocking on my door until Deirdre came. She tried to smooth the hair away from my eyes and calm my sobbing. 'I've lost the baby,' I finally managed to tell her. No one really knew what to say. It was a double shock for them. 'Maybe it was for the better,' they tried to be encouraging, but I locked the door of my room and stayed there for three days.

I had never felt so low. It seemed as though everything I did went wrong and now I couldn't keep a baby either. What was going on with my life? I was a complete failure and felt the whole family should be ashamed of me. I punished myself with such thoughts until they were veiled in a shroud of numbness once more. I just lay on the bed in front of the TV. Night turned into day, but the heavy curtains of my room denied any break of daylight. I drifted in and out of sleep, my eyes sore and heavy with crying. The handkerchiefs Deirdre had given me were sodden and I rummaged in the drawer by my bedside for more. My hand fell on a book. I picked it out and held it to my breast. It was an old prayer book of my grandmother's. If she could see me now, what would she think? I missed her so badly. I missed home and everything it meant to me. I longed to be young and free again, running on Donegal's beaches without a care in the world. Tears came and I clutched the book tighter. Oh God, what should I do?

Strangely enough I found myself reading from the book, rubbing my eyes with salty hands to help me focus. For a short time the words seemed to offer a little comfort, not especially because of what they were saying, perhaps more because they were half familiar. They took me back to a time when life was sweet. I found myself saying the prayers out loud and concentrating, trying really to feel what they were saying.

> *. . . O Mother of Mercy have pity on me . . .*
> *I bless and thank Almighty God my refuge and my hope . . .*
> *I know that with thy help I will be able to conquer but I fear of*
> *danger that I might lose my soul.*

There was no dramatic flash of light or word from God – I didn't expect it – but I did find myself smiling as I remembered my time at the Royal Irish Academy, how when I went into that church and asked God to help me with my lessons, somehow I always got through. It was as if God heard my prayer and answered. Was God with me now? Did he hear these prayers? Was he with me in the depth of my despair and darkness?

'Máire, Máire, are you awake?' Pól's voice at the door made

me jump. 'Máire, won't you come down? Greg is here and he wants to meet you. Come on, we really need you, this is going to be great.'

Greg Ladanyi was charming, with his smooth Californian drawl. He must have wondered what on earth he'd let himself in for when I came downstairs to meet him. I'd combed my hair and applied a little make-up, but months later Greg confessed what a dreadful and sad figure he thought I made at our first meeting.

I found it very hard to be motivated in the weeks that followed, but the boys were encouraging and I was swept along in their excitement and enthusiasm for this new project. We worked hard and by April we were ready to head over to Rockfield, the residential studio we'd booked in Wales. It brought back memories of our early album, *Dúlamán*, but of course this time we were in the big studio. We had a lovely time there and it lifted my spirits. Russ Kunkel, a well-known drummer was to produce our album with Greg. He had a natural inclination for our music and we were very happy to work with him. (In fact, in many ways, he was probably the saving grace of the album since we discovered Greg was very much a rock 'n' roll guy.) The recording sessions went well and there were plenty of fun moments. Ciarán and I even rented bicycles with the intention of cycling around the Welsh countryside, but it was a skill I had never mastered as a child and the others thought it was hilarious to see me launching myself around the studio courtyard in a bid to conquer the two-wheeled terror. It was no good. Once more into the ditch and I resolved to give up. Can't I do anything right!

After a couple of weeks we moved the production down to a London studio to do some overdubs with different musicians. Then it was off to the States where we would do the vocals and mixing in the Complex Studios, Los Angeles – a great recording facility that Greg part-owned with George Massenburg at the time.

It was very different to our last trip to the United States. Back in 1979, before our days with RCA, we'd hired a couple of cars and driven from the West to the East Coast, playing coffee bars and clubs. It had been a huge adventure. We had little money and stayed in cheap motels along the way. My brother Leon and

John McFadden came with us to drive and help us with the equipment and we must have looked quite a motley crew – a bunch of broke Irish musicians making their way across the States. Life was rough then, but I think we all look back nostalgically on the laughter and good times we all shared. Many a time now we recall the incident where we nearly got arrested in Canada. It was Halloween and, as is the tradition in Ireland, we bought fireworks to celebrate. That day we drove over the border into Canada where we were to play in a small industrial town called Kamloops. After set-up and sound-check we decided it would be fun to let the fireworks off. Within less than five minutes we were surrounded by six police cars, full of angry-looking officers with guns at the ready. We were completely shocked. We had no idea that Kamloops was a place renowned for its refinery and that the setting-off of fireworks was completely illegal. Of course, the look of us and our Irish accents didn't help. They couldn't believe we had acted in complete naivety. Thankfully one of the officers was himself Irish and recognised the tradition of fireworks at Halloween. It took a bit of doing but finally he persuaded his colleagues that we were innocent, naïve tourists rather than trouble-makers or terrorists, and they let us off.

This trip to the States was somewhat different. We stayed in a top-notch hotel and were surrounded by LA's beautiful people. It was a bit of a shock to the system. For the first time in my life I found myself in a beauty parlour having my hair and nails done. For what seemed like hours I was fussed and pampered by tousle-haired blondes who cooed over my pale skin, suggested a tanning bed and talked endlessly about the virtues of cosmetic surgery.

LA was vibrant and exciting and something of its spirit rubbed off on me. It was such an alien culture and I felt very much like an observer on life, amused by the behaviour of the cartoon-like characters that often crossed our paths. But we also made some very good friends and met loads of musicians. Toto were recording next door and there was a constant flow of musicians, some who ended up putting a vocal down with us. Even Jackson Brown dropped into the studio with his then girlfriend, Daryl Hannah, for the end-of-album party and playback. One of the highlights for me was when Bruce Hornsby came in and recorded a song with us. We'd met him during our recording in London and ended up going to his Hammersmith show. It turned out to be a great song. We spent our days between the glorious hotel pool and the studio and at night we were never short of a dinner invitation. LA is certainly a place to party, but for me there was something very unreal about it. I enjoyed it for what it was, knowing that we were only there for six weeks. That was time enough. Though I loved meeting new people, and the zest of the place had somehow broken through the heaviness of my soul, it was also a rather frightening experience that I think helped bring me to my senses. The people used coke on a whole different level. It was everywhere, and it seemed that everyone had a habit. Back home and in Europe it had always seemed so much more discreet. Even at my most indulgent time it was, for me, more for occasional, social use than an all-consuming habit. But in LA, no matter where you were, people would be going back and forth to the toilets all night. I found it hard to take in. Champagne ran like water and the 'get-togethers' were never-ending. This was just the ordinary way of life. There were beautiful people, but also some very sad cases. It made me want to stand back and take stock of what I was doing. I indulged, but not in the same way. I was beginning to want to look after myself again.

In my room alone I would sometimes turn to the prayer book. Something had made me push it into my suitcase. It was largely ignored, but I found myself muttering the occasional prayer. The partying took its toll and there were times in the studio when I really felt I needed some help with my confidence and my voice. It was strange. I'm not sure I was even fully aware of it at the time, but I would find myself asking God to help me and guide me. Sometimes when I was out I would get scared. It was such an alien environment, all too indulgent, and I felt it would be easy to lose control.

Six weeks was enough and I was glad to touch down on Irish soil. The August sun shone over Dublin and the streets seemed to be full of happy, fresh-faced people. Our time in America had gone well and we were especially happy with our new album, *Sirius*. Though quite removed from what we thought was the 'Clannad sound', it brought out the rockier side of our music and we were all quite proud of it. I was beginning to smile again and come to terms with my plight. I reasoned with myself that, after all I had done in my life, I had little right to expect fulfilment in a happy relationship with a family of my own. Even so, I began to want to make the most of my life. I wanted to be liked. I had a lot of love inside me and I suppose I wanted to show people I could be a caring, worthwhile person. I would change, I would watch my temper, I would be a better person.

There was excitement among the band and, for me at least, a certain sense of change in the air. I had no idea what was ahead. Something kept drawing me to my grandmother's prayer book and I even found myself wandering down the hill from Woodtown and into the Catholic church. I sat in the back and found myself talking to God again. I had been brought up to use the set prayers to the saints or to Mary. Now I found myself, almost in desperation, saying straight to God, 'Please, if you will hear me, please help me.' I felt so unworthy; I just sat in the back of the church, believing I had no right to take part in the ritual, but somehow it was right to be there. I spoke to Jesus, to Mary, to God. It didn't matter who or how. I'd ask God to help me to sleep, to help me pay an outstanding bill, to help me get through an interview. 'Help me, guide me, make me strong.' I felt I'd caused so much damage to my family and all I wanted to do was put my life back together and be strong for them. I didn't deserve it, but as the days went by, my prayers were more resolute and I was beginning to get a sense of real living again.

With the recording out of the way I was also able to enjoy more regular visits to Donegal. Deirdre had finished in Dublin and got her degree and Mammy loved having me back home more often. Along with teaching music she was also busy with the church choir and whenever possible I would join her there. It was comforting to be back in our chapel again and I was happy to attend mass. One particular day I found myself on my knees pouring my heart out to God. The priest was going through the ritual prayers but I wasn't listening to his words. In my heart I was humbling myself before God, somehow knowing that I had to seek his forgiveness. As a nineteen-year-old I had tried to justify the abortion to myself, yet over the years, though I had tried to push it out of my life, it had always been there. I suppose that was the time I was beginning to turn my back on God. I didn't feel he could forgive me for what I had done – and how could I even ask him to? Now I had a catalogue of failure to my name. I had done so much wrong – the abortion, a broken marriage, promiscuity, drug abuse. Looking up towards the front of the church my attention was fixed on the statues of Jesus and the Virgin Mary. Closing my eyes again I visualised them, not as icons, but as real human beings – a man and woman who knew what it meant to cry tears of anguish and live with extreme pain, people who had been beaten and broken on the wheels of life. Could it be that they were looking down on me now, understanding my pain, my loneliness, my frailty and fear? 'Lord Jesus, if you can, please forgive me.' I repeated the words over in my mind and began to feel a certain warmth running through my body, as if someone had laid a hand on my troubled heart and soul and with the most tender of touch had healed the hurt and turmoil inside. In that moment I felt forgiveness. The priest's monotone broke through my peace when I realised that Mammy had stood up beside me, ready to receive communion. I too got up off my knees and for the first time in my adult life took the sacrament with a pure heart.

# Chapter 17

On our return from America we faced the usual round of promotion work that would launch the *Sirius* album. There were some major music magazines interested in us and our record company decided it would be a great idea to bring the journalists over to Donegal where they could meet us in our home environment. It was an expensive venture, but it made a lot of sense. Our music is so heavily influenced by the experience of Donegal – its rugged coastline, barren beaches, mountain mists and the warmth in the language of the Gaeltacht. Somehow the place speaks of our sound and people get a better understanding of Clannad once they've spent time there. Even now I like to bring my music to Donegal, 'road-testing' it as I drive around the mountains and walk the beaches with the music in my ears.

Our final appointment of the week was with the *New Musical Express*. We were surprised at their interest in us – their reputation is for reporting on more 'indie' and rock music – and were a little apprehensive as to what kind of coverage they might give. Still, when I got word that the journalist they were sending was Alan Jackson, my concerns were laid to rest. I had met Alan some time ago and knew that he was a fan of our music.

We discovered later that there was a last-minute change concerning the planned photographer. Seemingly, the original guy was suddenly unable to make the shoot and, on Alan's recommendation, a certain Tim Jarvis received a late-night call asking if he would accept an assignment in Donegal, Ireland, to photograph a band called Clannad. He knew very little about us, but when his flatmate mentioned the lead singer's 'beautiful eyes', Tim instantly was intrigued.

We'd arranged to meet at a local hotel. I was sitting drinking tea and chatting to the make-up woman when Alan and Tim arrived. They were both good-looking guys. Alan, the shorter of the two, and Tim with an instantly infectious smile. As we were introduced I took in more of Tim's warm, open face, his slim frame and twinkling eyes. His wavy hair was a short style, but growing long and he had several moles that added a certain interest and charm to his features. He wore a red polo shirt, casual trousers and . . . terrible shoes. They were green slip-ons and looked quite out of character with his otherwise 'cool' appearance. I smiled to myself. He looked good. Shame he was the photographer. I had little time for photographers; I'd heard too many stories. I checked myself quickly. What on earth was I thinking about? I had resolved to stay away from men for a good long time; now here I was taking in every detail of the guy in front of me.

I turned my attention to Alan. He was friendly and very easy to talk to. It would be a good day. We shared a few glasses of Guinness then headed out to take some photographs around the area. Our first stop was Bloody Foreland, one of my favourite places in the world. As a child Gog would tell us the story of the two giants who fought each other with rocks and boulders in days gone by. 'That's why there's so many huge rocks around, Máire,' he would tell me, 'and you see the way the rocks have all those red streaks, well that's where the giants' blood ran into the rocks.' It seemed that Gog had a story for every area around our home. All through my teenage years I enjoyed wandering in this remote stretch of cliffs, finding refuge at Bloody Foreland, watching the waves dash against the rocks and feeling the spray on my face as a torrent of weed and foam fights its way through the rock pools and carvings of previous seas. Standing in this fury of nature, looking out across a torrid black sea, one feels alive in the power and magnificence of creation – and yet, sometimes, as small as one of the tiny pebbles on the turbulent shore.

Even on the warmest and calmest of August days the waves can be quite wild and Tim had come from London, completely unprepared for north-west Ireland's winds. A down of hair stood up on his arms and eventually he confessed to struggling with the cold and borrowed a sweater from Alan. I smiled to myself again as I watched him set up his camera. The sweater was a little small for him and the sleeves rode up his arms.

Later on Tim wanted to do some portrait shots so we all went back to the hotel. While Alan relaxed in the bar with the boys, Tim, myself and the make-up woman set ourselves up in a room to take the close-up shots. I sat on the bed while Tim moved some of the furniture around to get the lights in and Mairéad touched up my make-up. By this time I was talking twenty to the dozen. I've never been comfortable having my photograph taken in this way. It always feels so uneasy – all make-up and styling. I was conscious of my long painted nails, still manicured from my time in LA. They looked good, but it wasn't me at all. My hair was permed, with fair streaks and I knew that I looked somewhat out of place in this, my true home environment. We kept the conversation going all the time he was taking pictures. Aware of the excess moisture on my palms and a nervous giddiness that had come over me, I subjected the poor guy to a kind of inquisition. I genuinely wanted to know about him, but more than that, my barrage of questions deflected the attention from myself. Tim, it seemed to me, remained calm and collected. He had a gentle manner and put me at ease as much as possible. He recognised my dislike of strongly posed pictures and got me to smile naturally by making me laugh just as he took a shot.

The session over, we went back downstairs to join the others. Ciarán and I went to a quiet seat in the corner to do the interview with Alan and I found myself constantly looking over to the bar where I could see Tim and Mairéad laughing and chatting together. I couldn't help wondering what they were talking about. One time he looked over and caught my eye. I turned away quickly and concentrated on the interview.

Before dinner we all gathered together and relaxed over drinks at the bar. The chat was light-hearted and, for some reason, we got talking about horoscopes and star signs. It was no big deal to me, but I commented that I often read my stars and it always seemed that there was something in it.

'You shouldn't be taken in by such a load of rubbish,' piped up Tim. For I moment I was a little taken aback. It was such an assertive comment.

174

'No it isn't,' I said back, 'it makes a lot of sense to me.'

'No, no,' he interrupted, 'you just think it makes sense . . .'

I interrupted back, indignant at his contradiction, asserting that nearly every member of my family was a different star sign and that I could quite easily recognise the personalities according to the horoscope's predictions. Meanwhile Tim sat with his arms folded, gently shaking his head in an unrelenting attitude as I tried to debate the point by going through the personality traits of some of my brothers and sisters. Suddenly something that had been only a mild point of interest for me had become something I was debating and defending vehemently. I was determined to make Tim understand what I meant, but he wasn't having any of it. I was fascinated that he would argue with me, and more than intrigued.

When it was time to go into the dining room I led the way and chose a seat beside the guy from the record company at the end of the table. Gradually everyone filtered through, with drinks still in hand, and took their places. Tim, I noticed, chatting to one of my uncles, meandered in at a point when there were just two seats left. One was at the other end of the table next to Mairéad and the other was right opposite me.

'May I sit here?' he asked, flashing his smile.

'Why not,' I said, trying to be cool, 'so long as you don't argue with me,' I teased.

Secretly I chastised myself. Why did I even think or care about where he would sit? But I did.

Throughout the meal I found myself strangely drawn to this man opposite me and kept deliberately talking to Alan who sat to my left, just to keep my attention intact. I played around with the prawns on my plate and was disarmingly aware of Tim as he tucked into his lobster.

After dinner we adjourned to Daddy's bar. This would be another piece in the jigsaw for Alan's story. Daddy was in fine form and had the whole place singing along. He got us up to do a short turn and from the stage I smiled to see Alan looking very relaxed and happy joining in with the locals. My eyes scanned the room. Tim was at the bar chatting again with Mairéad. As the evening wore on, everyone was having a great time and we decided to go to a local disco where we proceeded to dance the night away. The place was full of old friends and members of our family and it was great to catch up with everyone.

As the place was closing we were ushered into the back bar for late drinks and more conversation. By this time it was around two o'clock in the morning but spirits were high and no one was in the mood to go home. The little room was hot and crushed with people and I felt slightly dizzy with the drink and pleasure of the day. Again, while talking with the chap from the record company, I found myself picking Tim out in the crowd. He was sitting to the side with my sister Olive and at one time I noticed his hand rest on her knee. Without even thinking too much I extracted myself from the conversation and was over there like a shot. They were talking about cooking. Seemingly this was a big interest of Tim's and, Olive being a chef, they were deeply entrenched in the dilemma of making perfect rice or something.

Eventually I found myself in the middle of the room standing opposite this guy who had unwittingly courted my attention all day. We chatted for ages, oblivious to anyone else in the crowded room and I felt happy and giddy in his company. In what seemed like no time at all we realised that the little bar was beginning to empty. Tim looked at his watch. 'It's almost five o'clock,' he commented.

'Well, it's been a great day,' I said, and without thinking I stood up on my tiptoes and gave him a peck on the cheek. Our eyes met for a short moment, then I hurriedly turned away, looking for Leon or Olive. I was shocked at the tingle that ran through my body. What was going on here? I had a feeling that was beginning to bother me.

As dawn was breaking, my brother Leon drove our two guests back to their hotel, me in the front passenger seat and Alan and Tim in the back. It had been a good day and there had been much hugging goodbye, as the rest of the family took their separate ways home. But when it came finally to dropping off the two men, for some reason I didn't even get out of the car. That was strange for me. I'm quite a 'huggy' type of person, but something held me back and I left Alan and Tim to shake hands with me through the car window. I hardly dared to look Tim in the eye, but smiled openly at Alan and thanked him for the day. Then before I knew it, Tim had climbed back into the car and reached over to the front seat to kiss me goodbye. It was brief and friendly, but caught me off guard. 'Goodbye then,' he said, and before I could compose myself they were gone.

As Leon drove us away, my mind was in a daze.

'Nice guys. I think they had a good time,' said Leon.

'Yeah, we did,' I said.

Something strange had stirred within me and it panicked me a little. Never mind, put it behind me. It had been a good day, but it was just another interview. Another week would bring another journalist with another photographer. We'd probably never even see Alan and Tim again. Little did I know that Alan would later become a good friend and Tim, well, that's where someone had other plans . . .

A week later a letter arrived on my doorstep with a London postmark. I felt colour rise in my cheeks as I realised who it was from. It was two pages on crisp white paper with beautifully formed characters in strong black ink. It bore the signature 'Tim Jarvis' and I smiled to myself as I pored over its carefully chosen words. He excused himself for writing to me, and confessed that he'd taken my address in Dublin from Alan who had acquired it in order to send me an album we had been talking about. The letter soon got to the point. It told me how much Tim had enjoyed that day in Donegal and how he didn't particularly expect to see me again, but he had nothing to lose by telling me he thought I was the 'grandest lady in all of Ireland', and if I was ever in London and had an inclination to meet him, he would be delighted.

I gasped and couldn't help the broad smile that broke across my face. I read it again and then again as I sat at the kitchen table drinking my tea. Deirdre came in and wondered what I was smiling about. I showed her the letter. She squealed.

'What do you think, is this guy having me on?' I asked her.

'It's beautiful, how romantic! It's strange you haven't even mentioned him to me. What was he like? What went on? Did you like him?'

'Well, yes, but you know me, I can't get into something like that again. I've promised, no more men.'

'He sounds so lovely, and a gentleman.'

That was it – in Donegal Tim had been a real gentleman. He was unlike most men I knew. He had made me feel so special

and I was charmed by his letter. All day I couldn't get his words
out of my mind. Maybe I would meet him. I was due to go to
London the next week for more interviews and a meeting with
the record company. The next day I scribbled a note to Tim,
informing him of my visit and promising that I would ring him in
the next few days. I hesitated a little before dropping the letter in
the mailbox but reasoned to myself that I was doing the right
thing. At least I was giving him plenty of warning and he could
have an excuse prepared if he had changed his mind!

Picking up the telephone a few days later I felt like a teenager,
trying to rehearse what I would say when he answered. Tim
confessed to me afterwards that he had been in his photographic
dark room when the phone rang and, when he realised it was me,
he opened the door without thinking and ruined the pictures he
was developing.

I told him I was to be in London for only two nights. On the
Wednesday night I had to meet people from the record company
for dinner, but wondered if he might like to see me on Tuesday
when I had a free evening. There was a short silence on the end
of the phone.

'I'm really sorry, Máire, I'd love to, but I can't see you on
Tuesday night.' I was quite taken aback and even a little angry.
What was so important that he couldn't change his plans and
come and meet me? He'd approached me after all. Maybe I'd
got him all wrong. It might have helped if he had told me why he
couldn't meet me that night, but instead it was as though he was
harbouring some kind of secret. Perhaps he had a date with
someone else. I tried to swallow my indignation.

'Oh well, maybe some other time,' I said coolly. It would have
been like me to put the phone down, but somewhere between
irritation, embarrassment and intrigue, I longed for him to change
his mind. We carried on a short conversation and I went to my
room that night looking forward to meeting him for a short time
before my dinner appointment on Wednesday. I sat at my dressing
table staring into the mirror and running over the conversation
in my head. My face revealed an excited glow, but also a puzzled
frown. If Tim thought I was the 'grandest lady in all of Ireland',
what was greater in London that was to consume his Tuesday
evening?

On the Wednesday afternoon Tim and I sat in the bar of my hotel, looking out over Russell Square. I only had an hour before I had to meet the record company and it soon sped by. There had been a nervousness in our meeting, yet at the same time I felt instantly comfortable in Tim's presence and our conversation had evolved with the same ease as in Donegal. I longed to be able to stay and while away the evening in his company, but before I knew it my manager had come over to find out why I wasn't ready to go to dinner. It was an awkward moment. We were out of time and there was so much left to talk about. I thought I recognised the same sentiment mirrored in Tim's eyes and plucked up the courage to ask him to wait for me while I went up to get ready for dinner.

Back in my room I grabbed my handbag and jacket and put the comb through my hair, all the time wondering if I dare ask Tim to meet me after dinner. It would be late by the time I could get away, but something told me I could not go back to Ireland without seeing him again. Dare I be so forward enough to ask him? Back downstairs Tim lingered in the bar.

'So . . . it was lovely to see you again,' I offered.

'Yes. What time do you think you'll be finished tonight. I guess you'll be late, will you?'

I half smiled. Could it be that Tim was thinking the same as me? 'Well, yes, quite late but . . . are you doing anything tonight?' We both skirted around the issue with half questions, but it was clear that we both wanted to see each other again. I went off with my manager, promising to ring Tim when I was about to leave the restaurant.

Dinner that night might have been the usual light-hearted fun that I enjoyed with the record company, but my mind was neither on the food nor the conversation. My stomach was knotted with nerves and excitement at the thought of seeing Tim again later. I couldn't help frequently glancing at the clock, but there was a lot to talk about with the record executives and it was late when I finally extracted myself from the crowd and made my way to the bar where we'd arranged to meet. Tim was already there. His long frame stretched over a bar stool in relaxed poise, but his eyes were fixed on the door and when I entered he leapt to his feet a little too quickly, betraying his nerves and nearly knocking

over his pint. We greeted each other with a polite kiss and he
bought me a vodka and tonic. I drank deeply to help calm my
nerves and was aware of Tim's gentle gaze. I talked frantically
about the day, the interviews, the record company, the tour, my
brothers and sisters, in fact, anything that came into my head.
But as Tim listened and smiled I began to relax again in his
company and calm my gibbering. Our time together was short.
It was late and the landlord wanted to go home. Tim walked me
back to my hotel. There seemed to be an electricity between us,
but we parted company with a nervous embrace and Tim walked
off into the night.

Over the next few days I couldn't get Tim out of my mind and
I was thrilled when, within a week, another letter arrived,
thanking me for meeting him and asking if we could perhaps get
together again the next time I was in London.

We met up several times in the next few months and soon
realised that on our first meeting in Donegal we had both taken
in almost every detail of the other. In the same way as I had
watched him, Tim had noted my every move: what I ate, what I
said, who I spoke to, who I danced with. Something special was
developing between us. But I was cautious. I was starting every
day with a prayer from my grandmother's prayer book. It was
becoming an important ritual to me, almost as if I expected the
day not to go well if I did not say my prayer. That might sound
obsessive and dangerous, but it was helping to build my life
again. I was getting stronger day by day. My confidence was
increasing and I was beginning to take pride in myself again. I
needed something to lean on and the religious rituals of my
childhood gave me that.

Religion was a large topic of discussion for Tim and me and
the more I spoke of my Catholic faith, the more I recognised just
how real and important it was in my life. I had not attended
confession or regular mass in years, yet I was able to look back
on times when I had prayed in desperation and somehow I had
got through. Tim encouraged this kind of conversation. Through
it we realised our differences. I was an Irish Catholic, raised in
rural Donegal with little knowledge, or indeed respect, for
Protestant religion. Tim was a middle-class Protestant from
Cambridge whose father had been a missionary in India. He had

Arriving at Los Angeles airport on our first American tour, 1979. From left to right: me, Pádraig, Nicky Ryan, Pól, Ciarán, John McFadden and Leon.

The 'Harry's Game' homecoming party at Leo's Tavern (Daddy's bar), 1982.

Performing at the Self Aid concert in Dublin, 1986, with Bono,
Bob Geldof and Chris de Burgh.

With Bono during the filming for the 'In a Lifetime' video, 1986.

Me on the day I met Tim Jarvis in 1987.  He took this photo.

Clannad celebrating the 21<sup>st</sup> birthday of Leo's Tavern, 1989.  From left to right:
Pól, Noel, me, Daddy, Ciarán and Pádraig.

Sisters are doing it for themselves: singing in
Leo's Tavern with Deirdre, Olive, Eithne and Brídín.

Clannad at the Royal Albert Hall, London.

With Paul Young during the
recording of 'Both Sides Now', 1991.

Tim and me on that wonderful day
of 12 January 1991.

Working with Deirdre, Olive and Brídín on vocal arrangements
for *Máire*, my first solo album.

Tim took this lovely photo of Aisling and me. It ended up as the cover shot for my *Máire* album – minus the nappy!

The day of Paul's dedication at St Mark's Church, November 1993.

A family gathering, Christmas 1995.

Olive heading off to Australia: Daddy, Andrew (Olive's husband), Mammy, Olive, Aisling, Paul, Tim and Bríd, with me and Brídín in front.

Singing in Leo's Tavern with Ciarán and Noel.

Our party piece at my brother Leon's wedding, 24 March 2000.

The Jarvis family.

been raised by a conscientious, fervently Evangelical mother and had grown up with an intense familiarity of church life – Sunday school, church choir and Bible classes – but had arrived at adulthood neither rejecting nor fully embracing a 'living faith'. Seeing his two sisters, Anne and Joy, follow in their father's footsteps on the mission field (in South America and with the London City Mission, respectively), with such strong motivation through their faith, made Tim aware of how little his own spiritual life and commitment had developed in comparison.

We realised that, though there were large cultural divides between us, there were also many parallels. I told him about the way I had found myself turning again to my prayer book and about a new longing I had to explore the way I seemed to be coping better with my life, as if my prayers were being answered. Similarly he spoke to me of a new fellowship he had joined in London and of a new discovery of faith. He'd even recently been baptised, and I was intrigued at the way Tim spoke of a God who was real to him, whom he spoke to on a regular basis through prayer, not from a book, but through a conversation as one might talk to a close friend. Maybe this wasn't so new to me. It reminded me of my own experience as a student in Dublin when I used to sit at the back of the church looking for comfort. To hear Tim speak of God with such intimacy was strange, almost weird. Tim was clearly nervous as he tried to explain to me what it meant to him to be a committed Christian, but he also spoke with a certain assurance and I was intrigued by his passion and commitment to his faith.

It was during such a conversation that Tim revealed that the reason he had been unable to meet me on that first Tuesday night in London was because of a weekly church house-group he attended. He spoke quietly, sheepishly and apologetically, confessing that he thought it might put me off meeting him if he told me the real reason. At first I was a little taken aback. Yes, it sounded strange, almost cult-like to me, but somehow I found his commitment and loyalty to his church endearing. Our conversations about faith would go on for hours as we learnt from each other's experience and ideas. In many ways it seemed as though Tim had God 'all worked out' and at times I found him rather dogmatic about the whole thing. But he was also ready to confess his worries. He found himself struggling to fully combine his faith into his lifestyle. Working for the *NME* didn't always sit right with the path he believed he should be walking as – what he intriguingly called – a 'born-again Christian' (a phrase that nearly turned me off), and I know his struggles with certain aspects of his lifestyle were a recurring burden.

We spoke often on the telephone and my trips to England to promote the *Sirius* album took on a new light for me. It would mean Tim and I could snatch some time together. We talked on the phone and became friends, but when we were together the passion would ignite and we soon became lovers. It was wonderful, but all too soon he was taking me to the airport bound for Dublin. We kept the relationship secret from most people at first. My brother Leon was the first to know about it. He would often accompany me on my trips to England to promote the band and he respected what Tim and I were finding together. Part of me wanted to shout Tim's name from the rooftops, but much of me was still cautious at the way he made me feel. I could not handle another failed relationship. I wasn't even prepared to acknowledge it as a relationship and announce to my family that I'd been seeing this wonderful man. I couldn't bear the thought of their sympathy as once again they watched it crumble. Each time I left him or put the phone down after a conversation, my heart would ache, but still I kept telling myself this would only be an affair. Yes, it was dangerous, but still, we were having fun and I felt more alive than I had been in years. Where was the harm in that?

Tim, it seemed, was also having similar misgivings. He was a nice guy. He could be a lot of fun, but he was serious in nature. He had not had many serious girlfriends and I knew that, while he was enjoying the thrill of our relationship, he wondered where we were going. Having this kind of affair did not sit well with him. Neither of us were teenagers and I don't imagine I was the kind of girl with the kind of circumstances he imagined himself settling down with. How had he managed to find himself sleeping with a separated – yet still married (divorce wasn't available in Ireland) – woman, living a musician's lifestyle, with a trail of disaster in tow and meetings snatched between publicity jaunts?

It was difficult, with so many miles between us, but the more we got to know each other, the more our relationship developed. Together, we were distracted with passion, but the telephone's separation helped us share more of ourselves. By Christmas I had revealed much about my life. I was ashamed of many things and I wanted to be gentle with Tim. If our relationship was to develop beyond an affair I wanted him to understand all that I had been through. I was drawn to explore more of the faith that meant so much to him and the deepening spirituality I was beginning to experience in my own life. He came over to stay with me in Dublin a couple of times and we went together to the local Catholic church. When I announced on the phone to Tim, however, that the next time I was over in London I wanted to go to his church I think he was quite horrified. His church, St Mark's, Kennington, had been in the vanguard of Anglican charismatic renewal in the 1970s and 1980s, developing a style of worship far removed from the traditional Church of England service, and certainly a million miles from the ritual-based mass of my experience. He tried to make an excuse for us not to go, but I was intrigued and determined. This was a part of his life that was alien to me and I wanted to understand more of it. I think he thought it might scare me or emphasise the difference between us and he tried to warn me what it might be like. I wondered why he was making such a fuss. It was just one hour out of one day – or so I thought. What could be so surprising?

But in a way he was right. Even his warnings had not prepared me for what I discovered the Sunday morning Tim walked me into his church. I was amazed at how casual it seemed. Everyone was really friendly, laughing, chatting, hugging each other, and the Vicar, Nicolas Carnac, had a hard time getting everyone's attention to start the service. When the music started I didn't know what was going to happen. There was a proper band playing and in minutes people were singing, dancing and throwing their arms in the air. Some were speaking out prayers and praises to the Lord, and young children ran up and down the aisle while others were fed by their mothers. It was all very noisy and free-form. Tim stood beside me, straight and cold, his eyes fixed on the words on the overhead projector screen. I felt for him. He must have suffered at the thought of what was running through my head. It was very weird, but I didn't feel too worried, just so long as they didn't expect me to behave like that. I followed the words and, in parts, joined in with the songs. They were very simple songs that for some reason the band repeated over and over again. The more they repeated, the more the people responded in worship. While the music was upbeat they danced and clapped, then the worship leader brought the music down. There followed about twenty minutes of gentle songs that seemed to stir people's emotions even more. I looked around. Some were crying, others just stood with their eyes closed and their hands held up towards the ceiling. Over to my right I watched one of these women start to shake, then before my eyes she collapsed backwards and lay on the floor. It made me jump and I was amazed that the people around just left her lying there. Another woman respectfully pulled her skirt back down below her knees and then carried on with her own impassioned gazing at something I couldn't see. There was also a strange muttering coming from some people, like a different language. I didn't understand it. I wondered if this was how Tim normally behaved and felt sorry if he was intimidated by my being there. I wanted to reassure him, to tell him not to worry. It was very strange to me, quite mad in fact, but I was interested in what was going on and what was being said, especially when the Vicar gave his message. He spoke with power and passion about the love of God, how Jesus died to take on our burdens, to wipe away our sins, to be our personal saviour. It was a new language for me, but I found myself quite gripped by what he was saying.

I came out of the church with many questions that kept the debates and explorations between Tim and me alight. I had never heard people talk about Jesus in such a close and loving way and as Christmas approached I was beginning to look at the nativity story, that I knew so well, in a new light. Tim had spent some time in France and had a friend there who was a very fine icon-maker. For Christmas he gave me one of his friend's pieces. It was a beautiful bronze and enamel image of Jesus. I don't think he intended it as any kind of heavy message, it was just a lovely piece of art, but it meant a lot to me. I suppose I was seeking a deeper meaning to my life and through the faith of my childhood and my meeting Tim I was beginning to find it.

During Christmas that year my family witnessed a smile on

my face and lightness in my spirit that they had not seen for years. There were still many clouds overshadowing me, but as I lived each day I found myself looking ahead with anticipation and hope, perhaps for the first time in my adult life.

# Chapter 18

At the end of February 1988 Clannad embarked on an extensive European tour with the *Sirius* album. It was a big show. The album was of much heavier rock influence and we needed a full band – saxophone, keyboards, drums, electric guitar – with an elaborate sound and light show. It was good to be back in places throughout Germany and Italy where we had not toured for a couple of years, but the response was quite mixed. Year after year they had welcomed Clannad as a five-piece band, and although we'd always used drums and keyboards on our albums, the new fuller band on stage proved a disappointment for some. Were we going off the tracks just a little bit too far? These uncertainties caused a few tensions among us. *Sirius* was heavily produced and, though it had been a valuable experience, we realised that it had pandered to an American radio format that was further removed from the original folk roots of the 'Clannad sound'. Still, it was something new for us and we all enjoyed the feel of a bigger band on stage.

I looked forward to the English leg of the tour when I knew I could meet with Tim. We'd kept in constant touch on the telephone and I was eager to see him again, even though one of our phone calls had deeply disturbed me. We had become embroiled in the kind of conversation that lovers enjoy through the distance of the phone. I was missing him badly and, by then, was secure enough in the relationship to imagine he felt the same way. 'You mean more to me than anyone else in the world,' I told him. 'I want to know that I am number one in your life,' I said softly and tenderly. There was silence at the end of the line.

'Tim?'

'Máire, you know how much I care about you,' came his retort after an awkward pause. I felt my body and mind spasm in shock. There was a 'but' coming next and the fearful anticipation of what Tim was about to say cut me to the core. I waited. I could sense Tim drawing a deep breath.

'Máire, you need to understand that you mean the world to me.'

I said nothing and waited for the final blow.

'But God comes first.'

I didn't know whether to laugh or cry. It wasn't the blow I had feared, but what did he mean? I knew Tim was serious about his faith, but how could he put it above our relationship?

We ended the conversation declaring our love for one another, but I was still troubled. Tim's words occupied my mind, spinning around in confused turmoil to the point where I stayed in my room all night, missing dinner with the boys. I needed time to think, to ponder, to control the anger and jealousy that were beginning to well within me. I was angry at Tim's words and jealous of God for the place he held in my lover's heart. I had a lot to try to understand.

Within a few days I had managed to put the troublesome conversation behind me and was desperate to see Tim again when our schedule allowed. We had a day off when the tour rested in Bournemouth so Tim and I made the most of it. It was a wonderful time. We wandered around the gardens and walked along the beach. The seashore was still wild with winter and we snuggled into each other as we chatted and caught up on the close companionship we'd missed. In the evening we went to a lovely restaurant and just as I was tucking into a plate of mussels, Tim dropped a bombshell.

'I've told my mother,' he said. I stopped, mid mouthful.

'Told her what?'

'About us.'

'Well, what did you tell her?' A knot tightened in my stomach.

'Everything.'

'What's everything?' I said, slightly panicked.

'Well, she had an idea I'd met someone and the other day it was her birthday so we had all the family together. When I had a moment alone with her I just told her about us.'

By this time I had put my fork down, pushed the mussels aside and was perched anxiously on the end of my seat.

'Did you tell her I am Irish?'

'Yes.'

'Did you tell her I was brought up as a Catholic?'

'Yes.'

'Did you tell her I am in the music business?'

'Yes.' Tim was looking at me almost in amusement while my mind was racing.

'Did you tell her I was married?'

'Yes.'

The conversation went on in this vein with me listing out many of my insecurities about the relationship as Tim just smiled and reached for my hand across the table.

'Máire, she is thrilled for me,' he said, 'and, of course, she wants to meet you.'

That was it. The mussels nearly came up. Meet Tim's mum? No way. Tim was her only son. They were different to me. Different class, different culture, different everything. She'd hate me, I was sure. How could she watch a married Irish Catholic woman take her precious son from his nice middle-class lifestyle and get him mixed up in the notorious undercurrents of the music industry?

Tim found my reaction very amusing. 'Don't worry,' he tried to reassure me. 'I love you and she will love you.' So that was that. I had little choice. Our relationship was real. It was official, and I was terrified.

When the fateful day arrived I busied myself around Tim's flat all morning. It was a council flat, that he shared with his good friend Len, but they had made it quite homely with lots of Tim's own photographic work around the walls. I was ridiculously on edge and kept making cups of tea in a bid to deny my craving for a vodka. Tim had been given a model car kit and to occupy my mind I started putting it together, yielding myself to the intricacies of the instructions that seemed to be losing something in the Japanese-to-English transcription. By late afternoon Tim announced it was time to make a move up to Cambridge.

'Oh Tim, I don't think we should go now,' I said. He wasn't

interested in my protests. 'Máire, you'll be fine. Mum's expecting us, come on.'

'But what about the model? I should finish painting it first.' It was a feeble excuse and I could do nothing but let Tim bundle me into the car.

The journey was horrible. I felt sick with nerves. There I was, a 36-year-old woman, absolutely terrified of meeting Tim's mother and sister. His father had died in India when Tim was only a year old and his mother was pregnant with his younger sister Joy. It was 1956 and, in deep distress, Mrs Jarvis took Tim and his older sister Anne back to her home town in Wales. Later she moved to Cambridge and, when Tim was twelve years old, she met and married Dr Ivan Sharman, whom the family knew as Docco. Though Tim seemed to live in the shadow of his dead father, they were obviously a close family and Tim's apparent respect and admiration for his mother's strength only intimidated me at that time. His younger sister Joy was married with two young boys. I'd already met her in London. She was very warm and pleasant and the presence of the children detracted any intensity from our introduction. In no time I felt as though I'd known Joy for years and we could become close friends. It was the eldest sibling, Anne, whom I most feared. She was about the same age as me and Tim spoke of her with great respect and admiration. Anne had obviously inherited her mother's strength and father's religious commitment, making her home for a time on the mission field in Peru. Everything I knew about the family painted a picture of middle-class perfection that tortured my mind. How disappointed they would be in me.

'Are we in Cambridge yet?' I asked Tim.

'Yeah.'

'Tell me when we get near your street won't you?' A few moments passed. Tim was quiet and smiling. 'You will tell me, won't you?' I insisted. 'And tell me when we get near to your house.'

All of a sudden Tim swung into a driveway off a leafy suburban avenue and we were facing the front door. I tried to compose myself. At least it was late in the evening. I could meet his mum and Docco, exchange pleasantries and then hopefully go to bed, ready to face meeting Anne in the morning.

His mum greeted us both with a hug. I instantly recognised Tim's warm smile on her lovely face. That helped. She was softly spoken and fussed around trying to make us feel welcome. Docco met me with a firm handshake. He had laughing eyes and the same kind of warmth that seemed to permeate the house. I was trying to be polite and, more than ever, became aware of my deep accent. Docco was intrigued to know about my career, but this comfortable sitting-room, full of china and photographs of family, seemed far removed from the music business and in a way I tried to make light of it. I was still terribly tense, and Tim's mum frequently asking if I was all right only added to my nerves. She kept refilling my tea cup and insisting that we had to have something to eat. I caught Tim's amused glow as he tried to keep me from a firing-line flow of questions. Just then there was the sound of a banging door coming from the area of the kitchen.

'Hello everyone,' a voice sang out.

'Oh lovely, here comes Anne,' exclaimed Tim's mum. I froze. What I hadn't realised was that Anne lived in the house just behind her mother and she had been keenly awaiting our arrival. It was almost too much. I clung tight to the little china tea cup to stop it rattling on the saucer. I wasn't ready for this. Anne burst in with that same Jarvis smile. I needn't have worried. She was lovely, not as I had imagined, and we got on instantly. She was interested in genealogy and had traced the family tree back to Ireland, so she was fascinated by the things I was able to tell her about my homeland. Anne had many great stories herself and as we talked I found myself easily laughing and feeling a little more comfortable in the family environment. I kept glancing over to Tim and saw a certain pride and pleasure in his expression.

That night I lay in a strange bed in this strange house. Tim's family were lovely and I had been more than welcomed. But could I ever fit in here? It was so far removed from what I knew and they were still to find out about me. How would they feel when we got beyond the pleasantries. Tim was the apple of his mother's eye. She doted on him. How could I be the kind of girl she would want as a daughter-in-law? Tears pricked in my eyes. How could I even afford myself such thoughts? I was a married woman. I had no right to be thinking these things. I wondered if Tim was lying awake in the room next door. What did he want?

Did he really imagine we could have a future together? In the dark loneliness of night the demons are all too ready to run wild. The house was still and quiet but my mind raced and the events of my past haunted shallow-sleep dreams.

I awoke early and took some moments to take in my surroundings. Sunlight streamed in through the red velvet curtains and its rays danced around the room resting on the little vase of freshly picked flowers that Tim's mum had thoughtfully placed on the dressing table. What would the day bring? I was anxious for the security of Tim's presence. Should I get up? What if Tim was still asleep? I would be left to make conversation with his mum and Docco until he could rescue me. They might find out too much about me. Thankfully it wasn't too long before I heard Tim's voice.

Later that afternoon we had tea in the garden. It was immaculately kept. Pretty flower beds and shrubbery, all colour co-ordinated, bordered a grand lawn and we sat in comfortable sun chairs, drinking our tea from fine china cups and saucers. Tim's mum was in good spirits and she continued to fuss around us both, filling us with sandwiches and delicate cakes. As she busied herself she sang 'in Dublin's fair city, where the girls are so pretty . . .'. It made us smile. She was trying hard to appease my nerves and show me her approval. I still found it difficult. Little did I realise that in the years to come I would grow very close to Margaret Sharman, and Anne and Joy would become like sisters to me.

My own family were thrilled to meet Tim. I'm sure they must have feared that it was just another affair, one of my whims, but as time went by they could see a change coming over me. They could see how happy I was when Tim was around and how much more settled I was with life in general. Mammy must have begun to thank God for answering her prayers. Yet still I had the ability to hurt her deeply. Tim and I continued to explore our faith together and I will always remember one horrible time when I tortured my mother with my tongue. I started criticising the religion she held so dear. I blamed her for the fact that I didn't have a Bible and that all my life I'd been raised to understand that God had no time for me, that I had to pray for his mercy through the saints or the Blessed Virgin. I riled at her that there was no joy in Catholicism, that we were burdened by the whims of the priests and bound in chains of guilt. I will never forget her face as I ranted and raved. A temper came over me, and though I knew I was crippling her inside, I could not stop. I just went on about how I was finding a new way, the 'right way', and maybe if I had known it from the start my life wouldn't have turned out as badly.

Mammy stood and took it all. She held onto the kitchen table and her lip quivered with pent-up emotion as my anger flowed. In the end she could take no more and walked out of the room. I sat at the kitchen table and cried. How could I be so arrogant and so cruel to my mother who had stood by me through everything. She'd never passed judgement and spent years praying for my life. I had been so caught up in my new fundamentalist view of Christianity that, before her eyes, I had rebuked all her prayers, and those of my precious grandparents who had held us all daily before God, seeking his protection on our lives. It must have been like twisting a knife in her heart.

I doubt my mother has forgotten that episode. But through God's grace that so evidently flows through her, I am forever thankful that she could bring herself, yet again, to forgive me.

I had a lot to learn. I realise now that it was the faith of my childhood that probably saved me. At the time of the miscarriage I hit rock bottom. I didn't feel that I could go any lower and I knew that it was going to take some kind of supernatural strength to put my life back together. Thankfully, because of my upbringing, I knew where to look. I had no doubt in the existence of God, but what I had to grasp hold of was the fact that he heard my prayers and cared enough to pull me through. It didn't matter how I prayed or whether my prayers were directed through someone else, the fact is, I knew that handing myself over to his mercy was my only hope. When you get that desperate the rules and trappings of any kind of religion disappear. There was no dramatic experience or great spiritual awakening, but I was beginning to understand that the God who had watched over me since my birth was carrying me now. My family had stood by me, even when I had barely communicated with them, and somehow I had been given this wonderful man whom I was beginning to trust and love deeply. Despite our differences, he seemed to be loving me back and helping me open my eyes to a whole new hope.

But it wasn't just spirituality that was being revealed. I had a lot to learn about myself, to confront things that I didn't like, or didn't think I could change. Tim and I wrote letters to each other. He was a wonderful writer and we found ourselves able to express many things on paper that we might not have spoken of to each other's face. Many of Tim's letters were wonderfully poetic and romantic, but some of them made me face a harsh reality. Although I was generally drinking less, I could still be terribly indulgent. I was still smoking the odd joint and taking an occasional line of coke, and I know it worried Tim. At first he hadn't tried to stop me, but he never joined in himself. I could see the disappointment in his face. Sometimes when I went over to England I would have a drink at the airport, then a couple of vodkas on the plane and by the time Tim picked me up I might be well on the way to being half-cut. More than anything, I suppose it hurt him and he didn't understand why I had to behave like that. It also didn't help my temper. Tim is not an argumentative man and sometimes I could be terribly cruel to him when I was not in full control of myself. I know he worried about what I might get up to on tour. He knew that I was committed to our relationship, but everyone can be tempted when they've had a few drinks and I didn't exactly have a good track record when it came to men. Sometimes he would pour out his feelings about my behaviour in a letter, many of which he did not post. He'd tell me about them and of course when I next saw him I'd insist on seeing them. Some of them were devastating. I guess he feared what I might do if I received such damning words through the mail. At least if I read them in his presence he could see my reaction and pick up the pieces. I would read the letters with trembling hands. They always spoke of his love for me, but went on to tell me how hard he found some of my behaviour. I would be angry. But beyond that I recognised a truth. Was this how he really saw me? Is this how I appeared to other people? It wasn't like sitting and having a conversation with someone where you can argue back. I had to sit quietly and read, letting the words penetrate my being. They made me face myself for the first time in my life. I began to see that I had spent years living from moment to moment with no sense of control on my life or regard for the future. Things happened to me. I was always a victim of circumstance. I rarely made a decision or followed anything through and I had little sense of direction.

It was hard to swallow. I knew that there were many contradictions in the way I was living. I wanted to lead a better life and enjoy a good and honest relationship with Tim. But I was still letting my bad habits get the better of me. They hadn't seemed so wrong before. Drinking heavily, smoking dope and taking the odd line was just part of my lifestyle. It came with the music industry and the people that surrounded us. But it wasn't Tim's way and it certainly wasn't God's way. I knew I had to decide what was most important in my life.

Somewhere in the middle of all this was Clannad. Our success was beyond anything we could have hoped for. But it wasn't necessarily bringing happiness. The boys were also drinking more heavily and musical tensions were becoming increasingly apparent. Still, we were achieving broader professional acclaim and we were thrilled to be approached to do a soundtrack for a BBC documentary about the Atlantic Ocean. Both Ciarán and Pól took on the writing, but it seemed to become Pól's project and through it he met Peter Gabriel in whose studio he produced the piece that became 'Atlantic Realm'. It was mainly instrumental so I had little involvement. That was OK. I was still doing the odd publicity date with *Sirius* and trying to snatch as much time with Tim as possible.

As autumn approached, the record company suggested we should do a compilation album of favourite tracks, plus a couple of new songs. Ciarán and Pól got together on the writing and we headed back to Rockfield studio in Wales to start work. It came together well but we only had limited time there and decided to complete the project – *Past Present* – at Peter Gabriel's studio just outside Bath in England. This was great for Tim and me because it was nearer London and meant we could see more of one another. It also was a wonderful studio to work in. Peter was just back from his own tour and often joined us for dinner with his two daughters. Meanwhile, Eithne had been working on her album and the single, 'Orinoco Flow', was released while we were in the studio. We were so excited for her. It was already at number eleven in the charts and we felt sure it was going to go up. We'd watched her on *Top of the Pops* the week before, so come Sunday evening we expectantly gathered in the house near the studio to listen to the Top Forty. Our youngest brother, Bartley, was working in London and he came over to be with us to hear the news. Flicking between the BBC charts and the independents we held our breath as the countdown continued. Number two in the independent chart. Brilliant. Then the BBC. Number one! We were all shouting and screaming and hugging each other and you couldn't have heard the record playing above the din in the room. First we spoke to Eithne on the phone. More squealing. She was so happy and we knew that sharing the moment with us, even over the telephone, was very special. Then we rang Leon who was over in Donegal. He'd been driving Mammy to church and they'd been frantically trying to get the station on the car radio so they could hear the result. The whole family were over the moon. That evening at dinner Peter presented us with a bottle of champagne and we all celebrated Eithne's success.

# *Chapter 19*

The *Past Present* album was something of a milestone for us. It represented a breadth of our work spanning the albums from *Magical Ring* to *Sirius*. It mirrored the developing sound and rise of Clannad and, with each song, I reflected on a season in my personal life, the deep downward spiral and the more hopeful spirit I was beginning to realise in the past year.

Still I was vulnerable. During the time of recording *Past Present* there was increasing tension between myself and Tim. We'd been together for more than a year and a half and though our love was deepening, there were some cracks beginning to show in our relationship. He knew me well and I recognised he'd taken on a lot. I think the ups and downs, and uncertainties presented by my being in the music business, were finally beginning to get to him. We were both scared. The love we shared was special and the more we explored our faith together, the more we wanted our relationship to develop on solid ground. This is where we both recognised that we were living a lie. We wanted to live as Christians, but there was the issue of our sexual relationship. We knew it didn't sit right with the spiritual walk we wanted to pursue. Though our backgrounds were different, we were both raised to respect the sanctity of sex within marriage. It was something we had both rejected in the heat of our passion, but now it seemed to have become an issue. We turned to the Bible to seek justification for our behaviour, but it didn't come. God's word was clear, and what struck us both the most was the fact that I was still married to someone else. In sleeping with Tim I was breaking my marriage vows and committing adultery. Heavy stuff. Why was this thing that was so beautiful and so natural, so wrong in God's eyes? It wasn't easy to reason, and yet something deep within me understood. I only had to look at my past to see the consequences of sex outside a steady relationship. Yes, sex is natural and children are a natural consequence. And, sure, there are many single-parent families who are doing fine, but when I look back on my own childhood I realise how precious it was to be brought up in family security and fed with love from two parents who were devoted to each other and bound by sacred vows that kept them together through the hard times and the good.

We knew we couldn't go on the way we were. It was as if we were living two separate lives. We were a couple, now going to church regularly and seeking blessing on our lives, but we were also caught up in our sexuality. Drink and drugs were still a part of my life and certainly Tim did not feel he could trust me with the way I conducted myself sometimes.

We decided to be celibate. It was a decision not taken lightly or easily and we fell along the way, but, almost immediately, something new happened. It was as if we had an assurance that we were choosing the right path. Our relationship took on a whole new dimension and our love and trust in one another seemed to deepen dramatically. More than anything, our friendship blossomed. Our time together was always short and therefore very precious and we had spent it embroiled in love-making. Now we had time to talk and 'play' together. We even spent time trying to read the Bible and it started to become a precious source of inspiration and strength. At our first Easter together Tim had offered to buy me an Easter egg. I'd asked if he would get me a Bible instead. He had been thrilled and inside wrote some words I have always cherished:

> To dear Máire,
> Never forget how much God loves you. May He always give you strength and encouragement and may you always be able to show His love in your life.
> From your dearest friend
> Tim (March 1988)

My Bible had become a treasured companion, along with my

grandmother's prayer book. I had taken it on tour with me, quietly and shyly seeking my way on my bunk in the bus while the others played cards or watched videos. My relationship with Tim was enriched beyond what we could imagine. Yes, the celibacy was a hard vow to keep, but somehow we had been given so much more. It proved to be an excellent test of the relationship. As in many new relationships, the sex was wonderful, but so often there is a danger that the partnership is built solely on physical attraction. When that wears off – as I'm sure it easily can do, especially when children come along and life in general gets busier and more pressured – you have to question what you are left with. A good relationship is built on friendship, companionship, care and trust. That was something I had taken for granted in my parents, and realised it had been sadly lacking in my previous marriage. With Tim, I was learning more of a love that is patient, kind, accepting, trusting and non-judging. It was a much higher love, and celibacy, in the greater realm, was a small sacrifice that would help us ground and prove the worth of the relationship. It was so immediately and obviously worthwhile and we blossomed through it, even though we knew not what lay ahead.

As well as earning Clannad an ardent following in America, *Sirius* also broadened our fan-base in Australia and New Zealand and so we were keen to embrace a tour of the southern hemisphere. It was an exciting prospect, even though it meant being separated from Tim. There would be quite an entourage on the road with us and Tim might have had reason to be nervous at my going. But this new level that our relationship had reached seemed to bond us in trust. I also promised I would take it easy with the drinking on the tour. 'That's something that is up to you', he had said, and I knew my vow was more of an important test for myself than a declaration of loyalty to him. I saw it as a new start, the rise of the new me.

After more than twenty-two hours on a plane we arrived in Sydney at seven o'clock in the morning. The air was warm and the morning sun felt good on my skin. As soon as we checked into our rooms I went down to the hotel reception and asked if they could tell me the whereabouts of the nearest church. I didn't care about the denomination or type of worship. All I knew was that, even after a long-haul flight, with little sleep, it was Sunday morning and it was important for me to get to church. It wasn't out of any guilt-bound duty, or even a promise to Tim. Something inside me simply longed to be in a place of fellowship. I was thankful to have been given the opportunity to travel and arrive safely. I was thankful that I was here with some of my family, that we were doing the music we loved, that we had so many good things going on with the band. I was thankful that I would go home to a man I was in love with. More than anything I was thankful to be alive.

I started to value my life and look after myself. Australia was a sunshine-infested, fresh place and I found it easy to eat well. I swam a lot and exercised. Within just a few days of being there and not drinking I could see a difference. My skin was clearer, the dark rings around my eyes were beginning to fade and I had an energy that made me want to dance and sing and throw my arms around as I walked in the fresh air. The flight had stopped over in Singapore and I had bought a portable CD player with little speakers and some classical CDs. Each morning I would start by reading my Bible and then make time to do some exercises to music before I took on the day. I wrote loads of letters and cards to Tim and telephoned him as often as possible. I wanted to reassure him that I had control of my life. I'm sure he could tell by my excited babbling down the phone that I was well, happy and, best of all, completely sober.

The Australian crowds were superb. We couldn't get over the vastness of the country. Sometimes we would travel for hours by plane to get to the next town. You get quite a kick when you realise that these people, across the other side of the world from Donegal, know your songs and appreciate your music. We made many friends and had some of our best concerts.

I loved New Zealand even more. Where Australia struck me as being very American-influenced, New Zealand seemed more British. The people were welcoming and homely and showed us the kind of hospitality that our own country is renowned for. All through the tour I made sure that I went to a church regularly. The others never took much notice. Sunday morning was usually the time to catch up on sleep and they rarely missed me.

Sometimes it would be a Catholic church, other times Protestant – whichever looked the most inviting. One of my visits took me to a large cathedral church in Christchurch. The worship was wonderful and it was a great service, but it is neither the music nor the teaching that lingers in my memory. Something happened that day. I came out of the cathedral feeling more alive than ever and I couldn't wait to speak to Tim. I stood in the telephone box lining up my coins and dialled the code for England. Within a few moments the line connected and the receiver purred in my ear. 'Come on Tim,' I said under my breath, 'pick up the phone.' It was late evening in England, but I knew Tim wouldn't have gone to bed. Click. There it was, Tim's familiar 'Hello'. He sounded distant, but the line was good and he was delighted to hear my excited voice. We exchanged the usual pleasantries, then I told him about the church.

'It was a great service,' I said.

'Oh yeah?' replied Tim, sounding pleased at my enthusiasm. 'What was the sermon about?'

I paused and realised I didn't really know. I felt slightly stupid, but there was a giddiness about me.

'Tim, don't laugh at me,' I said, 'but I think God has spoken to me.' I went on to tell him what was going on in my head. It was hard to explain. There had been no audible voice and it wasn't even anything the preacher said, but somehow I felt God was telling me that I would be used to help break through some of the barriers of prejudice in the Northern Ireland situation. I realised how vague it all sounded, yet it seemed so real and strong. At the other end of the phone Tim listened intently and was very encouraging.

'That's really something, Máire,' he said; 'you should remember this and wait to see what happens.'

Tim was right. I spent the next few days in an excited daze, wondering what might develop. But time went by. Weeks, months and even years later I still remembered what I felt so strongly at that time, but somehow it became less real. I told no one else of it. They would have probably thought I was mad. I had no imagination for what might be. How could I, a singer in a band, get involved in any kind of peace work? I didn't even fully understand the situation. Sometimes I would feel guilty about it.

What if God really had spoken to me and I had let him down by not doing anything about it? I had a lot to learn about his timing.

The New Zealand dates were drawing to a close. One of our most memorable concerts was up in Auckland where we played for the large Irish community. After the show the Ambassador for Australia and New Zealand presented us with gold discs. The people there were so friendly and welcoming and I left my disc with them. I believe it still hangs on the wall in the Auckland Irish Centre today.

From New Zealand Pól and I went off to Japan for a short promotional tour. We received an invite to the Irish Embassy there, and who should we meet when we walked through the door but the Ambassador who had hosted us in Auckland. Seemingly he had come to the end of his term there and was taking on a new post in Japan. I think it was he who arranged our invitation to the Embassy. It was a lovely occasion and Pól and I ended up doing a few songs there.

It was good to be away with Pól for a few days. Times were changing for Clannad. Towards the end of the tour in New Zealand Pól had called a meeting in his hotel room and announced that he intended leaving the band. In many ways we should have seen it coming, but it was still something of a shock. Ciarán, especially, took it badly at first and there were angry words exchanged. I suppose he felt let down. Pól and he were the main writers. It didn't have to be the end of the band, but Ciarán felt that with Pól gone, he would really have his work cut out to keep things going. Pól wanted to experiment more with different styles of music and pursue his work in production. He'd spent a lot of time with Peter Gabriel who had set up WOMAD, a company to help bring world music to greater prominence. This was something that Pól was keen to get involved in. It would mean he could broaden his musical horizons and flex his imagination. Clannad had come a long way in the last twenty years. Now *Past Present* was in the charts and 'In A Lifetime' – rereleased to coincide with this new album – was winning greater chart success than when it was first put out. We had toured a lot in the past year and Pól thought it appropriate to leave the band at a high point. Ciarán and Pól, in terms of writing and production, were a great team. They shared a lot of similar ideas and when they came together on a song it could be brilliant. But they were also quite different as individuals and the more they developed their own musical identities, the greater the artistic divide. New opportunities were arising and Clannad's path was set to continue with the boys going their separate ways.

Strangely enough, when Pól made his announcement, I wasn't unduly concerned. A year ago my temper would have flared, but I felt very calm about the situation. My own life was starting to change. My focus was on my relationship with Tim and I was on another cloud. I was also beginning to be quite philosophical about life. Instead of flying off the handle I reasoned with Ciarán and told him that Pádraig, Noel and I would try to help him with the pressure of writing. We were able to complete the *Past Present* tour in good spirit.

When we returned home we had to go straight into the studio to complete the soundtrack to an animation we had started called *The Angel and the Soldier Boy*. Ciarán took control of the project and it was the last thing Pól worked on. We completed it by Christmas and as 1990 dawned Clannad embraced the new year with the remaining four founder members – myself, Ciarán, Noel and Pádraig.

# *Chapter 20*

For me the dawn of a new decade meant tremendous hope and possibility. The eighties had been a rollercoaster of professional successes and personal traumas. I looked back at the girl I was then and I didn't like what I saw. Now I was in control. I had a wonderful man in my life and the possibility of our getting married, which was something I could hardly hope for. Towards the end of 1989 we had talked over the subject but it was a difficult area because I was still technically married and divorce was not allowed in Ireland. Tim couldn't propose to me, but we were at the point where we both knew that our relationship was special and if it was meant to be, we would be together. We didn't know how. Neither did we know that there was another test ahead.

I set about applying for a divorce through an English solicitor. Many Irish people at that time were going across to England to get legally separated. Strangely enough, if you did this it was kind of recognised in Ireland. We set the wheels in motion and waited. I knew I wouldn't face any opposition from Pat because a few years previously he had been very obliging when I had asked for his co-operation in trying to get our marriage annulled by the Catholic Church. To our disappointment this was not granted.

With Pól leaving the band Ciarán was anxious that we recorded a new album as soon as possible. His idea was to go back to our roots, writing and recording new songs more in the style of our early days. We appropriately called the album *Anam*, which means 'soul'. Over the years we'd become very used to spending indulgent amounts of time and money on our albums.

We used expensive studios and of course ended up paying for it in the long run. Even after all the years and all the success, none of us had much money to show for it. Everything had gone back into running the band – tour buses, sound systems, management, secretaries, stylists. We had garnered many trappings and a multitude of people, all of whom needed a salary. We didn't even own a car between us, yet somehow the staff who worked in our office were driving around in 'company-owned' vehicles.

We hired a nice little studio called Woolhall in Beckingham, just outside Bath. Spending time in England was convenient for Tim and me but I suppose I found the recording experience quite difficult. The boys were very laid-back and we found ourselves not starting until late in the afternoon and then working until two or three in the morning. A few years ago I would have just gone along with it, but I was trying to live a healthier life now. I wasn't interested in going to the pub, but the boys could always enjoy a pint and the start times got later and later. I felt that I never really knew where I was with them. One day I tried to talk to Ciarán about it, suggesting that we start work at a more reasonable time so that we could finish earlier. Nothing changed. It particularly upset me when I found myself still doing one of my main vocals at four o'clock in the morning. It was the end of the album and the boys and a bunch of friends had already begun to celebrate downstairs while I was up in the vocal booth struggling to finish the recording. I was disappointed to say the least.

Tim was wonderfully supportive. He would come over to the studio as often as possible and spent many hours hearing me spill out my frustrations of the day. I suppose it was at that time that another seed was sown. I knew I loved singing and recording, and realised my frustration was because I had little control of what was going on with the band. For years I had happily sat in the shadows. I just turned up to sing and had always done as I was told. I'd never had any confidence in the past, but now I was beginning to have ideas, both about songs and how my voice could be used differently. *Anam* provided a good opportunity to try my hand at a bit of writing. Ciarán was grateful for the support. He missed Pól and was feeling the load, especially since this was the first album on which he carried the full work of the production. I proudly put my mark on three of the songs, 'Poison Glenn', 'You're the One' and 'Rí na Cruinne'. It felt good. Maybe I could do it after all. And if I could write, maybe I could look at doing something by myself. How wonderful it would be to have charge of a project, to record when and how I wanted. Sometimes I would let myself dream a little. It appeased the frustration I was feeling. I was stepping into deep water, but it thrilled me. Tim was very encouraging and suggested I should, one day, think about doing a solo album. No. That was just too terrifying. But the idea was planted in the back of my mind.

During the time we were recording *Anam* there came another great confidence-booster. I took a call from a producer friend, Chris Hughes, who told me he was working on Robert Plant's new album. He knew I'd always been a fan of Led Zeppelin and I assumed he might be inviting me down to the studio to meet Robert himself. I was nearly blown away when Chris told me he was ringing to see if I would be interested in doing a vocal. It was so daunting. What would a folk singer from Donegal be doing with one of the greatest rock singers of all time? I cross-questioned Chris. Was he sure Robert hadn't got me mixed up with someone else? Was it really my voice he was after?

A couple of days later I found myself on the train to London. I was terrified. It was good to see Chris again and Robert Plant was charm itself. I tried to control my nerves. I had never been in the studio before without my brothers telling me what to do. I had sung with other people before, but Ciarán or Pól had always been there to guide me. It was as if I didn't think I could sound like myself without them. Now I was alone. This could be embarrassing. But it wasn't. We had a wonderful time and I ended up doing two songs with Robert. I left that day with a huge grin on my face and a spring in my step. This was just one of several other little projects I ended up doing that gave me another notch of confidence on my belt.

At the time *Anam* was released, however, I had to deal with some difficult news. A letter came from my solicitor informing me that my file for divorce had been refused. It felt like the bottom had fallen out of our world. I plunged into a pool of resigned despair. I had no right to be angry. It was what I deserved. When I looked back at the mess I had made of my life, there was little wonder that I had been denied this opportunity of happiness. How could I have let myself presume that I might be given another chance? I could punish myself easily. This was obviously a kind of divine retribution. I had made my bed and now I had to lie in it. But I felt so bad for Tim, bad that he had got mixed up with me, only to have his dreams shattered. It had been tough on him from the start and now he was suffering for the things of my past. Yet as I wallowed in my misery, something inside told me not to despair. I had experienced a new joy and some kind of release when I had addressed my burdens in prayer. I was learning new things about the God of my childhood and recognising something of his grace and mercy in my life. The decision about the divorce seemed so final, but we still felt sure that we were meant to be together. We'd never actually voiced it to each other, but knew that we were not prepared to compromise ourselves by just living together. Perhaps we would have to face up to this, but still, we hung on to our faith in the belief that our happiness would eventually be complete. It was a hard decision, but if we were to be together at all, it had to be in a marriage blessed by God.

I appealed against the court's decision. I knew I was a victim of the authority's clampdown on Irish people seeking divorce in England in false pretence that they were going to reside in the country. My case was genuine. I had an English boyfriend and fully intended to live in England. There was lots of paperwork to be completed and an affidavit signed to seal my intent not to return to Ireland as soon as a divorce was granted. A promise and a prayer, now it was out of my hands. All we could do was wait.

A few weeks later a letter dropped onto the doormat at Woodtown Manor. It bore my solicitor's stamp and my hand trembled as I tore at the seal. It was a short letter informing me that it looked highly possible that the divorce would go through before the end of July. I slumped down on a kitchen chair. Maybe I should have leapt around the room in joy and relief. This was what we had been waiting and praying for. But I could hardly feel euphoric. Divorce is a bitter thing. Pat and I should never have been married, but I had cared for him and we had hurt each other badly. In my heart I whispered a prayer of thanksgiving, and a prayer that one day our wounds would be healed. I rang Tim and shared quiet comfort.

My thirty-eighth birthday was on 4 August 1990. Tim and I walked hand in hand in a Cambridge park. We'd spent the afternoon with Tim's family and as the heat of the day lost its sting the two of us took a walk through Jesus' Green, down by the River Cam. We knew that we were now free to be together, but still, when Tim turned and asked me there and then if I would marry him, it somehow took me by surprise. I just looked at him. He had that same assured smile and twinkle in his eyes that I had fallen for the first time I met him. It had been love at first sight, for sure, though we hadn't realised it at the time. We had already been through so much together. He knew me so well, yet here he was, the man I loved, asking me to spend the rest of my life with him. I swallowed hard a few times. I could hardly believe this was happening. Of course my answer was a resounding 'Yes'.

By the time we got back to Tim's parents' house we were brimming over with excitement. Margaret was hanging out washing in the garden and when we told her she dropped everything and threw her arms around us. She was so thrilled. That night Tim and I thanked God for his goodness and faithfulness. It was late and I was looking forward to ringing home the next day. I was so happy and went to bed that night with a whole new future in front of me.

The next day there were shrieks down the phone when I broke the news to my sisters and I could hear the joy in Mammy's and Daddy's voice's. They knew Tim was good for me and had seen such a change in me over the last few years. Their prayers had been answered. It must have seemed that, at last, I was finding the happiness they had wished for me all my life.

The following Monday Tim and I went out to choose a ring. I don't wear a lot of jewellery and I didn't want anything too big or fancy. We soon found what we wanted in a delightful little shop. It was a delicate band of emeralds, very pretty and not too overstated. It was perfect and we were on cloud nine all day. We didn't know where we were going to live, what we were going to do, how I would handle things with Clannad, whether we would have a family, or anything about our future. But it didn't matter at all. We were just so happy that we were going to be together. We had the rest of our lives to work out the details.

# Chapter 21

The days that followed were a haze of happiness. We decided we would like to get married in Cambridge. It would be a big church wedding, a celebration that all our friends and family could share in and witness God's goodness. Sitting in the Vicar's office we poured out our story, stressing to him how important it was to us to have a full church blessing. He was a wonderful vicar, Michael Farrer, who was very sympathetic to our plight, but knew that he could not grant us a church wedding because of my divorce. He would have to bring our case before the Bishop. More waiting. It would have been easier to get married in a registry office and then have a blessing in the church.

Sure enough, several weeks later we received permission for a full church wedding. It would take place in St Paul's Church, Cambridge, the following January. It was less than five months away and there was lots to prepare. There were also certain conditions we had to adhere to. One was that, before the wedding, Tim had to move into the Vicar's house for two weeks so that he could legitimately say he lived within the church boundary – seemingly, his parents' home was just outside. It seemed to me a strange Church of England requirement, all tied in with the announcement of the banns of marriage, but it was okay. We were just thrilled that our wedding would be going ahead in the church, and would be led by a man who recognised what it meant to us. Michael Farrer did all he could to help us organise things, especially when I promised that I would return to the church later on that year and do a concert to help raise funds for their community projects.

In the midst of our plans Clannad released the *Anam* album

and I found myself busy with promotion. It was a crazy time, but I was happier than ever and, before I knew it, Christmas was around the corner.

To say my life was transformed is an understatement. I felt young again, enthusiastic and wallowing in love. I had found a spiritual path and I was growing in strength. I had a great career. Things were looking positive for Clannad. We had our ups and downs, but I was enjoying getting more involved in the writing and discovering a new creativity that I never believed was within me. Then I had the man of my dreams, who loved me as I loved him. Life was indeed good and I was blossoming in every way. How was it then that I could still be so foolish and fallible?

Just before Christmas I was asked to appear on a television show in Dublin. Christmas spirit filled the air and everyone was in a party mood. Tim had come over to see me before returning home to spend Christmas with his family and after the show a whole gang of us were ready for a night on the town. We went first to a restaurant. We were all on a high with the success of the show and the drink ran free. Everyone was talking and laughing, trying to make themselves heard above the music and the atmosphere was wonderful. We were there for several hours and I lost count of what I had to drink. I'd started on the vodka, then as more and more bottles of wine and champagne were brought to our table, the evening lost itself to raucous giddiness.

'Máire, do you fancy a line?'

I turned to the guy who had come over and tapped me on the shoulder. What possessed me in that moment, I do not know. Perhaps it's just that old habits die hard and in the alcohol-infused pre-Christmas party atmosphere I found myself getting up from the table and heading off with this guy towards the toilets. I don't know what I was thinking of, but somehow I convinced myself that we wouldn't have been noticed, specifically that Tim wouldn't have seen me leave.

Downstairs there were two little toilet cubicles opposite each other. It was late in the evening and they had seen many a visit. As we crammed ourselves into one of them I was excited, nervous and anxious to suffer the delights before me. My tempter knew the weakness in me. I watched as he prepared the line, not thinking about what I was doing or considering the consequences.

Just then I heard a familiar voice outside.

'Máire, are you in there?' It was Tim. It shook me and caught me off guard, but somehow I wasn't in the real world. It should have been enough to get me out of there quickly, but no, I was drunk and stupid. I opened the door, and to this day I cannot forget the look on Tim's face.

'I'm just having a line of coke,' I said. 'Is that OK?' And in that moment I turned around and took it in front of him.

The silence was deafening. Then Tim spoke, quietly and purposefully. 'Well, I'm just going to go home now.' With that he turned and left. At that moment the horror of what I had done came flooding over me. I felt so stupid, cheap and dirty. What was I doing in the seedy toilet, with some man, taking a drug I didn't need and jeopardising my whole future? I couldn't get Tim's disappointed eyes out of my mind. They bored through my very soul, torturing me with my own disgust. He was gone and I was alone. I didn't know what to do next. I couldn't go after him. I stood there shaking and confused. What would I do? Nothing else for it. I threw my head back, straightened my clothing and headed back upstairs to the biggest drink I could find. It was time to get this party going.

Talk about falling! I leapt from a great height. I hit the clubs and danced into oblivion, returning to Woodtown Manor after four o'clock in the morning. Tim's jacket was slumped over one of the kitchen chairs and I knew he'd be in the spare room. At least I didn't have to confront him. My mother was also staying with me at the time. I dreaded her seeing me like this, but at that time in the morning, with my head spinning, my only thought was of sleep. Ghosts of the past haunted my dreams. In the early hours the heat of the nightclub made it easy to kid myself that I was having a great time. I could dance and laugh and drink with the people there, but in my dreams I watched myself from afar, tortured by the emptiness of it all, the false highs and very real lows that would always catch up with you in the morning. It was a scene I thought I had left behind. I had been free from its clutches, getting high on the reality of love and life and the many good things that filled my world.

It was around midday when I surfaced and I could hear Thomas and my mother chatting and laughing together in the

kitchen. They looked at me when I entered the room, obviously
appearing a little worse for wear. They asked no questions. I
guessed Tim had gone for a walk. There was no sign of the dog
and I noticed Tim's wallet on the table. At least he'd not left
altogether. Thomas presented me with tea and toast. My stomach
was so tightly knotted I couldn't face it and the milk of the tea
seemed to stick in my throat. I sat there staring into the depths of
the mug.

When Tim walked in my stomach clenched tighter. I'm sure
Mammy and Thomas must have sensed an atmosphere between
us, but they made small talk while the dog fussed around me
with muddy paws and wet hair. When Tim walked out of the
room, I followed. We needed to talk, but neither of us knew what
to say. We were both shocked at the events of the previous
evening. I was ashamed, and above all frightened at the re-
emergence of my old self. I really felt I had betrayed Tim. I
could barely stand to look at him, yet everything within me was
focused on keeping him there. I didn't care what my mother or
Thomas or anyone else saw, heard or thought. I was aware of
only Tim and the probability that I had destroyed all that was
good in my life. I loved him so much, yet in one stupid move I
hurt him deeply and risked losing him for ever. It was a pitiful
situation. We were to be married in a couple of weeks. He was
the best thing that had ever happened to me and I needed him. I
might have been worried at having to tell my mother there
would be no wedding, but this kind of thing did not enter my
thoughts. I didn't care about ceremonies and celebrations; all I
feared was Tim walking out of my life for good.

I ached to tell him how I felt, how ashamed I was, how I would
never, ever lose myself in that way again. I wanted to beg him to
stay, but all that came out of my mouth were stupid excuses. It
was Christmas, it was a party, just a bit of harmless fun, it didn't
mean anything. I knew I was lying to us both. I felt the burden of
my behaviour and I have never felt such disgust and fear in my
life. Tim knew me well. Though my mouth babbled pathetic
excuses, I'm sure he could see the truth of self-loathing in my
eyes. In that awful moment when he had caught me in the toilet
he knew that it was pointless to argue with me or try to stop me
taking the coke. I would have had no logic or reason at that

stage. He knew that it would pain me more, and hopefully bring me to my senses, if he just quietly left, leaving me to handle the weight of my shame alone. He was right. I had carried on with the party, but now I was having to face myself in the harsh and sober light of day. Though we sat opposite each other, I felt separated and isolated from him. With the full weight of my vice on my shoulders, I found myself nervously twisting my engagement ring, as if waiting to hear my sentence. Tim was quiet. He was hurt and wore an expression I had not seen before. It frightened me more.

I knew deep in my heart that I would never let him down again. I started to talk, telling him of my resolution never to touch any form of drugs from this moment onwards. I told him I'd understand if he wanted to call the wedding off, but begged him to give me another chance. I don't know if he believed I could keep my promises, but I think he saw that they were made not just for his benefit, but for myself. He could see that I was so frightened at my own vulnerability and shocked at how easily I could fall. Finally he spoke.

'I think you have to make a decision about what you want for your life, Máire.'

We talked more. It was time to re-evaluate our relationship and scrutinise ourselves, our behaviour and what we wanted our marriage to be. It was a time when I fully realised the value of life and the merciful provision of a second chance. We had built up a lot of trust over the last two years, particularly since I had returned from our first Australian/New Zealand tour. The trust had been damaged, but it had strong foundations and would not shatter. I was young in my faith and hadn't realised how easy it was to fall. I had let my guard down and had been easily tempted. Thankfully Tim recognised this and knew that I had been hit between the eyes with the consequences of my stupidity. The worst thing was the hurt. He was hurt to see me lowering myself like that and hurt that other people would see me in that state. A thousand things were said with our eyes in that dramatic moment when he first discovered me. Nothing needed to be voiced. We both knew what might or might not be.

Looking back, I still feel the horror of that night. It was so dark and seedy. For years it had been just my normal behaviour. But I had been given a second chance. Where I now stand, I see that it probably took this shock revisit to the depths of my past to make me realise the full worth and value of the new life I had open to me. I would chase after the things that were good and the love I had in Tim with all my being and never compromise myself again. To this day I have kept my promise.

Tim left the next day to spend Christmas in Cambridge, and I was relieved that we could look forward to seeing each other when he came over to Donegal for New Year.

Christmas that year was everything that a family Christmas should be. I enjoyed the journey down there, relishing every wonderful thing about the countryside around me. I had made the trip many times, and in far better weather, but somehow the landscape was crisper and brighter than ever. We passed smiling people in the villages, all preparing for the festivities and aglow with Christmas spirit.

My parents' house was also alive with the season. There was the smell of cooking and music coming out of every corner. The music room, as is the tradition in our family, was full of brightly coloured presents. Reds, blues, greens, silver and gold coloured ribbons adorning packages of all shapes and sizes filled every available space. Even though there were nine brothers and sisters we always bought something for each other. We each took our own little space in the room and in the days before Christmas there was always someone sneaking in to inspect their pile.

All the sisters were at home and, being a couple of weeks before I was to get married, it was more 'girly' than ever. They organised some school friends to come over to Leo's Tavern one night and we later ended up back at the house, dancing, laughing and singing, long into the early hours.

I spoke to Tim every day on the telephone and enjoyed the warmth and tenderness that had returned to his voice. I missed him, but it seemed fitting that we should spend Christmas with our respective families and look forward to sharing our New Year together.

On Christmas Eve I went down to help my sister Olive who was running the bar at the time. Daddy was on top form and the place, as always, was absolutely packed. Deirdre, Eithne and Brídín went with Mammy to midnight mass and joined the rest of the family in the bar later on. Every year, when the last customer has gone home, the family gathers together for a special Christmas drink. Ciarán plays the piano and we sing carols and enjoy the intimacies of the family circle. Then it's back to the house to open the presents. By this time it's usually two o'clock in the morning, but there's much noise and merrymaking as everyone exchanges gifts. Ciarán or Pól take their place at the piano and again the singing goes on long into the night.

On Christmas Day we go to mass. This year, as always, the church was packed and it was good to catch up with old friends. There were many faces from the previous evening, some with fragile heads from their indulgences, cringing as children belted around with new toy cars, dolls and space ships. As the priest performed the mass my mind reflected back on the miracles I had seen in my life. So much of me had been healed and restored. I thought of Tim and knew that he would be in church with his family, all those hundreds of miles away. Soon we would share our New Year together, in excited anticipation of our marriage.

Back at the house the traditional Brennan Christmas continued in full swing. It was wonderful that we could all be at home together. This was one of only two days in the year when the pub would remain closed – the other was Good Friday. The girls set about preparing the meal while the boys rearranged the furniture so we could all sit around the table together. The smell of Christmas dinner wafted through the house and the radio in the kitchen clashed with the sound of the traditional choir coming from the television in the sitting-room, all of which could just be heard above someone bashing out some refrain on the piano in the music room. Eithne had just got a video camera and was skulking from room to room trying to catch everyone at their most embarrassing. It didn't take much to get us to act accordingly, and the house was full of laughter and song.

Full with Christmas dinner and lazy with the day, we sat by the fire reminiscing and playing games. My mind wandered to Cambridge and I stared out of the misty window into the distance, wondering what the next few months would have in store. As I watched, beautiful little droplets of white snow began to fall and settle on the ground. A perfect end to a perfect day.

## Chapter 22

On Boxing Day we awoke to a snow-covered landscape. As a child I loved the snow and it was always a disappointment if a winter passed by without us being able to sledge and skate. As Christmas Day faded I had been warmed by the memories as the first gentle flakes graced a dreamlike scene. But when I drew back the curtains to deep drifts of white, my first thought was of Tim and the journey he would be making before the week was out. All day we watched as more snow fell and the television reports warned of unprecedented bad weather ahead.

Over the next couple of days I watched in horror as some of the worst weather in history descended over Ireland. Tim and I talked on the phone and neither of us were prepared to admit defeat and cancel his trip. We were desperate to see each other. Besides, our plans had broader repercussions. Tim was coming over with the car so that after New Year he could drive us both back to Dublin. There we would pick up as many of my things as possible from Woodtown Manor to take back to Tim's flat in London where we would be living after the wedding.

On 29 December Tim and a friend, Andy Martin, drove from Cambridge to Holyhead and took a rough ride on the ferry across the Irish Sea. He rang me throughout the day to report on his slow progress. As evening drew in I joined the family down at the bar for a couple of hours, but was anxious to get back to the house to await his arrival.

A couple of years earlier I had bought the little house next door to my parents. It had been built for an American couple who had spent many of their summers in Donegal and had decided to retire there. They had become good friends of my

Aunt Bríd and the family were happy to welcome them to the vicinity. Sadly, just as they were preparing to leave America, the husband had a heart attack and died. His wife was devastated and didn't feel she could make the move to Ireland by herself. She asked Bríd if anyone in the family would be interested before she put the house on the market. None of us were really in a position to buy, even though it was a bargain price. After much deliberation I decided to go for it. I was in my late thirties and didn't have anything to my name. It took some serious negotiation with the bank manager, but I managed to get enough together for the mortgage deposit and, as soon as the paperwork went through, I knew I had made the right decision. My heart was always in Donegal and it seemed only natural that I should want some kind of base there, next to my family. As it turned out, it also meant that the ever-expanding family gatherings could be more easily accommodated and I was certainly grateful when Ciarán, Lynda, Olive and Eithne came over to keep me company that night as I waited for Tim.

Every time I looked out the blizzards seemed to be getting worse. The television news tormented me with scenes of blocked roads and warnings not to travel. As the hours went by I grew more and more concerned. We didn't have mobile phones at that time, so he had been stopping along the way to make calls wherever possible. Now it was nearing one o'clock in the morning and I had heard from him only once since he'd landed in Ireland, over five hours ago.

There were no vehicles on the roads, but at three o'clock we heard the sound of a car approaching the house. Sure enough, skidding along the road came the white Ford Escort, the sight I had been waiting for. My heart leapt with relief and joy as two poor bedraggled travellers joined us to thaw out in front of the fire. Tim had driven at less than ten miles an hour all the way from Letterkenny to Gweedore. At times it had been virtually impossible to see the road and they had feared they might become stuck in a drift. To make matters worse Tim was beginning to suspect that there was something wrong with the car.

Once again, I had so much to be thankful for. Tim was safe and we were together. My prayers were answered

New Year's Eve in my father's bar is always a riot. Everyone wants to be there and the place is heaving with people from early evening. We had a fabulous time and even the two Englishmen were wished a 'Happy New Year' by the locals. Tim had always been aware of a frosty welcome by some of the older men. He often recalls one of his first visits when we had not long been seeing each other. The bar has a back room where the family often meet and some of the locals sometimes used to persuade my father to keep the drinks flowing there after closing hours. Of course the chat is always in Irish and Tim knew that some of the men were muttering to each other about the presence of the Englishman in the corner. Daddy heard the conversation and without further ado proclaimed, in English, 'If you don't mind, the Englishman is here as my guest. In fact that Englishman is my future son-in-law.' All went quiet among the men and of course Tim was absolutely stunned. This was the first time he had met my father and here he was being introduced as his future son-in-law. I might have died of embarrassment had I been there and we've had many a laugh about it since. It was as if Daddy knew something then that we were yet to discover.

These days Leo's Tavern is usually packed with people from all nations, especially in the summer when travellers from all over the world come to sample the infamous Irish hospitality. There's rarely a week goes by without a film crew from America, Japan or Europe wanting to make a programme about the place that launched the careers of Clannad and Enya, and of course Daddy is always happy to oblige with a singsong.

After New Year the party atmosphere continued among the family in anticipation of my wedding. But before I left to get married I had another recording session to squeeze in. It had all been a bit last-minute, but it was a project I was flattered to be invited to do. I had received a phone call in early December from Tony Adams – a friend of ours from recording *Sirius* – who was the producer of a new film called *Switch*, starring Ellen Barkin. He'd asked me if I would record the Joni Mitchell song, 'Both Sides Now'. Ciarán and I quickly put together a rough demo and when the production team heard it they decided they'd like me to try it as a duet with a male voice. The question was, who? Around the same time, Clannad's tour manager, Phil McDonnell, was working with Paul Young and he invited me along to one of his shows. I loved Paul's voice and was thrilled to get the opportunity to meet him. After the show we sat and talked and by the end of the evening he'd agreed to do the duet with me for *Switch*. It was another very natural collaboration.

The boys were anxious for me to do the session before I went off to get married and time was ticking by. Then a couple of days after New Year I got a call asking if I could go down to the studio in Dublin that Friday. It was short notice, but it coincided nicely with our plans to collect my things from Woodtown Manor before heading over to England. It would have been very straight-forward, except that Tim's car was increasingly unhappy and he booked it into a garage, only to be told that it needed a new part that would take at least another two days to get hold of. It was decided that I would head back to Dublin on the bus and Tim would meet me there later when the car was fixed.

I went straight from the bus station to the studio and spent two good days recording with Paul Young. It sounded good and, again, gave me one more notch on my confidence belt.

When I met Tim he didn't look very happy. The car had supposedly been fixed, but he was worried at the way it seemed to be overheating as he drove up from Donegal. Oh well, we had loads to do and no time to worry about it, just as long as it got us back to England in time for the wedding, that was all we cared about. On Monday Tim had errands to do around town, including collecting our Order of Service sheets from the printers. The bad weather seemed to be setting in again and we kept trying to get reports from the docks, fearing that our boat to England might be cancelled. Our worst fears came true. Just before lunch time we heard that no boats would be sailing from Dublin until the weather had significantly improved. We were stranded and our wedding was only five days away. A few phone calls later we managed to book ourselves on what was probably the last boat that left Ireland that week. It went from Rosslare, two hours south of Dublin, to Fishguard in Wales. That would be fine. Our next shock came when we headed out towards Woodtown Manor only to discover that we could not get near the house because of the snow. We had to get in. If nothing else, my wedding dress was in there. More hours were lost, but thankfully a friend with a Land-Rover was able to make his way up to the house and relay my things back to Tim's car.

So, we were on our way. In the car we chatted excitedly about the journey, both of us too scared to admit that we feared we might not even get through to Rosslare as the snow fell more heavily and the roads became treacherous with black ice. A few miles on, we both sat in silence as Tim concentrated on the driving, both of us praying inside for a safe journey. I tried not to think about Donegal, where the weather was probably even worse. What if the family couldn't get to Dublin airport and ended up missing the wedding? The car crawled along and I tried to stay positive. Rosslare might be only two hours from Dublin, but when you can only manage to drive at ten miles an hour, it's a whole different affair. To make matters worse, the car kept juddering and the dial showed it was dangerously close to overheating. The only way to keep it going was to have the heating on full blast. Yes, it was a freezing day, but even so, it's hard to breathe with a car fan heater blowing in your face, and it was making us both sleepy. The only thing to do was drive along with the windows down. We must have looked a curious sight.

By the time we reached Rosslare it was five o'clock in the morning and we were thoroughly exhausted. In the last couple of hours it had got so cold that we'd even wound the windows back up. It was absolutely freezing and we daren't turn the heater off, so we pulled up at the quayside, left the engine running so that the heater could keep going and promptly fell asleep.

I awoke with a jolt and a gloved hand banging on the window beside me. As I came round I realised we were surrounded by people. Tim was also trying to haul himself out of his slumber and immediately leapt up when he realised what was going on. Fumes and smoke filled our nostrils and people were shouting at us that the car was nearly on fire. It had been a narrow escape. The car had completely overheated and was probably close to bursting into flames. With the engine turned off and the smoke dispersed we still had another couple of hours to wait until the boat was ready to go. There was a stream of cars in the queue behind us, everyone hoping and praying that the weather would give them safe passage to England. With no heat in the car it was distressingly cold. We wrapped ourselves in coats and blankets and huddled together to try to keep warm, praying that the time would pass quickly. It did. Too quickly in fact. We must have both fallen asleep again and the next thing I knew Tim was saying, 'Oh no, I think we've missed the boat.' Cars were flying past us and as Tim struggled to start the engine I scraped at the ice on the inside of the screen, trying to see what was going on. Thankfully I could see the boat, still moored at the quayside. The cars continued to fly past. We had completely lost our place in the queue, but thankfully Tim managed to start the car and we limped along, laughing with relief and shock as we finally made our way into the depths of the ferry.

The sea was wild and it was easy to understand why all the other boats had been cancelled. I'm usually a good traveller, but on this trip many of us were ill as the boat lurched on the waves. It would have been a miserable time, except that Tim and I were together and kept warm with excitement and anticipation of the forthcoming days.

Still, our journey was far from over. Once in Fishguard we found that the weather was so bad, with high winds, that the Severn Bridge had been closed down to one lane. Everybody needed to go over the bridge and we found ourselves sitting in a stream of traffic for hours, again trying to prevent the car from finally giving out on us. It was a long and arduous journey. We had arrived in Fishguard mid morning but it took us until eleven o'clock at night to get into London. Cold and exhausted, we drove into Brixton, knowing that our final hurdle was just around the corner. Tim's flat was three flights up with no lift. There was no way we could leave all the stuff in the car, so there we were, feeling like death, hauling suitcases and boxes up the stairs to what would be my new home.

The next day was Wednesday. We were getting married on Saturday and I still hadn't completed my going-away outfit. I'd bought a jacket and skirt in Dublin, but still needed a blouse and persuaded Tim that I had to have a trip into the city on our way up to Cambridge.

London was packed with people shopping in the sales and it's unwise to take the car into Central London at the best of times. We decided that Tim should drop me off at Harrods and then go and find somewhere to park the car. We arranged to meet by a certain door and I would bleep him on his pager when I was ready. No problem. Harrods was swarming with people, everyone rushing around excitedly grabbing the bargains. The food halls were beautiful, full of Christmas fare, and the whole store still glittered with gold and silver decorations. I made my way upstairs to the clothing departments. Walking through one of the lingerie sections I spotted some beautiful cream silk stockings that were in the sale. They would be perfect for underneath my wedding dress. Smiling to myself I queued at the desk and I suppose it was then that I realised how unorganised I was.

The sales assistant commented, 'Oh, aren't these lovely, I've put some aside for my own wedding.'

'When are you getting married?' I asked.

She replied that her wedding was the following August and was absolutely flabbergasted when I said I was buying these stockings for my wedding which was in three days' time. She probably expected me to go next to the bridal department and buy a dress! But no, I had, thankfully, already got that arranged. I'd had it made for me in Dublin. It was a very traditional ivory wedding dress. It was so different from the way I felt preparing for my first wedding. Now I was brimming over with excitement and wanted to be very much the glowing bride in the beautiful wedding gown.

I continued around the store and found exactly what I wanted by way of a blouse, and also treated myself to a beautiful pearl necklace and delicate earrings that I thought would look lovely with my wedding dress.

Now to meet Tim. Perhaps things had been going too smoothly up until then, but when I tried to page him I got absolutely no response. I tried again and again and when an hour went by I was beginning to get seriously worried. Harrods is a massive store, and standing among the ground-floor throng of people I began to despair. Time went by and I began to feel really stupid. I wondered if people noticed the agitated way I kept looking around the store, moving between areas, hoping to spot him. There was nothing for it. I would just have to stay by one of the doors until Tim found me. Then – I'm sure by some miracle – I saw him making his way through the crowd to the very door where I was standing. He struggled with a huge box that he could barely carry under his arm and I realised that it was my wedding dress. A few months earlier a friend of ours had had her wedding dress stolen from her car and there was no way Tim was going to allow this to happen. He'd parked in a rather dodgy area and was aware that the car was packed with our things for the wedding and honeymoon. He couldn't bring everything with him, but if nothing else, he was determined that I should have my dress safe with me at all times. He looked quite a sight, damp with the weather and steam rising off him as he fought his way through the crowd.

Thankfully the car was still intact and we made our way up to Cambridge, arriving late in the evening. The trauma and emotion of the last few days caught up with me and I slept soundly until around lunch time the next day.

There was lots to do: cars, the cake and flowers to be checked, and arrangements confirmed at the hotel. I was still nervous about my family making it through the bad weather, but made sure that the hotel was expecting them. Then we had what turned out to be a mammoth task, of putting together the Order of Service sheets. We had decided that we wanted to include every single word of the service and all the words of the hymns so that people would have a full record to take away with them. This, of course, meant that there were several pages to be compiled together into the beautiful handmade covers that our good friend Carol Diver had designed. I loved the look of the finished piece. The front design was two cups in a beautiful Celtic art setting. Then the inside pages were tied in with delicate pink ribbon. Each one had to be hand-tied and by the time we went to bed on Thursday night we'd managed to do 150 between us.

The next day I took my dress and case and checked into the University Arms where I would spend the night before the wedding with my family. I was so excited waiting for them to arrive. I spoke to them on the telephone in the morning and knew that they'd agreed that the safest way, because of the bad weather, to get to Dublin was by bus. I was happy to hear from them later in the day. They'd made it safely to the airport and were on their way.

It was such a relief when they finally arrived at the hotel, much later than scheduled. Their journey had not been without trauma and the girls especially had very worried looks on their faces. The problems had begun that morning when they awoke to find the little shop that Bríd owned beside my grandparents' house had been broken into and vandalised. She was a bit disturbed by it, but the most pressing problem was that Mammy's suitcase, containing her wedding outfit and Daddy's best shirt, had been lost in transit. Much of the evening was spent making frantic phone calls to the airline to see if the case would turn up by the following morning. They didn't sound convinced. Still, there was nothing we could do at that time of night, so we gathered together and shared a lovely meal in the hotel. It was wonderful to be surrounded by all the family again and we were all in good form. Tim came over later to say hello to everyone and we shared a special moment as he kissed me goodnight for the last time before our marriage.

Then it was up to my room with Deirdre, whom I'd made promise to wax my legs before we went to bed. It was wonderful to be able to have this time together, just chatting about the events of the last few days and reminiscing about old times. Deirdre had seen such a transformation in me. I apologised to her for the way I had behaved, all those times I had dragged her out on my drinking binges. We laughed and cuddled and I screamed as she pulled the hot wax off my legs. It was one of those special times and Deirdre will always be so precious to me because of the things we shared. Things could have been so different. As she and the rest of my family had witnessed, the happiness I had found was nothing short of a miracle.

# Chapter 23

I awoke the following morning from a sound and peaceful sleep. It was 12 January: my wedding day. As winter sunlight softly pressed through a crack in the curtains I could see the form of my wedding dress hanging on the back of the door. Outside, the early morning shoppers and traders were going about their business and periodically a call of 'room service' could be heard in the corridor. I smiled. Today was the start of a new chapter in my life, a new adventure that I was ready to face head on. It didn't matter what trials were ahead or what the future might hold, today I would live my second chance. I had come so far in the last few years and my life had changed beyond recognition. Here I was, on the brink of a wonderful day, surrounded by the people who meant most to me in the world and marrying a man that I could only dare to dream about. Peace and overwhelming joy flooded my heart. In that moment I could barely find the words to give thanks to God.

There were still a number of last-minute chores to be seen to and I knew that the family would be in a panic about my mother's missing outfit. It would have been lovely to have shared the morning with Deirdre. She was my bridesmaid and there were plenty of duties I could have passed her way, but I knew that she'd promised to help Mammy, should the worst come to the worst and her suitcase not be retrieved from the airline. Sure enough, when I rang her room there was no answer. Nor could any of the other girls be raised. Eithne had gone off to the church early to practise her singing for the service and it seemed that every other sister had responded to Mammy's disaster and gone off on an emergency shopping spree. No use in getting flustered, everything would sort itself out. I spent the next half hour in a luxurious bath of sweet-scented bubbles.

Meanwhile, as the story is repeated by my sisters, my poor Mammy was in Robert Sayle's department store across the street. The sorry party of flustered women had burst through the doors not long after opening time and soon found themselves with the finest of the store's outfitters who valiantly rose to the crisis situation. Dresses, jackets, skirts, blouses, the finest of regalia was presented, tucked, pinned and fitted. Deirdre stayed with Mammy for opinion and moral support, while Brídín ran off to the nearest men's outfitters to try to replace Daddy's missing shirt. Meanwhile Olive was doing the rounds of the lingerie department looking for tights and suitable undergarments for my mother's sadly depleted wardrobe.

Back at the hotel, with hair still hanging damp around my shoulders, I was busying myself with the laying of name-place settings ready for the wedding feast. The clock on the wall ticked steadily, taunting me with the fact that in less than an hour I would be walking down the aisle.

Still, I was determined to remain calm and savour every moment, planned or otherwise, of this most precious day. Time to get ready. Before going downstairs I stood gazing at myself in the mirror. I wore a big, beautiful, flamboyant bridal gown of ivory satin and a little Juliet cap attached to a short veil. The perm and streaks that adorned my hair when I first met Tim were now completely gone and my dark locks hung loose and free. So, too, the garish nail varnish had been replaced with a delicate shade of unassuming pink and my fair complexion was enhanced with the most modest of make-up that I applied myself. This was my fairy tale, completed, of course, when I stepped into little satin slippers and placed the dainty string of pearls at my throat. I beamed, a big broad smile that hardly left my face all day. It was as much a part of the outfit as the intricacies of underskirting and delicate lace that adorned the bodice. The smile would remain long after the dress was packed away.

Downstairs there was still no sign of my family. I stood in my wedding gown, as the clock again called out to me. 'Five minutes to one, tick-tock, tick-tock, you should be there now, tick-tock, tick-tock, what will Tim be thinking, tick-tock, tick-tock.' Just then Mammy and the girls burst through the door, rushed passed me with shouts of 'You look lovely, Máire', and disappeared into the depths of the hotel. Meanwhile the chauffeur waited patiently. He was to do a couple of trips, ferrying the family to the church, before returning to pick up myself, Daddy, Deirdre and Tim's little nephew who was a pageboy. After what seemed like an age, the girls finally appeared, all rigged out in their finery and Mammy looking particularly beautiful in a new outfit. Even as they got into the car Olive was detaching a price label from Mammy's jacket, but soon they were off with shouts of 'See you at the church'.

By this time it was one-thirty. The wedding was supposed to commence at one and I was cringing at what Tim and his family would be thinking. Tim had always teased me about my 'Irish time', so I'd promised him that I would not be late on our wedding day. Standing there, helplessly waiting for the car to return, I knew that this was pushing it, even by Irish standards. At home it is almost customary for the bride to be at least fifteen minutes late. I smiled to myself remembering a wedding we were singing at in Gweedore. Since the bride never arrives on time, it is perfectly acceptable for the choir to be taking its place ten or so minutes after the scheduled commencement. This time the bride arrived bang on the hour, to astonished murmurs of 'Well, fancy!' and 'Imagine, arriving at the church on time!'

Over at the church, our own guests had started to murmur. I heard the stories afterwards from poor Eithne who sat alone on the left-hand side of the church, cringing and willing the family to arrive. She had been there for what must have seemed like ages, having rehearsed her song, and was now enduring the intensity of the wait as all Tim's family and our friends had arrived and taken their places.

Finally, I stood at the entrance to the church. Tim's friend Bob, our photographer, took a few anxious shots as I composed myself there. It was nice to see his familiar face. I was so happy and looking forward to the occasion that I could hardly imagine being nervous, but with the dramas of the morning and worry in being so late, my top lip started to quiver (a trait common to all the Brennan girls – including Mammy – when nervous) and my legs felt something akin to jelly. In that moment I was grateful for a long full skirt that couldn't betray my trembling limbs. Then it began. Daddy squeezed my arm and we set off walking down the aisle. A sound of celestial-like voices rang in my ears as the congregation sang 'Love Divine'. The church was a sea of familiar faces, applauding my entrance with their smiles and bringing a lump to my throat. I couldn't believe that so many people, from many far-flung places, had turned out to share our day. It was one of those episodes that seemed to unfold in slow motion and I could have wished its lasting for ever. I glanced at Daddy. His face was alight with pride and I swallowed hard, lest the emotion I felt towards him get the better of me. He had always been there for me, never judging, always graciously accepting and loving, despite my absences and the worries I had brought the family over the years. I was still his little girl and today was as special to him as to me. I was proud to be his daughter. There at the front of the church stood Tim. Tall and elegant in his new suit, he wore a look of delight and relief as I took my place beside him. The nerves subsided as I felt the heat of his touch, my hand clasped firmly in his. All through the vows we looked deeply into each other's eyes. He spoke his promises loudly and boldly, for all the church to hear, but in those precious moments, we knew only of each other.

The church ceremony was very much the focal point of our day. Sure, we looked forward to a grand hooley afterwards, but, for Tim and me, the service was the most sacred part and we concentrated on committing every cherished moment to memory. It was wonderful for me to have all my family involved. My youngest brother, Bartley, was an usher and Leon did a reading. After our vows Eithne sang a psalm. Then Pól on the flute and Ciarán at the piano played a traditional Irish air, 'Tabhair Domh Do Lámh' ('Give Me Your Hand'). Michael Farrer gave a wonderful sermon and I gripped a trembling hand as he spoke of Tim's father – whom he had known – how proud he would have been to have seen his son grow into the man now standing at the altar with his bride. Towards the end of the service all four of my sisters took their place in front of us and sang 'Close to You, Lord'.

*Yes you are always close to me*
*Guiding me on my way*
*May I be always close to you*
*. . . on my way Lord.*

It was a beautiful song, with words so meaningful that we were all in pieces by the end. As they began the song, they all stared straight ahead and I noticed more than one quivering lip. Then Deirdre looked at me and caught my gaze. Her voice trembled a little and I saw a tear escape down her cheek. That set Brídín off. She too glanced at me in a nervous moment and saw my eyes brimming over. Before long we were all just looking at each other, fighting not to lose ourselves too far in the emotion of the song, but already falling in unspoken love and choking with joy. I'm sure some of the congregation thought the girls were giggling, but the truth was that they were so overcome with emotion that they all but sobbed their way through the final chorus. Tim subtly handed me his handkerchief and smiled knowingly at the intimacy I shared with my precious sisters on this most celebrated occasion.

We walked out of that church the happiest couple on earth. There were plenty of jibes about being so late, but people were very sympathetic and admiring of my mother as we recounted the story of the emergency rig-out. There was much cooing and laughter and my mother fussed around me, sorry that she had not been there for me that morning. I reassured her that nothing on earth could spoil this day and that, on the contrary, I knew she would always be there when I really needed her. For the first time in my life, everything seemed to take its correct perspective. I simply had no worries about anything. I had no idea what was ahead. I had moved my things from the grandeur of Woodtown Manor to a council flat in Brixton, but did it matter? I was surrounded by people I loved and had become Mrs Tim Jarvis, in a marriage made possible and blessed beyond reason. As we stood for photographs I noticed the little buds of snowdrops pushing their way through winter soil. It seemed even they were celebrating our day and cheering us on. The air was full of chatter, crisp and lively with January's sharp hue. Though winter still wove her frosty fingered grasp over the land, it seemed that

life, in all its abundance, was laid out before us and it was ours
for the living.

# Chapter 24

Bombay's streets were hot, dusty, vibrant with life and abhorrent with squalor. Leaving England in the middle of winter for the more humid climes of a honeymoon in India was something of a shock to the system, but more of a blow was the extreme poverty that distracted our gaze. It was everywhere: the limbless, the hopeless, the helpless, all clamouring at the heels of the princely pale-skinned for a small donation that might buy the day's existence. We had been warned of the horror that would raise the philanthropic spirit in even the hardest hearts, but nothing prepared me for the heartbreaking sights of babies smothered by a life of squalor, maimed mentally, if not physically, by the cruel dealings of a caste system. We were told that to give money was not always the greatest of benevolence. Few of them could trade it for food from a bread-seller who was above them in caste. To him they were unclean, the 'untouchables'. Many were riddled with leprosy. The hardest thing was knowing that this is a curable disease, if only for the provision of those who would claim to place a higher value on life.

The heat of our first afternoon and the smell of the open sewers – that were home to many – soon got the better of us and we resolved to make our way back to our hotel. Not far from the relative grandeur of our residence we passed what appeared to be no more than a pile of rags, but closer inspection filled me with remorse, anguish and a deep sorrow, the picture of which I cannot rid from my being, though that day is long gone. The rags turned out to be two very young women, fast asleep under the midday sun. Between them lay a newborn baby, its eyes and face covered with flies. Tim held my hand tightly and prevented me from going too close. I longed to brush away the flies, to pick up the baby and cradle it in my arms. I wanted to soothe it, to tell it everything was going to be all right. The thought of what it would inevitably grow up to was unbearable. Beneath the flies lay the most precious, the most beautiful, the most miraculous of all God's creation – silky brown skin, perfect little toes and fingers with their own unique set of prints. I fought with myself to shut out the horrors of my knowledge. I had heard of the mutilations that often took place in these slums, how families were sometimes forced deliberately to maim their children in a bid to capture more of the sympathies of western visitors who might bestow more pity on them than their fellow beggars because of an ill-fated child. It broke my heart and took all my might and reason to walk away, back to the marble-clad, cool grandeur of our hotel.

We'd been given good advice before our trip to India and instead of giving money we stuffed our pockets with sweets and, where possible, bought bread and ice-cream to give. A horde of white palms and dark sorrowful eyes would follow us around: 'please auntie, thank you, thank you auntie' was their perpetual cry. Never have I seen such gratitude for a tiny loaf or a small sweet as on the faces of these children. As we took a rickshaw tour around the city, people would shout and wave in recognition and our tormented hearts were warmed by the broad, toothy smiles coming out of the most squalid of conditions.

Scenes like that will never leave me. Nor should they. I do not regret our stay in Bombay one little bit and would urge anyone and everyone to pay a visit there or to any other of India's cities. For there one sees human existence at its most base and most bleak. In comparison, all problems, difficulties and pressures of the western world fade into insignificance; it is in such places that the warmth and resilience of humanity is at its most frayed and most desperately needed.

It would have been much easier to have taken some nice little package honeymoon and start our married life on a beach in a cheery Spanish resort. But Tim and I were long past being rosy-eyed teenagers. We had been given a wonderful second chance and we wanted to face it head on, tackling the demons of our past as we soaked up every moment that life had to offer. Why India? Well, it was Tim's birthplace, the land where his father died and, to an extent, where his legacy had haunted Tim all through his growing up. It was time to face the ghost. Tim had never been back there, so he was apprehensive, yet pleased when I suggested it might be a suitable honeymoon destination. We were starting our new life together and I wanted to share the experience of the return to this land and support him in any way I could.

We had very little planned or booked ahead, only the first two nights in Bombay – the city into which we flew – and an India-Rail pass that, at a very reasonable rate, could take us the length and breadth of the country. We first headed south to Kerala where we spent six nights by the Indian Ocean. It was glorious.

Then it was off to Vellore. On our way we had promised to drop in on one of Tim's mum's friends in North Kerala. Mary George was a lovely Christian woman who was doing great work there. She introduced us to a local orphanage where we were greeted heartily and the children put on a special show for us, their 'guests of honour'. In material terms, they had so very little, but there was an almost tangible sense of joy, love and Christian charity at its most sincere.

In Vellore we wanted to visit the medical missionary hospital where Tim was born. Again we were greeted by wonderful hospitality and were thrilled to see the amazing work that goes on there. We happened to drop in on graduation day when up to ninety, mostly Indian, students were preparing to leave and make their way back to their villages as qualified doctors and nurses.

From there we moved further north to Vijayawada, where Tim's parents had lived. It had been Tim's first home and his father was buried there. Far from the usual tourist trail, this peasant city is probably typical of many in rural India. The poverty is still abhorrent, but the people know little else and we were met with genuine fresh-faced smiles, beaming with curiosity and intrigue at the two mysterious foreigners.

We felt we knew a little of the place from Tim's mother's stories. She had also warned us of what we might find as we sought her husband's grave. Margaret had kept up some contact with old friends from the area and had made a return visit herself in 1976. In more recent years she had heard that the land where her beloved was buried was no longer owned by the church and was fearful of the state in which we might find the grave, if indeed it was to be found at all. It was hard to know where to start. All we could do was head for the Church of India compound and hope for the best.

It was a hot day. I could sense a certain tension in Tim as the cab driver drew up outside a large set of iron gates. I too, struggled with an over-dry mouth and tightness in my stomach. What would we find here, and how would Tim react if our trip proved futile? Had it been enough that we had made this pilgrimage and he had walked the same land as his father, or would the absence of his grave leave Tim more desolate than ever? The gates opened the way onto a courtyard, where crumbling architecture and marble betrayed fading splendour.

'This would have been quite some place,' I whispered to Tim, gripping his hand tightly. Why I whispered, I do not know, but there was something of a nervous reverence about the place. It appeared largely deserted, but I couldn't help feel that we were intruders, about to be caught red-handed. Tim was silent, but his eyes exhibited a strange glaze and beads of sweat clung to his brow.

Tentatively we headed towards what looked like a small office. The door was ajar and once inside we were met with a dusty, high-ceilinged room that might once have been a fine entrance hall leading out into a further compound. It was a relief to be momentarily out of the sun, but the place had a smell about it which added to our sobriety. The walls were bare, except for two large portraits. With just one glance I recognised the Jarvis face, smiling down from one of the frames. I turned to look at Tim. He stood, transfixed, looking up at the portrait. It was a familiar picture, present, in much smaller form, in Margaret's Cambridge drawing-room. Here, though, was the place of its origin and I prayed a silent prayer of thanks that we had at least found the right place. Time seemed to stand still, but the moment was broken by the imposing frame of an Indian man, babbling at us in Telegu, the language of the area. As we turned to face him, clearly showing our non-understanding of his barrage, he tried to speak in stuttered broken English. We could only surmise he was making enquiry as to our business there. We barely knew what to say, or how to express ourselves, but in a mixture of sign language – which largely featured Tim pointing at the portrait and then to his own face – and the most basic of utterances, we managed to communicate that the person in the picture was Paul Jarvis, his father. The man squinted into Tim's face and then in a rush of delight almost knocked him over in a bid to shake his hand. It was an emotional reunion as, in pidgin English, he told us that he used to baby-sit Tim from when he was newly born. He was beside himself with excitement and Tim and I were laughing together in a mixture of relief and joy as he led us through into the compound to the Bishop's house. Whatever appointments the Bishop had planned that afternoon seemed to be pushed aside as the people of the residence were so thrilled to welcome us. They treated us like royalty, fussing over us, recalling stories of Tim as a baby, and, of course, speaking with the utmost fondness and respect for his late father. It was a wonderful time, and there seemed to be an endless string of people wanting to meet us, all with varying degrees of English language. Still, among the smiles, laughter and storytelling we also noticed a certain whispering going on behind our backs. We didn't instantly realise what it was, but it soon dawned on us that the debate concerned how they might break the news that we would not be able to visit Tim's father's grave. They were trying to come up with some kind of excuse, but Tim silenced them gently, explaining that he had been warned about the problem with the land, and knew that the grave was likely to be far from its sanctified state in a proper graveyard. At this they were sorry, but we could detect the look of relief on many an official face. It wasn't their fault they suffered from lack of funding and that land was becoming increasingly precious to the ever-increasing population. We explained that we had to leave the next day and, being anxious at least to try to find the grave, we would be grateful for any direction they could offer.

One of the men offered to go with us, explaining that we stood little hope of finding it alone. Bidding emotional farewells to our hosts we climbed into another cab and headed down the road. On the way our host got the driver to stop at a little roadside stall and insisted on buying flower garlands for us. It was such a sweet gesture and throughout the journey he continually spoke of the honour in meeting the son of Paul Jarvis. Tim was clearly very touched by the whole episode, but became quiet and pensive again as we approached what was once a graveyard.

We would hardly have known it, except for the bits of broken walls that had now become the mainstays of a shanty town. Pieces of gravestones and broken monuments were used to lay out washing, or as supports for makeshift shelters. In the heat of the sun there was an acrid smell about the place as pigs and children ran and slept side by side and little fires cooked some semblance of a meal.

As we picked our way through the stones and people I had a sinking feeling inside. This was going to be difficult. How dreadful for Tim that this would be the lasting memory of his father's place of rest. I prayed silently to myself and knew that Tim would be doing the same. Within minutes we were surrounded by a crowd of people. Few of them would have seen a white person before and they were intrigued at the way we moved around, turning over rocks, brushing away the dust and reading gravestones. Our guide shouted at them in their native tongue to leave us alone, but they did not go far, observing us with curious eyes, mutterings and suppressed giggles. There was a lot of ground to cover and we might have despaired, except that I'm sure we felt something of a supernatural protection. We decided to split three ways to cover a greater area.

What happened next can be best described as something like a scene from a film. Within minutes our guide was frantically beckoning and shouting to us. We ran over, Tim reaching the site first. As he brushed aside more of the rubble and dust, he unearthed a perfectly intact plaque bearing his father's name. It suffered not a crack and Tim slowly traced his fingers over the names: 'Here lies Paul Jarvis, beloved husband of Margaret and father of Anne and Timothy.' At that Tim broke down. The crowd of people had gathered round again and Tim became painfully aware of their intrusion. 'Please,' he begged of our guide, 'just tell them to go away.' The man roared at the crowd and they scattered like ants. Then he retracted to a distance, leaving Tim and I alone at the grave.

It was a significant moment for us both. Tim and I were one, and I shared his grief. I think it was the first time that Tim felt his Dad was truly real. All those years he had lived in the shadow of his father's legacy – the photographs, the stories, his mother's memories and the celebratory homage of those who had known the great man. Now the two men almost communed together, father and son, in a last resting place. It was a most precious and sacred time. We stood in silence, we cried, we prayed, we took photographs and cried some more.

The next day we rose early. It was Sunday and the people at the compound had invited us to a seven o'clock church service. It suited us well and we considered it a fitting end to our visit to Vijayawada. Of course the service was completely in Telegu, but the small congregation were full of joy and praise and we were warmly welcomed there. Though we didn't understand a word, we were in fellowship with other believers, and it was easy to imagine Tim's father smiling down on us in the presence of those in whom he had a hand in bringing to the Lord. We received Communion and both silently recognised a further, very special bonding between the two of us.

The emotion did not end there. An overnight train took us to Hyderabad where we met with Doctor John, his wife and extended family. They had been very close friends of Tim's parents. They were living in a factory compound, where their son worked, and they'd made a special effort in laying out knives and forks for our meal. We would have happily followed the local custom of eating with our hands, but it was a sweet gesture and they showed us tremendous hospitality. We enjoyed a wonderful day with them, but spent most of it consoling poor Doctor John's wife who kept bursting into tears because she could see so much of her dear friend Paul Jarvis in Tim. When we left she presented me with a beautiful string of broken pearls which I will always treasure.

The next day we headed off back to Bombay where we spent our last two days reflecting on our journey. We were sorry to leave India. It is a land of extremes, of obscene poverty, yet uncompromising hospitality. Devastatingly sorrowful, yet vibrant with colour and exotic invocation, it is a place that has hijacked a little piece of my heart and we have vowed one day to return.

# Chapter 25

Professionally, I was on the brink of another new adventure. Over the last year, with Tim's encouragement, a seed – sown during the frustrating sessions of recording *Anam* – had been germinating within me. I began to toy with the possibility of doing a solo album and as we touched down on British soil I was keen to try out some of the ideas and music that had been spinning around in my head.

Before I had time to change my mind or suffer another confidence crisis, Dave, our manager, had mentioned the idea to Clannad's A & R man and in no time the record company had a contract on the table for me. All I had to do was sign. It was a nerve-racking time for me, but I couldn't pass up the offer. It was probably now or never.

In April I would go to Dublin for a week of rehearsals with Clannad before a short British tour. I was itching to get back on stage again, but I didn't relish the thought of being away from Tim. We were still very much in a dreamy world of newly wedded bliss, and there was something else occupying our minds. Though we tried not to get too hopeful, we were both harbouring a dream that I would become pregnant. I was conscious of my age and knew that at thirty-nine, with an abortion and a miscarriage on my record, I could only trust in God for the provision of a family. We tried to prepare ourselves for it not happening, but couldn't help our disappointment as January, February and March slipped by with no sign that I might have conceived.

'Well, there's no way it's going to happen this month,' I said to Tim, as I prepared to go off to Dublin and then Los Angeles where I had a meeting planned with a record company.

The American meeting went well and before I knew it I was back on tour in England. By this time our younger sister Brídín was touring with us. With Pól leaving, we needed another vocal in the band and it was easy to draw on the family resource. Being her godmother, I had a very close bond with Brídín and it was lovely to have this special time together. One day, with a little time out in Manchester, Brídín and I hit the shops.

'I just want to nip quickly in here,' I told her, and headed into the nearest chemist. Of course Brídín followed me in and squealed in delight when she saw me pick up a pregnancy-testing kit.

'Oh, Máire, are you? Wouldn't it be fantastic,' she enthused.

'No, no, Brídín, calm down. I'm certain I can't be, I just want to make sure.'

But Brídín's reaction fuelled the excitement in me. That put paid to the rest of the shopping trip and we could hardly wait to get back to the hotel room to do the test.

To my absolute astonishment, as we both sat hugging each other, a little blue line appeared, indicating that I was indeed pregnant. It took more than a few moments to get over the shock. I had convinced myself that it couldn't happen that month and had expected that the absence of my period was due to the travel and general business of preparing for the tour. Ironically, it seems, the moment I resigned myself to it not happening, and relaxed about the whole thing, nature took its course.

The next thing was a phone call to Tim. My hands shook with excitement as I dialled the number, but I was met with something of a vacuous pause at the other end of the line when I announced my news. Then he seemed kind of distant. It distressed me; I thought he wasn't pleased, but I realised afterwards that he was simply in as much shock as I had been. By first post the following day I received a beautiful card from him, thanking me for being his wife and telling me how proud and excited he was. It was difficult for him to get away because of his work, but a couple of days later he joined me for a short visit. We decided not to tell anyone. It was very early days, and with my past history I wanted to be sure that everything was safe before we broke the news. Still, this proved impossible. Brídín all but blurted it out immediately and we were beside ourselves with excitement. By the end of the week the whole Brennan family were in the know.

Mammy and Daddy were thrilled to hear the news. I wanted to tell them myself, and they shocked me with the return news that they'd also just received a call from my brother Pól, announcing that Christine was expecting their first child. So began a new generation of the Brennan clan.

Thankfully the tour was only scheduled to last two-and-a-half weeks and I was pleased to be able to settle back home and spend time with Tim. His work took him away on odd nights, so our time together in our home was always precious. One month into the pregnancy I had a small scare, and with the trauma of my days in Woodtown Manor fresh in my mind I went straight off to the hospital for a check-up. Thank God, they were able to reassure me that everything was all right and that the slight 'spotting' was nothing to worry about. They advised, however, because of the circumstances, that I go home and take serious rest. I knew how crucial the first few months are in pregnancy, so although I was bored almost to tears, I adhered to the doctor's instruction and spent many hours of the day in bed, breaking the tedium only with the odd strum on Tim's guitar and the jotting down of a few ideas for songs.

I was still trying to behave myself well into the third month of the pregnancy and one particular day, lying in bed alone in the flat, I was feeling desperately bored and sorry for myself. I hadn't told my mother about the scare because I didn't want to worry her. In all her pregnancies she had not experienced these kinds of symptoms and I knew she would fear a repeat miscarriage. Still, I longed to pick up the phone, just for a chat. Maybe I would give her a call, but first another trip to the bathroom.

I sat there, frozen, gripping the side of the bath, horrified by what confronted me. Red blood, and not just a little spotting.

The next few hours were spent hugging myself on the bed, sobbing my heart out. All the horror of my time in Woodtown came flooding back and I felt sure that I had lost my chance of ever carrying a baby. My whole body ached and I wailed like a hurt animal, longing for Tim to come home and at the same time dreading telling him the news. When he did eventually come through the door he did nothing for the first few minutes but hug me. There were no questions, he just held me in my distress and waited until I could compose myself enough to tell him what had happened.

Sitting in the car outside the hospital was excruciating. I was cold and numb. It seemed as though going through the doors would only serve to confirm the news that I didn't want to hear. To make matters worse, as Tim finally cajoled me out of the car, a young couple came out of the hospital, smiling with pride as they carefully placed a new bundle into a car cot for his trip home. Tim squeezed my hand tightly, ushering me past and into the warmth of the waiting room. I don't know what was going through his mind at that time. I clung to him, but at the same time was lost inside my head, resigned to my old feelings of failure.

The nurse ran the scanner over my stomach and listened carefully for any sign of a heartbeat. If she was anxious at my symptoms, she did not show it, and her softly spoken ease gave me a little comfort. 'Please, please, please make it all right.'

'Well, Máire, I'm happy to say that everything still seems to be fine. Baby is alive and well and probably wondering what all the fuss is about.'

Hit by a wave of relief and joy, Tim and I were left again to hug each other and thank God for his hand on our unborn baby.

Back home I occupied myself with ideas for the album. I was now under contract to the BMG record label for my solo project and knew that I would have to work quickly to get it together before my baby was born. I still wasn't confident that I could write a whole album myself, so I gathered together cassette after cassette of a wide variety of songs, most of them from Irish writers. Listening through them gave me something to do from the confines of my bed, but song after song passed by and little seemed to be suitable. In the end only one song stood out – 'Jealous Heart', by Christie Hennessy. I decided I'd like to use the song on the album, but otherwise resolved that I would have to put in the hard work of writing the rest of the repertoire myself.

Our flat had three bedrooms. One was used by Tim as a dark room, but after a little rearranging, we were able to set out my keyboards, a microphone, an amplifier, a couple of speakers and an eight-track machine in the spare 'box' room. It was inordinately primitive – I had worked in some of the best studios in the world – but I was as excited as a child with a new toy. Hours were spent – interspersed with plenty of rest, of course – laying down chords and writing chants that, in my head, I heard being sung by my sisters. I really wanted the girls to be involved on a couple of the songs. We had always sung well together and, with all the harmony work with Clannad being male voices, I imagined my sisters would provide a unique and distinctive direction.

By August, we were getting restless in the confines of the flat and Tim managed to organise enough leave from the *NME* to allow us to go over to Donegal. I was excited at the prospect of finally getting together with the girls to try out some of my ideas. With the car fully loaded with music gear, plus Tim's bike, we headed off to get the overnight boat. I'm sure, by now, you're expecting to hear of another disastrous journey, and yes, you'd be right. Not helped by general holiday traffic, it took us a good seven or eight hours to drive from London to Holyhead and, to our horror, the boat was absolutely packed. It felt as though the entire population of England and Wales were heading over to Ireland on that one boat. There was nowhere to sit, let alone lie down, and I was growing increasingly uncomfortable. I had a nagging ache in my lower back, and, as the shoreline faded into the distance, the pain became worse. I soon became desperate to lie down. It was noisy on the boat, with children crying and running around the decks, while the bar areas bulged with over-zealous holiday-makers, anxious to make the most of the duty-free liquor. An hour into the trip and the exhaustion of the journey and pain in my back got the better of me.

'It's no good,' I told Tim, 'I simply have to lie down.'

Tim was anxious and tried to clear us space so that I could lie on the floor. Protectively, he stood over me, as people pushed and shoved their way past. Meanwhile I felt increasingly ill. Though Tim wrapped me in his coat, I was freezing cold and the smell of stale beer, cigarettes and overused toilets filled my nostrils, adding to the general sickening motion of the boat. 'Please, just get me through this journey.'

I have never been so thankful to get to dry land. Instead of staying in Dublin, Tim was keen to drive the five hours to

Donegal. Finally, home was in sight, but even the thrill of seeing my family and the welcome of our little house could not distract me from the ever-increasing pain. Mammy's face tightened with worry when she saw the state I was in and I had a sleepless night, clutching a hot-water bottle and facing the fear that such pain could mean only one thing.

I can't imagine anyone ever being grateful for a kidney infection, but as the doctor examined me the next day he announced that a simple course of antibiotics and a few days' bed rest should see both me and my baby fit and healthy again. Yet again my fears were dispersed and as the doctor left I hummed a little melody of love to my baby, a lullaby that would become the song 'Oro'. I often found myself talking and singing to my growing bump; being pregnant seemed to open my eyes more to the world around me. I was acutely aware of nature, and especially the suffering that seemed to fill the television screen. The news became a strong focus of my attention. At the time it was full of stories of the Eastern Europeans fighting for greater freedom as the Communist state hung in the balance. Faces of hungry people fighting for justice and humanity struck a chord within me and I was intrigued at the way they found strength in each other when they united to stand against their oppressors. It inspired a song called 'Against the Wind'. More than ever I found myself enjoying the writing process, and the beauty of my homeland surroundings served as strong inspiration.

Getting the girls together was no mean feat. Olive was running my father's bar at the time and she couldn't join us until after work. As soon as she could get home, usually around half-past midnight, we would start working on vocal arrangements and recording. Our sessions rarely ended before the full flush of morning, but there were many laughs along the way and some very special work came out of it. I loved the way my sisters' voices blended together and soon realised that I wanted them to be an integral part of the album.

As the weeks went by the deadline loomed heavier than my growing middle and I knew that I needed to complete the basis of the recording before Christmas. I also knew that I would need a lot of help with the recording process and it was important for me to work with people whom I thought might understand where

I was coming from with my music. As far as I was concerned, the obvious man for the job was Donal Lunny. He had become something of a guru in Irish music and it was he who captured the early Clannad sound, producing our second album. At the same time I was a big fan of Calum Malcolm's work with Blue Nile. I went up to meet him and we clicked instantly. He had a wonderful new studio just outside Edinburgh. To my delight, both men were keen to work together and I thought it would be an interesting collaboration. They had never met each other before, but became good friends and have since worked together on a couple of other projects.

At the end of October I went up to Scotland to begin work. The surroundings were idyllic. Calum's studio was a converted school in a little village called Pencaitland and I stayed in a nearby hotel in North Berwick. Every day Calum would pick me up at eleven o'clock and we would work through until eleven at night, barely breaking for meals. It was hard, but I was having the time of my life. Calum and Donal seemed instinctively to know what was in my head and were brilliant to work with. For the first time, everything about the music was my decision and I was pushing myself to new limits. Tim came up as often as possible and we attended a local antenatal class. Once we had the basic instrumentation down, Olive, Brídín and Deirdre came over for a week. Layer after layer of harmony was laid down, and we had tremendous fun together. The hotel was in festive spirit and we got to know the staff, who treated us really well. I was the size of a house by then, and everyone was very attentive and wanted to know what we were up to. One day we were all exhausted with work and decided to take some time out to have a meal at the hotel. They were fully booked with office Christmas parties, but set up a little table at the back and served us extra-generous helpings of scrumptious Christmas fare. I have wonderful memories of that day. The comedian hosting the party was terribly rude and not at all funny, but my sisters and I were in such high spirits that everything around us seemed hilarious and we enjoyed a riotous afternoon in sisterly communion, eating far too much and generally making merry. Inside, my baby wriggled to the rhythm of my laughter and my heart was alight with joy.

Two weeks before Christmas, I returned to London with the recording complete. I was absolutely elated. We had worked hard and, for the first time in my life, I felt as though I had really achieved something, and realised how much my heart was in music. The project was left for Calum to complete the mixing in the New Year. Meanwhile I could concentrate on my next release – our baby.

So began what felt like an eternal waiting game. Tim kept his diary free from work and we packed a bag ready for the hospital. Days went by. My official due day came and went. On 13 January we heard the news that my sister-in-law Christine had given birth to a baby girl, Sara Kaya. Surely my time would come any day now. We waited, and we waited some more, and day by day I grew more uncomfortable. The pregnancy had given me licence to eat (so I believed) and I foolishly ate my fair share and probably enough for triplets. I would regularly consume whole tubs of Häagen-Dazs ice-cream just through boredom, so in the latter stages of the pregnancy I felt, and probably resembled, something akin to a whale. Sitting was uncomfortable, walking was more uncomfortable, and sleeping at night time was a complete non-event. The flats were noisy, but it never really bothered us. One evening we had an invitation from our neighbour downstairs to his wife's birthday party. We always got on well with Arty and his family, but the thought of a crammed, hot and noisy party was just a little too much in my condition, so Tim and I took ourselves off to see a late movie. On our return we were barely in sight of the flats when we heard the music. Loud reggae beats thumped out across the compound through a speaker system more fitting for the Albert Hall. The smell of West Indian food filled the air and the party only slowed down after six o'clock in the morning. Still, we didn't mind. The sounds of laughter and celebration only fuelled our excitement and we longed for some sign that I would begin the labour.

The next night followed our usual routine. We sat up watching a Jack Lemmon movie and by three o'clock I began to feel that I might be able to sleep. Setting the video to record the end of the film we finally went to bed. At five o'clock I awoke with serious cramping pain. This might be it. I don't know if many women feel the same, but I had a very real fear of going into hospital to find it was a false alarm. I didn't want to cope with the embarrassment or disappointment. Also, Tim had mentioned that if you take the car to the hospital you are allowed to park free of charge if you go in and have the baby. But if you're sent away as a false alarm you have to pay for the parking. The things you think of! The cramps were getting heavier and more frequent. But maybe it was a false alarm. I decided to have a bath and try to count the time between the contractions. Tim heard the commotion and eventually persuaded me to ring the hospital. The nurse didn't sound too sure when I told her what was going on, but when she heard I was already two weeks overdue she suggested that I make my way to the hospital.

By the time I got dressed and gathered my things together I was sure that the labour was starting. The contractions were getting more frequent and I was having to concentrate on my breathing exercises to control the pain. Tim gently eased me into the car, but by this time it was rush hour. The traffic was horrendous and I could see Tim's face was tight with tension as he battled his way towards St Thomas's. As we drove through Kennington and around The Oval the car hit a huge pot-hole, sending what felt like hammer-blow spasms right through my body. Yes, this baby was definitely on its way.

We got to the hospital. I could be brave no longer and was crying out for an epidural. In a way that turned out to be a mistake. It slowed down the contractions and they never reached the same level again, so at one o'clock in the afternoon my beautiful baby girl was born with the help of forceps – hardly the most comforting way to come into the world.

I cannot even attempt to put into words the joy of holding my baby. She was perfect in every way and we couldn't take our eyes off her beautiful little face and mop of dark hair. Another wonderful surprise was the midwife, whose little fish badge and familiar accent told us she too was a Christian from my homeland. She was really great and found us a little room where we could share a few hours' peace and get to know our new daughter. We still didn't really have any particular ideas for names so we continued to call her 'Precious', as she had been affectionately termed throughout the pregnancy.

Later in the day I was moved to a ward with other new mums.

It was a good place to be, with everyone sharing their experience and helping each other. But that night, while most of the other babies settled, my darling Precious just wouldn't stop crying. I kept her in the bed with me all night. There was no way I was going to let her go, so each time a nurse came around, I pretended I was breastfeeding her, so that I wouldn't be told to put her back in the cot. All night I soothed her, talking and singing lullabies, but when Tim and my brothers Leon and Bartley arrived the next morning I was almost delirious with lack of sleep. It was wonderful to see some of the family so soon. Both brothers were working in London at that time, but I think they got a nasty shock when they saw the state of me that day. It had been days since I had slept properly, and it was lovely when Tim's mum came down in the afternoon and took the baby for a little wander so that I could get some rest. The second night both Precious and I slept heavily and the next day I felt completely revived. It was wonderful. Tim and I were closer than ever, but there was one person I was desperate to see. I had just become a mother and the person I wanted to be with most – next to Tim – was my own mum. She had been through this nine times and I wanted to fling my arms around her and thank her for the life she had given me. Now I understood how, no matter what I put my mother through, I would always be her baby.

A couple of days later I got my wish. Tim and I were just leaving the ward with our new charge when who should come walking through the doors but Daddy and Mammy. It was an intensely emotional moment. We just held each other and cried with joy. No words were necessary.

So began our family life. My parents stayed with us a few days, so the baby slept with Tim and I on the pull-out bed in the sitting-room while we insisted Mammy and Daddy had the bedroom. It was cramped and not very comfortable, but we simply didn't care. Nothing in the world could have made me any happier.

Everyone was fascinated by my baby's full head of hair. Unlike most babies, Precious had thick, dark locks and Mammy said she looked exactly like me when I was born. To Tim and me, she was the most beautiful-looking baby ever and we wandered around in a starry-eyed glow, not caring about anything else going on around us. Meanwhile I think people were beginning to wonder if we would ever give our child a proper name. I liked 'Aisling', pronounced Ashleen. I realised that, as with my own name, people would always struggle to know how to pronounce it, but we both liked the idea of christening our baby with an Irish name. The name means 'a dream' or 'vision' and she was certainly that for us. Much to the approval of the new grandparents we announced that our baby would be called Aisling Ann Precious. It was perfect.

# Chapter 26

Aisling Jarvis was born on 21 January 1992 and by the end of the month my record company were anxious that I take my album to the next stage. I had given Calum the go-ahead for the final mix in the few days before Aisling was born and BMG seemed happy with the result. The next thing was photography and, the thing I dreaded most, a video.

There ensued a very depressing session in front of the mirror. Nothing fitted me except my dreadful maternity clothes and breastfeeding was only making matters worse. Thankfully the record company were happy for Tim to submit some shots, so he set up some pictures with me and my sisters. It was a riot having them over and it helped me stay relaxed and happy. We couldn't resist taking pictures of Aisling so we could share the joy of our new arrival with our family and friends. One of them turned out to be a beautiful, very natural and spontaneous picture as Aisling, in my arms, turned towards me. I expressed my wishes for it to be included on the back cover of the album to complement the song 'Oro', the lullaby dedicated to Aisling. A few days later the record company called to say how much they loved that photograph and asked if I would consider it for the main cover shot. Of course we were delighted.

It was decision-time again. The release of the album meant lots of promotional work and Atlantic records had committed to promoting it in America. I was breastfeeding Aisling and needed her with me. We looked at the possibility of hiring a nanny. Then, after much contemplation, we agreed that Tim would put his work on hold in order to travel with me. It was a big decision, but it meant so much to us to be able to be together as a family, and Tim was such an encouragement to me. Aisling was a wonderful baby. I vividly remember making the video for 'Against the Wind'. It was in a studio in London and there was dry ice and dancers everywhere. Music blared out over the speaker system, but Aisling slept peacefully through the whole event, only stirring for the occasional feed.

Before she was a year old, Aisling had travelled forty or so times to Europe and America. We have pictures of her at seven months at the top of the Empire State Building in New York. I was working hard, but having Tim and our baby with me was my joy.

I also used the opportunity of time in America to promote the Clannad album *Anam*. It had not yet been released in the States, but around the same time we had also been approached by a film company over there who wanted to use the 'Theme From Harry's Game' in a new movie, *Patriot Games*. The film was highly successful and the record company suggested putting 'Harry's Game' on the *Anam* album and releasing it to the American market. The timing was perfect.

It certainly turned out that 1992 was to be a big year for us – releasing a solo album, giving birth to Aisling and moving our home to Dublin.

Early in the year Tim and I had begun to wonder about whether we should consider moving over to Ireland. We had been happy in the flat, but couldn't afford a larger house in London and imagined that Ireland would be a nicer place to raise our family. For me it was home, but I didn't want to push Tim into anything. We resolved that we would move over to Dublin temporarily to see whether we might settle there. We had just three days free over the Easter period to find somewhere to live. On the very last day we found a house that we instantly and instinctively knew would become our home. It was a beautiful Georgian house near the canal and the landlady lived next door. She was about my age, and, like me, had started her family later on in life. In the two years that we lived there we became close friends and I was thrilled at how easily Tim settled. His family love Ireland and made many visits. Within a short time we knew that we wanted to make Dublin our permanent home.

One of the most important things for us was finding a church.

Churches in Ireland can be so tied up with 'being Catholic' or 'being Protestant', and we were keen to find somewhere we could feel comfortable and worship without any of the denominational trappings. Through friends we heard of a church called St Mark's and one Sunday we decided to make a visit. We arrived early and as we stood in the corridor we could hear the worship band rehearsing. As we stood, hesitating as to what point we should go in, a woman came out of the ladies' cloakroom. To my absolute shock and delight I recognised her as Pauline Ryan, my school friend from the Ursuline Convent. We had lost touch and it had been almost twenty years since I had last seen her. She was so excited to see me; her eyes filled with tears as she told me how she had followed my career and often prayed for me over the years. Now here I was, walking into the church where she – now called Pauline Bradshaw – and her family worshipped. It was like a confirmation that this was to be our spiritual home.

Pauline and her husband Peter became great friends and also helped me resolve a spiritual issue that was beginning to prey on my mind. For some time it had intrigued me that, despite our dedication and the support from our record company, Clannad had never quite enjoyed the exposure or acclaim that was expected. We always seemed to go so far, and then it was as though something was blocking our path to the next level. Throughout that summer, both at home and abroad, I seemed to find myself in meetings or reading books that carried a theme – that of the reality of the power of a curse. It was something that I had always shunned. It was never an issue in my Catholic upbringing but, now with my revived and very real faith in God, I kept wondering about it. Down through the years I knew there had been strong ill-feeling and jealousy towards the band. Could it be that something like this had engaged some kind of dark spiritual power? When I tentatively shared my thoughts with Tim he suggested it was something we should seek advice on.

I was still feeling embarrassed and a little unsure when we gathered together with Pauline, Peter and a couple of other elders in the church. Yet, the feeling that I might have hit on some kind of truth was growing stronger within me. We began to pray together, asking God to release me, my family and the band from anything that might be binding our lives, whether it be an actual curse, or simply ill-feeling or envy. I began to feel an overwhelming sense of peace, and a feeling that we were doing the right thing. Previously, I assumed that when I chose to walk with the Lord he had automatically cleared my life of any kind of binding and the rubbish of my past. But now I began to understand something of the freedom we have in Jesus. I have little knowledge of theology but I began to realise that God has the power to move in our lives, but does not take over our free will. He wants good things for our lives but needs us to come to him out of free choice. Sometimes we simply have to voice our concerns and ask in a very specific manner. It taught me a lot about prayer.

Soon after that, certain amazing things began to happen. Many remain personal to the family, but I am delighted to share the way that Clannad, after more than twenty years together, suddenly began to take off. By Christmas, the 'Theme from Harry's Game' was filling the airwaves of America. It had been used on a Volkswagen advert and the ad agency found their lines alight with queries regarding the music. In the end they even had to set up a dedicated hotline telling people who the band were and where they could get a recording of the song. It completely exploded; we were in huge demand to do the rounds of promotion and all the major US chat shows. Walking down Sunset Boulevard we were met with a huge billboard of a car with a 'Clannad' number plate. The funny thing was the kind of questions we were being asked in interviews. Although we'd toured in America several times over the years, we were largely unknown. People had no idea that 'Harry's Game' was actually eleven years old and frequently asked us if we were influenced by Enya. They hadn't realised she was our younger sister and had started her career with Clannad.

As the promotion wagon rolled with both *Anam* and my solo album I came under a certain pressure to change my name. Eithne had done this early in her solo career, changing the spelling from its original Eithne to the phonetic spelling, 'Enya'. In the same way, the record company wanted me to become 'Moya'. It was a suggestion I turned down. My identity was very much Máire Ni Bhraonáin, although I had happily anglicised my surname years before, to save too much difficulty.

The end of a whirlwind year found Clannad back in the studio recording our next album, *Banba*. In the meantime we'd also been asked to write a track for a movie, *The Last of the Mohicans*, which we included on the *Banba* album. Things were going great and the album was due for release in the early summer of 1993. It was decided that I would go over to the States to do some promotion, in preparation for a major tour in September. The success of 'Harry's Game' gave us household name status in America and I was thoroughly looking forward to being back there. However, a delightful hitch came our way. Tim and I would have loved a large family, but were very conscious of my age. Still, we threw caution to the wind and secretly hoped that it might happen one more time.

To our sheer joy in January of that year I fell pregnant with our son Paul.

Everyone was delighted for us, but of course, it had serious repercussions for our plans. Our US tour was scheduled for September, but Paul was due to be born in October. At this time there was a lot at stake. I'm sure there were some disgruntled words behind record company closed doors, but I didn't care. The boys were thrilled for me, and we've always made it a precedent that 'family' comes first. The tour was brought forward to begin in April and we worked right through to the end of July. Thankfully it was a wonderful pregnancy. This time I was careful about what I ate and really looked after myself. I felt great, and had to keep reminding myself I was actually pregnant. I did as much as possible, up until the last time I could fly when we made a fleeting trip back to do America's Jay Leno show.

Back on Irish soil I was still full of beans, with a couple of months to go before the birth, so I involved myself in a few other projects, including a fashion show for a charity called Cradle. They were raising money for children in Bosnia and among all the waif-like models I waddled down the catwalk with Aisling holding my hand and my growing bump in front of me.

Our son, Paul Leo Jarvis, was born on 6 October 1993 at Holles Street Maternity Hospital, Dublin – the very same place where I was brought into the world. In many ways it was a perfect birth, all over with very quickly. I had gone into hospital late the night before, but when everything seemed to calm down

Tim was sent home with the assurance that he would be telephoned as soon as anything started to happen. In the morning when my waters broke I found myself being pushed on a trolley into the delivery room yelling at the nurses to phone my husband – there was no way I was going to let him miss it. From then on everything seemed to happen in slow motion. The pains got stronger and stronger and I desperately wanted to push, but there was still no sign of Tim. The hospital was frantically busy. Dublin is just that kind of place. There are three dedicated maternity hospitals in the city, but that day, as many others, there were babies being born in corridors. I was one of the lucky ones who got a delivery suite.

'He's here, he's here, Máire. Just hang on now.' The nurse was waving frantically at Tim to hurry down the corridor. To my great relief he burst into the room, breathless with running.

'You'd better take that sweater off,' I remember saying to him, 'this is going to be quick.' Three more contractions and Tim was holding our son in his arms and cutting the umbilical chord. We were in bits. A son. A beautiful, perfect son.

The staff at the hospital were wonderful and brought a telephone into the room so that we could ring our parents. Tim phoned Gweedore and I could hear Daddy shouting to everyone else in the house: 'It's a boy, Máire's had a baby boy!' Then Tim handed the phone over to me as I cradled Paul in my arms.

'Hello Daddy,' I said. There was a moment's pause.

'Who's this?' came my father's hesitant voice.

'It's me Daddy, Máire.'

Another pause, then he shouted, 'Baba, come quickly, it's Máire on the phone and she's just had the baby.'

It was a strange and delightful experience. Somehow Daddy couldn't grasp that I could be speaking to him from the delivery suite. Times had certainly changed since he had anxiously paced the corridors of a maternity hospital, barely allowed near his wife and child until they were presentable.

A couple of days later Tim arrived at the hospital with the Moses basket my parents had bought for Aisling. I enjoyed a lovely, restful stay, but I couldn't wait to go home. I couldn't believe my eyes when we got outside the hospital entrance. Tim had hired a limousine to take us home and when we drew up outside the house, there was Brídín and my friend Carol with Aisling waiting to welcome us. She was all dressed up and gave me the most beautiful smile as I ran to her, with Paul still in my arms. My heart melted. Our family was complete.

Some of the best songs written come out of tragedy and heartbreak, but in my case it has been my joy that has fed my creativity. In early 1994 I started to work towards my second solo album, *Misty Eyed Adventures*. The title track was written for Paul and I included a song inspired by the relationship and love Tim and I have found together. The song 'Mighty One' was inspired after I had been watching a documentary about the first Irish man to conquer Everest. The mountain was often referred to as 'the mighty one', but by the time the chorus of the song was put together it was very much from my own heart, singing out in praise to the true Mighty One.

Again I wanted Calum Malcom and Donal Lunny to record the album with me, so in April, with our little family, we went back up to Calum's studio in Scotland. Life at that time was busy enough, but by then we had decided that we definitely wanted to make Dublin our home and had set about looking for a house to buy. Only two days before heading off to Scotland we had our offer accepted on a beautiful Victorian house in Dun Laoghaire, county Dublin. The house had been on the market for over a year and was in need of renovation, but it stood tall and proud, looking out over the sea, and we fell in love with it instantly. As we walked around the cold rooms I imagined what it would be like as our family home.

Recording *Misty Eyed Adventures* was a thoroughly enjoyable experience. I rose at seven each morning so I could spend a couple of hours with Aisling and Paul before going to the studio. Then during the day Tim would bring them over to see me in my lunch break and we'd go to the playground opposite the studio or take a wander down to the beautiful nearby beaches. I always found it hard to leave them and go back to work until the late hours.

We spent most of May and June up there and I was thrilled with the final result. For me, it celebrated a breadth of influence and was very much a family piece. Tim had co-written several of the songs and my sister Deirdre had contributed a track. I'd also included a song I had recorded with Davy Spillane and a cover version of Joni Mitchell's 'Big Yellow Taxi' with Blue Nile. My record label, BMG, had been very encouraging about the project and released it in October 1994, but I couldn't help feeling that very little was done to promote the record. Then, to my utter disbelief, 'Big Yellow Taxi' was all over the airwaves – a single by Amy Grant. Who would have believed another artist would have recorded the very same song at the same time? Amy's version enjoyed massive promotion and was a hit both sides of the Atlantic. As the weeks went by I realised that my album was being lost in the usual Christmas compilation rush and by January it seemed that BMG had all but dropped the project. Then came the news that they were releasing me from my contract and wouldn't be considering me for any future solo projects. It was like a bolt from the blue and I was bitterly disappointed. It was a good album, I knew that, and I was more confident in my own musical ability than ever before. It had taken courage and energy to step out as a solo artist and fortunately I was mature enough by then to recognise my own worth. I consoled myself in the knowledge that I had been in the music industry long enough to realise what a fickle beast it can be.

My disappointment was eased when within a few days of being dropped by BMG I was asked to do a song for the movie *Circle of Friends*. It was a duet with Shane McGowan, produced by Trevor Horn, and when the call came through it required me to get on a plane to England the very next day to start recording. It turned out to be a wonderful song that everyone agreed should be released as a single. Again, however, it suffered a certain lack of backing. There was a lot going on at the time in terms of record company and management politics and an amount of bitterness from certain individuals towards this collaboration for one reason or another. Needless to say, a great song was lost.

In buying the house I had been forced to investigate my financial business and had employed a reputable music business accountant, O. J. Killkenny. Serious losses were brought to light and after all the years of touring and selling albums I had very little to show for it in terms of personal financial reward. It made me stop and take stock of my career. It was at this time I took the opportunity to release myself as a solo artist from Clannad's manager, Dave Kavanagh. At that time I had little idea where my music was heading, but I knew that whatever happened I wanted to be more in control.

The following year the boys also came to the same decision and finally separated Clannad from Dave's management. Meanwhile, we were at the point of releasing a new album, *Lore*. With my new writing experience I threw myself into its making and when it was eventually released in March 1996 we were all thrilled with the result and looking forward to taking it on the road.

*Lore* received fantastic reviews and took us on a grand-scale British tour. By then I was taking on some of the band management duties myself, sharing the load with Shane McDonnell, the brother of our tour manager, Phil. (Shane later went on to manage Clannad full-time.) Tim brought the children out to see me in London at the Royal Albert Hall. By that time Aisling was four years old and not very subtle in her regular announcements across the auditorium of 'That's my Mummy'. Tim apparently became so embarrassed that he practised all sorts of distraction tactics – including getting her to suck ice cubes – during the quiet lulls between songs. It was so special to have them with me for a week. I loved touring but it was always hard to leave them. I was just so thankful for Tim's full-time commitment. One day, while on the tour, Paul developed a nasty cough and I was up all through the night trying to comfort him. The next day was horrible. I still had dates left to do in England and the sound of Paul's racking little body filled my ears long after I kissed my little family goodbye and waved them off on the flight back to Dublin. The day's rehearsals and sound-check seemed longer than ever and I was anxious to hear from Tim later that evening. To my horror, Tim told me that Paul's cough had grown more disturbing and he had finally taken him to the doctor. From there he was sent for an X-ray at the hospital where it was announced my precious little boy was suffering with pneumonia. He was only two years old and I was beside myself with worry. There I was on tour, hundreds of miles away, and my little boy needed me. My mind was a fury of distressed despair as I pictured him all alone in a huge hospital bed. Thankfully moments of reason did break through and I clung to the comfort of knowing that he was being well cared for, and the hospital had allowed Tim to stay with him. In actual fact we were well provided for. We had taken on a local young woman, Margaret Deveraux, to help look after Aisling and Paul so that Tim could get on with some of the heavy-duty DIY that the house needed. Margaret is wonderful with the children and at that time especially I was relieved to know that Aisling was being well cared for while her Daddy was at the hospital with her brother. The worst thing for me was not being there. I was committed to two more concerts, then there was a free day in the tour schedule and I was able to get a flight out from Leeds.

My heart ached to see Paul and I spent all day at his bedside. Tim brought Aisling in and I savoured every single minute with them. That night I slept at the hospital, cuddling Paul through each passing hour and dreading the morning. Leaving my children then was the hardest thing I had had to do for the sake of Clannad. If I had not been so assured by the doctors that Paul was on the mend and was in such good hands I would have been willing to jeopardise the tour, but I was persuaded that my only option was to go back and do my job. It was difficult as the taxi pulled away and I could see Tim holding Aisling and Paul up to the window to wave goodbye. Tears rolled down my cheeks and I stared back through the misted screen until the hospital was well and truly out of sight.

A couple of days later Clannad were heading out to Holland. By that time Paul was at home with Tim and Aisling, but I knew that something was going on with my own health. My throat burnt and my voice was very inconsistent. I must have picked up some virus in the hospital. Everyone was worried; the press interviews were cancelled and I lay resting, eating garlic and gargling with cider vinegar. I did the shows, but I was extremely nervous – not the usual pre-show tingle of anticipation, but a very real fear in recognition that I was not in full control of my voice.

Several days later I was well on the road to recovery and thrilled to be heading back to Tim and the children. Home never felt so good and I was determined to have time out with the family. It was at that time we established one of our favourite family pursuits. We bought a big tent and took ourselves off down the coast of Ireland. No telephone, no recording studio, no press, no record company calls, just me, Tim, Aisling, Paul and our freedom. It was truly wonderful, even when it rained. Playing Scrabble by torch light with the gentle purring of sleeping children can be more romantic than any weekend in a top Paris hotel. We cherished every thankful moment of our harmonious, wellington-boot-clad, well-deserved break.

# *Chapter 27*

One of the most amazing things about life is that you never know what's around the next corner. In many ways my life was complete, happy and fulfilled. I had a wonderful family, I had my career with Clannad and I was enjoying church life at St Mark's. One day my dear friend Ann Trainor, who leads one of the worship teams at the church, invited me to sing a Gaelic Psalm for the morning service. By that time we had been attending St Mark's for three years and I had valued the fact that I had been welcomed and accepted into the church as just a member of the congregation, rather than as 'Máire Brennan of Clannad'. We had many friends at the church with whom I could relax and share my everyday experiences the same as any mother, wife or struggling Christian. So when Ann invited me to sing I saw it as a lovely opportunity and gradually found myself becoming a regular member of the worship team. When Ann discovered that Tim played the cello when he was younger she eventually coaxed him into the team as well.

There was the odd occasion when someone might make a comment about me making a Christian album, but the idea had no appeal whatsoever. In fact, I'd go so far as to say I hated the thought of it. Years before, I'd seen some so-called 'contemporary Christian music' on American TV shows and the whole thing made me cringe. I have always been uneasy about the perception people have of performers, as if you're somehow better than anyone else because you're on stage or your name is in lights. In church circumstances the same can apply. It wasn't easy for me to stand up as part of the worship team. My fear was – and to this day remains – that people somehow imagine you are a more holy person, or you have your faith all worked out and are more worthy than others. They don't always understand that you suffer the same insecurity as everyone else. I grew to love singing in church again, but as far as I was concerned, I was a musician who happened to be a Christian and not a 'Christian musician'. I felt at peace with the whole issue.

Then one day I came across a band called Iona whose music was billed as 'Celtic Christian' and something about it intrigued me enough to go along to the Dublin gig of their tour. I really enjoyed it and after the show got talking to their singer, Joanne Hogg. I discovered the band were Clannad fans and she asked whether I would be prepared to help out with a Gaelic song they were recording for their next album. I was more than happy to go along to the studio and even ended up doing a little vocal work and harp playing. It was lovely working with them, but I found myself almost shy and embarrassed to admit to other people that I was involved in a 'Christian album'.

As 1996 progressed, life was busy with Clannad. We continued to tour with the *Lore* album, but thankfully there were enough breaks in the schedule to be able to get home on a regular basis.

One Sunday morning in church, after the service, I was chatting to our pastor over a cup of tea.

'Well, y'know Máire, we've got to get you doing a Christian album one of these days,' he said with a half wink. I glanced at Tim, who I knew would recognise my look of resignation. Couldn't people understand what I was about? Pastor Gary had always been very supportive and accepting of my work. I really thought he knew where I was coming from, so I couldn't help but be slightly niggled at his suggestion that day. Funny, though, how God works in mysterious ways. Looking back now it was almost as though my pastor had a prophetic hotline! I didn't want to think about it at the time, but the longer I live the more I am beginning to understand that there is a time and season for everything. The only thing I would admit to myself back then was that I was beginning to get itchy feet to rediscover my solo career – I had no idea what change of heart really lay ahead.

One day Phil McDonnell, a long-standing friend of the band, came for a visit. He got chatting with my brother Leon about various bands and managers and talked about a guy, Peter

Carson, in America whom he had worked with for years.

'He was a musician himself, seems to know the business, and has done a bit of producing and management,' I heard him say.

'He sounds like someone I would like to meet,' I said, taking more notice of their conversation.

'Yeah, maybe,' said Phil, 'I know he's a big fan of your voice. I could give him a call if you like.'

Within a week I had chatted on the phone to this Peter Carson. I was impressed by his track record in band and artist management and he seemed very interested to talk further with me, no strings attached. I was due to head off on the next leg of the world tour, taking in Australia, New Zealand and Japan, but before I left, Peter arranged to fly over from his home in St Louis to meet me in Dublin.

We had a good couple of days together, talking about my career and listening to my solo albums and I appreciated in him what seemed to be a very genuine love of my work. If things were going to progress any further it was important to me that he should also spend some time with Tim, so on our second evening we took him to one of our favourite local restaurants where we could all relax and enjoy getting to know one another better. I was also careful casually to mention the faith Tim and I shared. We didn't need to make a big deal out of it, but from the beginning I wanted him to realise that there might be certain work that I would not be comfortable with. Peter had no problem with that. The conversation progressed, then at one point he took us by surprise.

'Máire, have you ever thought of doing a Christian album?'

There it was again, the same question, but this time it was as if something inside had clicked. Tim and I just looked at each other. I spoke to Peter about my reservations, but as we talked I knew that I was somehow becoming a little more interested in the idea.

We said our goodbyes to Peter with a good feeling in our hearts, agreeing that he would explore a few possibilities in the Christian music world on my behalf. Maybe he was going to become more involved in our lives.

Six weeks in the southern hemisphere left me pining for my family and as we flew back from Japan I could think of nothing other than getting home to Tim and my precious Aisling and Paul. Despite the difficult time differences, there had been plenty of telephone chats (I always try to speak to Tim and the children before they go to bed, no matter where I am in the world), but we avoided in-depth conversations about business; so although Tim had mentioned that Peter had been in touch with him in my absence I was yet to hear the detail of their discourse.

As it turned out, Peter had arranged a meeting with Word Records Nashville – one of the leading record companies in the 'Christian market'. Seemingly, a couple of the executives were fans of Clannad, and were intrigued to meet me but were uncertain of my potential as an artist for them because of my apparent 'New Age' association. In many ways it didn't surprise me. I knew that Clannad were very much seen as a 'New Age' band, simply because of our style of music. Often people assume a certain 'spirituality' in our music – probably just because of its ethereal styling – and over the years I have frequently been asked by fans about my interest in paganism, druids and the like. Such things really annoyed me and it is perhaps this that ultimately encouraged me to discover more about my Irish Christian faith through my music. Strangely enough it was something I had found myself contemplating more and more on the *Lore* tour. I was intrigued that simply because Clannad drew inspiration from the heritage and folklore of Ireland, it was assumed that we nailed our spiritual colours to the New Age mast. Yet even from my school history lessons I could remember learning of St Patrick, Ireland's greatest missionary, who brought Christianity to Ireland way back in AD432, and of the many great people who were encouraged to follow on this path. Indeed, at a time when the 'Dark Ages' spread across Europe, Ireland was flourishing both academically and spiritually and thus earned its reputation as the 'Land of Saints and Scholars'. There are so many wonderful stories about the men and women who lived a life of deep Christian faith from around the four corners of Ireland. Such legacies should not be forgotten.

I had often sensed, during my twenty years or more of singing, a fascination with how the Irish had gone through so much pain and been subjected to so much tragedy, yet still had songs which displayed a sense of encouragement and were never dark. But I have recently become perplexed as to how we Irish have managed to mix up our ancient, Celtic mythical legends with the more recent traditional culture of the last four hundred years. In doing so we have also blurred the distinctions between our pagan heritage and that which is firmly based on the cross. We shouldn't be ashamed of our spiritual heritage or try to disguise it all as folklore and mythology. In looking at the traditions and cultural influences of the last few hundred years I have discovered how real and important Christian faith was to our recent ancestors, giving them a strength which they carried with them into the communities wherever they were. It played a vital role in their lives and I feel passionately that we should never lose that faith and should always regard it as a cornerstone of our Irishness.

My interest in the history of the early Irish Christians was stoked further when I met a guy called Gordon Moore during our tour date in Brisbane. He was a very well-respected pastor who I knew had visited Ireland several times, and I was thrilled to get the opportunity to meet him in his homeland. We spoke for hours and as he shared his knowledge and vision for what he called 'Celtic Christianity' I realised that he was helping me to set my heart and inspiration towards what was becoming a very real – and, I believe, God-given – calling. I resolved to explore this further on my return home and soon immersed myself in books on the early Celtic Church and the new wave of Celtic spirituality that seemed to be capturing the imagination of many people in the late 1990s.

Several weeks later Peter Carson had arranged for two of the American executives from the Word label to come out and see me at a couple of Clannad shows in Holland. They were great gigs that they seemed to enjoy. I was honest and open with them regarding my concerns at being labelled a 'Christian artist', but by that time had a firm concept in my head that my next solo effort would be a 'Celtic Christian' record. I could tell that this was something a little beyond the realm of the Nashville scene, but my two new friends were at least graciously interested and we agreed to pursue the idea further.

At the beginning of 1997 I got together with a producer, Denis Woods – who had worked on several Clannad albums – and began writing songs. Was this a step of faith? Everything seemed so right and my passion was growing for the project. By August I had signed the contract with Word but it appeared that I was faced with some obstacles. My deadline was 12 December and at the same time Clannad were working on the next album, *Landmarks*. Practical things got in the way. I was using some of the band's recording equipment, yet it was needed up in the house we had rented to record with Clannad. I found myself struggling to split my time between the two projects and in a complete panic about what to do. Then one Sunday morning in church a woman stood up at the front and told us that she felt God had given her a message she must share. As she spoke I knew instantly that the message was for me. She talked about how it is important to trust in him and to accept his perfect time for everything, rather than trying to make things work out in our own strength. It was as if a great weight had been lifted from me and I knew that my solo project would be by his hand.

I went home and later worked on a song called 'Perfect Time', not knowing then that this would become the foundation stone for the whole album. When I look back over my life I see so many times when I was nudged in the right direction and the right doors opened for me. Over the years I have become very aware that no matter how much things bewilder me or are beyond my understanding, along the road they eventually become clear. That's the essence and beauty of faith – not knowing what is around the corner, and yet being able to trust that because your life is in the hands of the Man Above, nothing is beyond you.

Clannad's *Landmarks* album was completed at the beginning of December, and sure enough, I met my deadline for *Perfect Time*. It was released the following spring. Here were two projects of which I was very proud, that came together under seemingly impossible circumstances. Like our two previous Clannad albums – *Banba* and *Lore* – *Landmarks* was nominated for and won a Grammy in the 'Best New Age Album' category. I never felt particularly comfortable about being in this category for reasons I have already mentioned but the irony really struck home to me when I found *Perfect Time* having a far more visible impact in the New Age charts than in the contemporary Christian equivalent.

*Perfect Time* opened up a whole new realm for me and I spent much of 1998 travelling, especially to America, promoting the album. I made many new friends who had loved Clannad and were now appreciating the transcendent calm of my new project. More and more I found myself talking about my faith and the Catholic roots that I still hold precious. Yet, even among the Christian community, I often detected a certain intolerance of Catholicism. Indeed within the Protestant Church I became very aware of the disparity and lack of respect between different denominations. Coming from Ireland, and seeing the misery caused by such factions, I am ashamed that such obvious bigotry still exists among those who profess to love and serve the Lord. Is there any wonder that the outside world looks at the Church with a certain disdain? The impression so often is of a body of people who wallow in self-reflection and are bound by guilt and rules. Yet the reality of Christianity is that Jesus Christ, the man from Nazareth, blew away the rules and regulations and replaced them with love – a love that does not condemn and judge, but breaks down barriers and unites people in what is far more important than rules about being a 'good person'.

Thankfully this is the heart of some people I have met around the world. Towards the end of 1999 I found myself performing at a Presbyterian church in the Loyalist stronghold of East Belfast. I had to double-check that the pastor knew what he had set up. There I was, with my band, our traditional Irish instruments and Gaelic songs in a place that traditionally has had no tolerance for the things of Irish culture. And yet that night the church was alive and electric with joy as I performed in concert. It is in arenas such as this where the seeds of unity are beginning to flourish. As the politicians struggle to bring peace to Ireland, the people of God – from all backgrounds, denominations, classes and walks of life – are seeing their prayers answered, and I cannot help but remember the conviction I had all those years ago in Christchurch. Once again, he is working out his perfect time in my life and I am honoured and privileged beyond words to be able to play a small part in uniting God's people in my music.

# *Afterword*

My grandfather was a great storyteller. As a girl I loved to sit on his knee while he filled my head with legends and fables, rhymes and allegories. In my dreams I chased the rainbow, ran with rogues and danced with leprechauns. There were stories of wise men and fools, the broken and the brave, the shipwrecked and the saved. Some have faded, but many remain, bringing smiles, sometimes tears, and often a certain wisdom that fuels the fires of perseverance and hope in troubled times.

Many lifetimes ago a fugitive lay in hiding on a remote island off the north Irish coast. Downtrodden, defeated and hopeless, the sanctuary of a cave encased this heavy heart and almost broken spirit. Little light broke through the cold grey stone, where no human soul should ever rest, but one day Robert's heart was strangely warmed as a spider sought to make its home. More than once it fell, and yet again, it rose, fighting against the odds, persevering in the storm, patiently weaving and threading . . . falling and getting up again, falling and getting up again, falling and getting up again . . . until finally the victorious web was spun.

Gog loved to tell the story of Robert the Bruce. The history books testify to the valour of this king who, with renewed courage to go on, overcame his fear and went forth to win the battle against his oppressors. It's a story that speaks in triumph of the Celtic spirit and I guess that through it, Gog hoped to plant the seeds of perseverance, patience and hope amid adversity, in the children he loved.

This is my own story, an adventure that is still being lived. My concern throughout has been to portray this tale with honesty

267

and dignity, recognising myself as the catalyst for my own downfall, and ever seeking the forgiveness of those I have hurt along the way. Far from looking back with regret I set my eyes forward with firm roots, proud of my 'Irishness'; thankful for my upbringing in the Catholic Church; and ever grateful for those who preserved the songs and arts of my heritage – without whom and which the Clan As Dore would never have got out of the Donegal kitchen.

During the writing of this book I have completed my second solo album, largely inspired through the faith that lives within me – that same spirit who motivated the hearts of Ireland's great saints and scholars in years gone by. *Whisper to the Wild Water* is full of the sounds of my homeland. In the grand scheme of things my voice is nothing but a mere whisper against the mighty force of a wild and torrid landscape. And yet it continues to speak. It may only be heard by relatively few, yet its message, I pray, is one of hope and peace that will be encouragement to all who care to listen.

I have never been a chaser of dreams nor have I burned with ambition for success or riches. I have stumbled through each chapter of my life and fallen many times along the way. And yet, through some great mystery, the rainbow's end has found me.

Recent days found me looking through my grandmother's old Book of Remembrance. A loose leaf floats to the floor and I smile, hearing Gog's voice reciting this, one of his favourite pieces of verse:

*Not till the loom is silent and the shuttles cease to fly*
*Will God unroll the pattern and explain the reason why*
*The dark threads are as needful in the Weaver's skilful hand*
*As the threads of gold and silver for the pattern He has planned.*

By Diana Leatham

# They Built on Rock

## Stories of the Celtic Saints

*They Built on Rock* tells the stories of the men and women who brought light and hope to the world of the Dark Ages. They are tales of miracles and crusades, intellect and passion.

St Martin, St Ninian, St Patrick, St David, St Columba, St Cuthbert, St Brigid, and others: these are the heroes of the Celtic Church, upholders of a vibrant faith that still transforms lives today. Strong in both word and deed, champions of Christ's gospel of love for all people, their characters and achievements are related here in enthralling style.

> *'This wonderful book shows the true depth and power*
> *of the Celtic way.'*
>
> Máire Brennan

Hodder & Stoughton
ISBN 0 340 74627 0

By Ray Simpson

# Soul Friendship
## Celtic Insights into Spiritual Mentoring

'No-one is an island' and 'everybody needs somebody' – phrases we know well but do we recognise the wisdom behind them?

To become fully human and realise our individual potential as we journey through life, we need support at many different levels from: best friends, soul mates, spouses, mentors, sponsors, counsellors, prayer partners, spiritual directors. Spiritual growth is something many seek and the tradition of soul friendship is recognised as a valid and successful way in which to achieve spiritual balance and growth. It is a tradition which is challenging, heart warming and holistic, weaving together evangelical, catholic, charismatic and postmodern strands.

The author is Guardian of the Community of Aidan and Hilda. He lives on the Holy Island of Lindisfarne where he facilitates a new cradling of Celtic spirituality providing soul friendship, retreats and resources for churches.

Hodder & Stoughton
ISBN 0 340 73548 1